D1235362

A SEASON OF HOMECOMINGS

LIVING, LEARNING, & LOVING
Every School in the SEC

RON LANG

RJL

No part of this book may be used, represented, or reproduced in any manner without the express written permission of the publisher. The only exceptions are for small samples to be used in writing reviews.

All photographs are the exclusive property of the author.

The stories in the book are from my experience traveling around the Southeastern Conference.

This book is not in collaboration with the Southeastern Conference or any of its member institutions, nor is it meant to represent the ideals and interests of any of those entities.

Copyright © 2020 Ron Lang
All rights reserved.

ISBN: 978-1-7338893-5-3
ISBN: 978-1-7338893-7-7 (paperback)
ISBN: 978-1-7338893-9-1 (e-book)

Cover Art: Eden Graphics, Inc. - Francine Eden Platt
Editing: Dave Holcomb - @dmholcomb
Interior Design: Rachael Cox

This book is dedicated to college football fans and alumni of the many wonderful schools around our great country.

To the loyal fans of the Southeastern Conference — Your passion and enthusiasm is what takes SEC football to another level.

To my grandfather "Pap" who introduced me to SEC sports. Thank you for being a great example of hard work and for always providing a positive environment.

FRONT COVER

The array of pictures on the front cover show an image representing each school. The following list is alphabetical and explains each image:

ALABAMA   An overhead view of the plaza containing the statues of the national championship coaches.

ARKANSAS   The "Wild Band of Razorbacks" monument outside the stadium.

AUBURN   Inside Auburn Arena, looking up at the War Eagle with championship banners streaming down.

FLORIDA   The Century Tower on campus.

GEORGIA   The Arch on the north edge of campus.

KENTUCKY   An end zone view of Kroger Field.

LSU   A view of Tiger Stadium from the upper deck.

MISSISSIPPI STATE   The statue of Bully at the entrance of "The Junction."

MISSOURI   The famed "Columns" with a homecoming banner in the middle.

OLE MISS   The "Walk of Champions" arch on the edge of The Grove.

SOUTH CAROLINA   The "Cockaboose Railroad" just outside the stadium.

TENNESSEE   The "Vol Navy" on the Tennessee River.

TEXAS A&M   The "Aggie Ring" statue outside of the Alumni Center.

VANDERBILT   The statue of "The Commodore" - Cornelius Vanderbilt.

IN THE BOOK

*When you see an asterisk (*) followed by a reference to "fan favorite(s)," then the following lists contain results of surveys I completed with fans on campus.

**Many schools proclaim to be "Running Back U" or "Linebacker U." At the end of every school's chapter is my choice of the best position group on each side of the ball for that program. It includes 10 players (in alphabetical order) who were major contributors through the years.

*** "My favorites at other positions" is not an example of the most talented players, but lists players that I enjoyed watching compete during their career.

Contents

1. WELCOME HOME - Introduction 1

2. ANCHOR DOWN - Nashville, TN 7

3. HOTTY TODDY - Oxford, MS 29

4. MY OLD KENTUCKY HOME - Lexington, KY 51

5. IT'S GREAT TO BE A FLORIDA GATOR - Gainesville, FL 73

6. HERE'S A HEALTH, CAROLINA - Columbia, SC 95

7. GOOD OL' ROCKY TOP - Knoxville, TN 117

8. M-I-Z, Z-O-U - Columbia, MO 139

9. HAIL STATE! - Starkville, MS 161

10. HOLD THAT TIGER - Baton Rouge, LA 183

11. ON THE HILL - Fayetteville, AR 207

12. ROLL TIDE ROLL - Tuscaloosa, AL 229

13. THERE'S A SPIRIT CAN NE'ER BE TOLD - College Station, TX 251

14. GLORY, GLORY - Athens, GA 273

15. THE AUBURN FAMILY - Auburn, AL 295

16. 2019 SEC CHAMPIONSHIP GAME - Atlanta, GA 317

    AFTERMATH - Atlanta, GA and New Orleans, LA 332

    NATIONAL CHAMPIONSHIP GAME - New Orleans, LA 337

17. SUNDAY SUPPER 345

    ACKNOWLEDGEMENTS 359

    ABOUT THE AUTHOR 363

1

WELCOME HOME

The Southeastern Conference is one of the most polarizing entities in all of American sports. SEC fatigue, SEC bias, and SEC envy are all very real sentiments among fan bases in collegiate sports. People outside of the South perceive the SEC as a bunch of rogue schools that will do whatever it takes to place a competitive team on the field. The conference and its member institutions are proud of their athletic successes, but they are so much more than sports. The conference produces leaders in the classroom, in the community and in the business world. *A Season of Homecomings* will walk you through each campus. It will reveal the culture, traditions, and atmosphere all throughout the SEC. It will give you a better understanding of what makes the SEC so special.

I have been an admirer of the Southeastern Conference schools for forty years. Since 1980, I have followed or participated in every SEC football season. Long before the national championship game participants were both from the SEC and even prior to the SEC winning seven straight BCS National Championships. Even before there was an SEC football Championship Game, I supported the SEC.

I have seen the SEC evolve and expand. When I started following the SEC, fans were lucky to find any of the conference's teams on television. Now, every game for each team is broadcast in some form of media. The football games are great, but there is so much more to each school.

The SEC takes great pride in its athletics, but as Southerners, our passion is much deeper than wins and losses. We appreciate the accomplishments of the universities, the history in the towns, and the contributions to the culture. I picked football season to visit each school because I am a football guy, but also because so much activity is based around the SEC football season. It has been years since I have visited some of these SEC campuses, and it's time for a homecoming.

Actually, it is time for fourteen of them. An anomaly with the schedule provided us with a fourteen-week regular season in 2019. It offers us an opportunity for *A Season of Homecomings*! This is the year for me to share the immersive experience of a game week in all fourteen SEC towns.

A Season of Homecomings conveys the quintessential passion and pageantry of a football season in the SEC for all of those who are either skeptical of it, deprived of it, or addicted to it. For readers to understand why well over 150,000 show up, when barely more than 100,000 (at most) will make it into the game. It's about letting everyone experience or recall the unavoidable anticipation, inevitable festivities and ultimate delights delivered every week in our conference.

It is a request for you to immerse yourself into the SEC for a full season. *A Season of Homecomings* will provide the encouragement to find a connection to the towns and schools that we call home. It's an attempt to absorb and decipher the particular dialects and beliefs. It's an invitation to walk through the stately columned campuses. It is the motivation to meet new friends who will be courteous and entertaining at the same time. It describes the lure of the beautiful countryside, delectable cuisine, remarkably elaborate celebrations, exalted traditions, and supremely talented teams. It is rare access to the biggest events of the year in the south.

In other words, *A Season of Homecomings* is the majesty of an autumn in the Southeastern Conference.

My coaching career took me from Maine to Texas, and many states in between. I've seen some beautiful places and met some wonderful people. Through it all, I've always stayed abreast of the SEC. I even had some recruiting battles against SEC schools. You already know how that went. During recruiting trips, wherever I'd be, I inevitably ran across alumni and fans of Auburn, Florida, LSU, Tennessee and all the rest. They are omnipresent and ready to vocalize the pride they have in their team and conference.

Alumni associations have chapters in most states, with some of the stronger associations being outside of the Southeast. In places you wouldn't expect, there are bars who dedicate fall Saturdays to SEC patrons. While in Austin, Texas in 2007 (five years before Texas A&M joined the conference), I learned that a large city park hosted a pre-season picnic for SEC fans. There are revivals all throughout this land, and they are growing in numbers every year. SEC football has always been played at a high level and the loyalty of the fans is just as intense.

You have all heard it. Many of us have voiced it. The Chant - S...E...C, S...E...C, S...E...C! Most outsiders think that it's done antagonistically, or that it is downright arrogant. It's not. At least, not in most cases. It is done out of pride! Pride for our conference. Pride for our teams. Pride for our region. Pride for our family. Yes, you read that right, pride for our family. The SEC is a family!

The SEC has its spats and rivalries. We've called each other names, tattled on one another, and given each other beat-downs. We've been aggravated by one another, and we've been jealous. In our family, no team likes to be outdone, but outside of the family, one can bet that we want our siblings to succeed. We are proud of their accomplishments, and we've got their back too. So, if you tussle with one of our brothers, and they whoop you, then get ready for it. We'll show our appreciation. We'll show our pride.

S...E...C, S...E...C, S...E...C!

Would you ever believe that Ohio State fans would genuinely root for the Michigan Wolverines in a non-conference game? I don't think so. Do you think Florida State folks watch every Miami play hoping they earn one for the ACC? Not likely. How about the UCLA supporters showing up to their home stadium to cheer on Southern Cal in the Rose Bowl? Doubt it. Can you envision Texas followers being happy about the Sooners winning anything? No chance.

Please don't misunderstand me. I don't mean that there is a total absence of pride for those conferences. That would be like saying there is a total absence of selflessness in Washington D.C. It does happen in those conferences, but only at a small collective fraction compared to that in the SEC. The dynamic in the Southeastern Conference is different than any other conference in America.

I've heard Bill Walton declare "The conference of champions" during those (with my best Bill Walton accent) *horrible* weeknight PAC 12 basketball games. Actually, I don't hate. Thank you, Bill Walton! I am glad you do it. I appreciate the loyalty that you show your conference. But, can the fan base in Eugene explain why you say it? Will the people in Tucson care enough to make a case as a testament to their sports? Do the fans in Berkley honestly proclaim they believe that motto deep in their souls? The supporters of the Southeastern Conference can, will, and do assert that passion for their conference.

In the Southeastern Conference, the atmosphere is utopia, traditions are law, coaches are legends and coeds are beauty queens. The stadiums are cathedrals, fans are zealots (especially when bourbon is involved), players are unconquered warriors and rivalries are epic battles. Even when they're not, they still leave an indelible impression on our hearts.

There is always a devotion to our team, and we always have a reverence for our conference. Southeastern Conference athletics is as much a staple of Southern culture as Sunday services, southern hospitality and sweet tea.

There are more than a few reasons why you continually see Top 25 polls littered with SEC teams. There are more than a few reasons why "it just means more!"

A Season of Homecomings presents stories from campus at every school in the SEC. It gives the reader historic tidbits about each institution and its football program. There are detailed versions of game day and results from fan surveys that reveal some of the most popular players and favorite home games. It puts you right in the middle of the conference action throughout the season. The chapters of each school conclude declaring the schools' best position groups, which includes 10 examples of some of the best players at that position through the years.

The SEC masses routinely believe that their coaches, players, and teams are unequivocally the best in the nation. Sometimes that belief is miscalculated, but more often than not it proves to be prophetic. Whether it be the indulgence at The Grove or watching the Gamecocks' entrance set to the theme of "2001: A Space Odyssey." I want you to be able to absorb it, feel it, and even have respect for it. I'm attending these reunions, and I am taking you with me.

Hopefully, you will develop a new understanding and possibly an affinity for the wonder and passion of SEC football. Some of you have never been to an SEC campus, while others haven't been able to see their team play away from home. Still, others are transplants that yearn to once again see the fall foliage, breathe the southern air and be welcomed back to our favorite family tradition: SEC Football! So, come up here on the porch and have a seat on the swing. Enjoy the southern breeze while I get you some sweet tea. Welcome Home!

2

ANCHOR DOWN

Week of the August 31, 2019 game against Georgia

There was only one game between Southeastern Conference opponents in the first week of the 2019 regular season. I was fortunate to have that because most schools rarely have a conference game to start the season. Not only was the Georgia at Vanderbilt contest a conference game, but it was also a division game in August. It was all set. I was starting *A Season of Homecomings* in Nashville, Tennessee at Vanderbilt University.

Vanderbilt is a private institution on the west side of Nashville. Founded in 1873, the school would eventually be named for its largest initial benefactor. Cornelius Vanderbilt was the country's wealthiest person at the time. He made his money in the inland water trade and the railroad industry. As an influential entrepreneur in the steamboat industry, he was commonly recognized by his nickname "The Commodore." Vanderbilt participated in many profitable business ventures, but he is most widely recognized as the owner of the New York Central Railroad. He invested heavily into the country's railroad infrastructure, but that wasn't his only financial venture.

His $1 million gift to help establish the school was meant as an olive branch to help heal wounds from the Civil War that remained in the South during the Reconstruction Era. According to Vanderbilt University's web site, Holland McTyeire, a Methodist Bishop from Nashville, sold Vanderbilt on the idea of building a university in the South that would "contribute to strengthening the ties which should exist between all sections of our common country."

McTyeire took a hands on approach to forming the school. He is credited with selecting the site and planting many of the trees on campus. Cornelius Vanderbilt died in 1877, but the university carries on his name (and nickname) to this day. Vanderbilt University's sports teams are known as the Vanderbilt Commodores.

Vanderbilt University continues to be a leader of higher education in the South. Vanderbilt has been designated as a Doctoral University, which signifies very high research activity. The school has the smallest undergraduate enrollment in the SEC. The 6,886 undergraduate students (as of 2019) benefit from a very personal education experience with a student-to-faculty ratio of 7:1. Vanderbilt ranks in the top 20 in five separate categories in the *U.S. News & World Report*. The recognitions include top 15 of national universities and even higher (No. 7) as a best-value school.

Vandy, as it's endearingly referred, has nearly as many graduate students as undergraduates. As of 2019, 6,245 graduate students attend Vanderbilt. The experts consider the Vandy graduate programs even more beneficial to its participants. Vanderbilt boasts a top 20 ranking of graduate programs by *U.S. News & World Report* in an eye-popping 20 different categories. Fourteen of those categories have Vanderbilt in the top five, and in half of those rankings, Vanderbilt sits either at No. 1 or No. 2 in the country.

The honors don't stop there. According to Vanderbilt's web site, the following accolades have also been bestowed on the school:

Reuters (2019)
- No. 19 - World's Most Innovative Universities

Kiplinger (2019)
- No. 10 - Best Value Among Private U.S. Universities

Money (2020)
- No. 15 - Best Colleges in America, Ranked by Value

The Princeton Review (2020)
- No. 1 - Best Quality of Life, Students Love Their College
- No. 2 - Happiest Students, Great Financial Aid
- No. 2 - College City Gets High Marks, Best Athletic Facilities
- No. 4 - Best Run Colleges, Most Beautiful Campus

Vanderbilt maintains its high standards with an intellectual focus. Throughout all disciplines, they maintain a low student-to-faculty ratio, which allows a more intensive educational pursuit. In fact, 91 percent of classes have fewer than fifty students. The quantity of teachers is deliberate, but so is the quality of the faculty. Ninety-six percent of Vanderbilt faculty members have earned terminal degrees (the highest degree awarded in a field).

Vanderbilt University is also very conscious of diversity and the caliber of students that are selected to enter into the school's programs.

For the 2019 fall semester, the university admitted less than 10 percent of the more than 37,000 applicants that were received. Of those that enrolled, the middle 50 percent had an ACT score between 33-35.

Vanderbilt has recruited some of the best students in the country along with a healthy number of pupils from international origins. The current student population includes scholars from all 50 states, and I don't have any doubt of the validity of that fact. During my first morning on campus, I was struck by the number of different states represented on license plates attached to vehicles on campus. Seeing states like Hawaii, Maine, and Montana made me decide to keep a running tab of which states were represented. The day ended with me identifying registrations from 31 distinct states outside of Tennessee.

Many of those transplant students were certainly attracted to the school because of the quality of education, but Vanderbilt also offers a gorgeous campus. I started my exploration by walking down West End Avenue to the entrance to the university. The first thing I saw was the Cornelius Vanderbilt statue surrounded by a magnificent setting. The bronze statue of "the Commodore" stood strong atop of the tall stone base. Behind him, I could see the top of Kirkland Hall's clock tower. The trees were filled with leaves at that time of the year, so I had to walk down the road to get a better view of Kirkland.

Speaking of trees, the entire campus of Vanderbilt University is considered an arboretum. It has been referred to as such since 1879. It officially became such when the American Public Gardens Association registered the campus as an arboretum in 1988. There are over 6,000 trees and shrubs that call the 333-acre campus home. The most recognizable tree is the Bicentennial Oak. This beautiful tree has been aged at more than 200 years old, and it's the only tree on campus believed to be older than the university itself. All of the different species of trees make the Vanderbilt campus a natural oasis in the ever-growing urban environment of Nashville.

I was really impressed with the elegance of Kirkland Hall. It has quite a storied existence. It has faced many years of wear and endured a devastating fire, but it wears its scars well. There are staircases on either side of the fantastic main entrance that curve up to their own magnificent entrances. The clock tower rises up from the left side. The building is an iconic landmark that is a storied part of Vanderbilt's history. The building is featured on many of Vanderbilt University's promotional items.

Just south of there is Benson Hall, which has a stunning steeple that adjoins two mirrored sides to the building. Benson is one of the older buildings on campus, but it too is very well kept. Outside of Benson is where one will find the Bicentennial Oak. From there, I went back north past the Rand/Sarratt complex into Alumni Lawn. It is a wonderfully green field with a flagpole proudly flying the American Flag. Students were all around as they stood and talked, threw Frisbees, and even sat on blankets reading. It looked like a good place to have a football game too. Just a week prior, Alumni Lawn hosted the Founders Walk, which welcomes all incoming students to Vanderbilt.

I walked through nearby historic Alumni Hall and then between Neely Auditorium and Kirkland Hall toward Bishops Common. Those of you familiar with the campus will wonder why I doubled back. Well, to be honest, I wanted to go to Alumni Lawn and didn't realize that it would have been in direct line with my return path. As it was, I went through Bishops Common to go check out the top-notch "Vandy" Law School. It is one of the oldest and most prestigious law schools in the South. The Law School has "V" doors that have handles in the shape of a thick "V."

After exiting the "V" doors, I walked past Curry Field and through Moore College. I was trying to get back to West End Ave to walk down to Centennial Park. It was a longer stroll on West End than I thought, but it sure was worth it. As I navigated through the hustle and bustle of a modern American city, I eventually stumbled upon the natural delights of the more than 130 acres of Centennial Park. As

Vanderbilt, Vandy, VU

School Colors:

Black & Gold

Traditions:

Anchor Down

V-U Hand Sign

Star Walk

Anchor Dash

Victory Flag

Spirit of Gold Marching Band

Fight Song - Dynamite

Spirit of Gold

Cheer for Old Vandy

Favorite Battle Cries:

Anchor Down

Go 'Dores

soon as you enter its perimeter, your anxieties and concerns exit your consciousness. The distractions melt away as the tranquility of the park fills your spirit.

It was as if even the day of the week was lost on me. The appointments, challenges and responsibilities were afterthoughts as I sauntered through the serenity of the expansive green space. I found many things that I really didn't expect like sand volleyball courts that hosted a hotly contested coed match that afternoon. Musician's Corner is another special place in the park. It hosts live music of all genres and is a great space for a concert. I was fortunate to be part of the audience for a young guitarist. He occupied our attention as he practiced his craft hoping to someday occupy the stage as the headliner. His delightful melodies transported me further from the everyday grind.

Lake Watauga is a welcoming man-made lake that sits inside the park. The one-mile path that surrounds it allows you to absorb many forms of nature's serenity. From the healthy trees and colorful floral gardens to the ducks, turtles and fish that swim in the cool waters, Lake Watauga is an intrinsic retreat. It was already past the lunch hour, but I saw people walking, jogging, reading and sitting in the natural beauty of the park. There was even a person taking a nap in their hammock. Many spots around the lake provide picturesque views of the Parthenon.

The Parthenon was originally built in 1897 and was an ode to Nashville having been referred to as the "Athens of the South." It is a full-scale replica of the original Parthenon located in Athens, Greece. There is now an impressive 42-foot tall recreated sculpture of Athena (the goddess of wisdom and war) that sits inside along with various other pieces of art. The columns and Greek frieze make the Nashville Parthenon very similar to its historic namesake in Athens. As Nashville's art museum, it is the focal point of Centennial Park.

I had an interview away from campus, and as the afternoon wore on, I decided to get something to eat. I didn't expect to have tacos, but I decided to try this interesting place called Tacos With A Twist located on Gale Lane. I am glad that I did. It turns out that they had only been open for a few weeks, but they were already in full swing.

It wasn't what I envisioned. It was better than that. The place had a fun atmosphere with great food. They have some interesting combinations that will pique anyone's taste buds. The food blended perfectly with the cold drinks that washed the day's heat away from me.

I started the following day around the athletic facilities. The McGugin Complex sits across the street from Dudley Field (football) and Charles Hawkins Field (baseball). The McGugin Center houses the athletic administration, most of the coaches' offices, the Stratton Foster Academic Center and many of the Commodores' sports teams. The outside features the "Star V" logo in full color. The glass had a white layer with "Anchor Down" cut out in block letters. The doors had the Star V etched into the white and the two door handles came together to form the Vanderbilt "V" similar to those at the Law School. As soon as you enter, there is a black and gold SEC logo.

Across the street at Hawkins Field, crews were hard at work replacing the playing surface. The stands surrounded heavy machinery, large dumpsters and mounds of gravel. I was surprised to see it like that, but I am positive that it will be ready in the spring. Just in time for Vanderbilt's national championship baseball team to defend its title. I turned down 25th Avenue South and walked past the outfield wall up the hill toward Memorial Gym. This is the unique venue where the basketball teams play their home games. I wasn't able to enter and see it from the inside, but there was a plaque outside that enlightened me on some of the history of the storied arena.

I strolled up Vanderbilt Place and then cut through Branscomb Quad. The students were constantly streaming in and out of the residence halls. Emerging from the area, I encountered Featheringill & Jacobs with its three stories of brick and stone exterior. The tower at one of the entrances helps the engineering hub stand out among its peers. I continued on through some of the medical buildings and across 21st Avenue S, arriving at the heart of Peabody.

Peabody is the College of Education and Human Development at Vanderbilt University. The school has roots as far back as 1785. It received funding from the Peabody Education Fund and was eventually called the George Peabody College for Teachers. The liberal arts institution was an illustrious school of education. There was so much collaboration between Peabody and Vanderbilt that Peabody students were granted the ability to participate on Vanderbilt's intercollegiate athletic teams. Peabody ended up having some financial issues in the 1970s and was absorbed by Vanderbilt in 1979.

The Peabody campus is delightful with charming older buildings and striking newer structures. The view from the Peabody Esplanade is captivating in every direction. Even with the construction occurring while I was there, the views were breathtaking. To the north is the beautiful expanse of Magnolia Lawn. To the south is the majestic domed structure of the Wyatt Center. I left Peabody and explored the other side of the medical facility.

It wasn't long before I encountered another one of Vanderbilt's highly-regarded schools. The Blair School of Music is renowned throughout the country. The school's building includes the Ingram Center performance Hall. I continued up Children's Way past some intramural fields and the recreation center. At Natchez Trace, I took a right and followed the road past the track and football practice fields. I had completed a long loop and learned a lot about the south side of Vanderbilt's campus. Now, it was time to learn more about downtown Nashville.

Music is a focus of Nashville visitors, especially in the vicinity of Broadway. The street runs from the Vanderbilt campus through downtown and is the center of the entertainment district in Nashville. A steady stream of restaurants and honky-tonks line the major thoroughfare's perimeter as it creeps toward the Cumberland River. Live music is ever-present in downtown Nashville. Whether it is a ticketed event or a musical entrepreneur on the street, there are always sweet notes floating through the crowds on either side of Broadway. There is a party every night, and it almost always centers around different styles of music. Broadway is "The Strip" in Nashville, and it helps validate the city's appropriate moniker of "Music City, U.S.A."

The city is home to the Country Music Hall of Fame, whose building has a look of a giant piano from the outside. A few steps away is the Schermerhorn Symphony Center. Continue up Fourth Avenue North and it will unveil the backside of the iconic Ryman Auditorium and eventually the Musicians Hall of Fame and Museum. That's just a few of the historic musical landmarks around downtown. If you want to create your own history, then Broadway offers more than a few options to do just that.

The entertainment choices in Nashville were certainly many of the reasons why so many Georgia backers were in town a few days before the game. Red-clad, barking humans had infiltrated the city and Vanderbilt's campus. The Holiday Inn, in the shadow of Vanderbilt Stadium, became a sanctuary city for the Bulldogs' supporters. On Friday morning, they were in the pool, at the bar, in the lobby and filling up the back parking lot. It reminded me of how the team hotel is on the road, yet the Georgia Bulldogs team was not staying at that hotel. In fact, the lobby restaurant was hosting a Vandy luncheon. The restaurant even had to turn some away as they prepared for the private Vanderbilt event.

Those folks made other plans, and for many, that meant heading over to where *SEC Nation* was set up. It was a significant walk from the hotel. I had already made the journey twice that week. It was all the way across campus on the other side of the Peabody campus at Ingram Commons. The stage and the demo field were constructed in the Lower Quad just outside of the Commons building. It's a scenic area surrounded by lovely new residential halls right off of 18th Avenue South. The temporary fencing was adorned with *SEC Nation* logos and the *SEC Nation* tour bus was parked just to the side of the makeshift studio.

Vanderbilt students were joined by some UGA fans of various ages. Some students paused to take in the scene while others hurried over to the location at the completion of the week's classes. Most people in attendance were on the lawn behind the stage where they might make an appearance on national television. I found one of the few shaded areas behind the cameras in the courtyard of Ingram Commons. A couple of things became apparent almost immediately.

The first is that most people (even many Georgia fans) love Tim Tebow. People interrupted their own conversations to say, "Hey, there's Tebow right there" or "I wonder if Tim Tebow is going to be here?" Female students occupied the remaining seats in my area to get a look at him. I heard them speak into their phone "Wait for me. I just want to try and see if Tim Tebow is here" and "I'm on the way. I just got a picture of Tim Tebow!" One student gloated about how Tebow had spoken to him and other students with disabilities earlier in the day. He was a freshman student at Vanderbilt, and he enjoyed heckling Tebow.

When Tebow came around to say hello to him, the student matter-of-factly told him "If I wasn't in this wheelchair, then I would tackle you!" Tebow spent some time with him, and brightened the young student's day. The second thing that was easily recognizable was that there are a lot of good people on *SEC Nation*. The "talent" films a segment or two on Friday, and they also meet with the press. This was the first week on campus this season, and the SEC couldn't have had better representatives.

Laura Rutledge is a wonderful person. She hugged and said hello to the people she was reunited with for the show. She greeted VU and media reps with a sincere smile. She cordially talked with fans and happily obliged when they asked to take a picture with her. I hadn't noticed, but Rutledge was nearing a full-term pregnancy. I heard a wife point it out to her husband. It was remarkable how personable she was with everyone, but it was extraordinary considering everything that she was dealing with at the time. Laura Rutledge may be the nicest person on television.

If Rutledge is the nicest, then Marcus Spears has to be the most real television personality I have seen in television. Spears is a genuinely good dude. His job on the show is to talk SEC football, and it is obvious that he loves it. He takes time to answer everyone's questions, and he doesn't have a problem giving his true opinion. It's refreshing to hear someone honestly reference his interests like hunting, fishing, music or hooping. Spears is a guy who just is who he is, and I appreciate that most of all.

It's fitting that some of the best people in sports television open fall Saturdays by talking about the best conference in America!

Saturday started early. I parked on 32nd Avenue outside of the western edge of campus. I walked all the way to the eastern edge to Ingram Commons. I walked into the Upper Quad as *SEC Nation* was about to commence with their first on-campus show of the 2019 season.

It started with a bang. Robert Randolph & The Family Band played the *SEC Nation* theme song live on the demo stage. Joined by the Vanderbilt cheerleaders, they belted out a rousing rendition of "Party Wherever We Go." On August 31, 2019 at 9:03 am ET, every SEC fan in attendance already had dopamine levels higher than they had all summer. The SEC football season was upon us.

The show was a good one. There was a nice energetic crowd, and they discussed every SEC team. It always feels like home when football season begins, but this was the season of homecomings, and it was starting off in a special way. Members of the Vanderbilt baseball team (including phenom pitcher Kumar Rocker) joined the crew on set. VU fans went wild, showing their appreciation for the 2019 National Champions while a Georgia fan held a sign that read "Kumar can't help this game!" The first week of the season and the SEC banter was already in full force.

I met Lanier, who is a Georgia fan who lives and works in Athens. His family had come to Nashville for the game. His wife is a Vandy alum, and they come to Vanderbilt games each year. They especially make it a point to attend the Georgia game every other year. Their boys want to attend Vanderbilt. Lanier feels that Georgia will win, but he is also quick to tell me that in 2013 Vandy beat Georgia in Nashville. He also remembers Vanderbilt won in Athens on Georgia's homecoming in 2016. His wife proudly admits that Vanderbilt is known for academics. She is also proud that their boys could witness the fun atmosphere. "At Vandy, we work hard and we play hard," she confirmed to the boys.

I went into the Commons to cool off and purchase some water. I was also hoping to watch some of the other games. It wasn't even 11:00 am ET, so there weren't any games underway yet. My oversight confirmed that I was still in pre-season form. Not to worry, I would be locked in within the hour before the games actually started. I left the Commons and *SEC Nation* and headed out to the tailgates.

As I approached Greek Row, the music was already blaring. They must have worked hard all week and now it was time to play hard. Cutting between Memorial Gymnasium and the Kensington Garage, I headed to the Holiday Inn to check on a lead for a ticket. The Nashville hotel had turned into "Athens North" during the latter half of the week. The ticket didn't work out, but I found Georgia fans having a heck of a party. UGA fans encircled televisions in the lobby preparing to consume college football. I joined steady flows of red rotating between the air-conditioned indoor social and the full-blown tailgate bash in the back parking lot.

Vanderbilt Stadium

Dudley Field

Surface: Fieldturf

Built in 1922

Capacity: 40,350

Record Attendance:

41,600 - multiple times

Nickname:

Commodores

Mascot:

Costumed - Mr. Commodore (Mr. C)

*Fans' Favorite Home Games:

Won 45-34 over Tennessee in 2016

Won 31-27 over Georgia in 2013

I walked up Natchez Trace toward "Vandyville," the part of campus that hosts most of the Vanderbilt tailgating scene. The road was blocked off and a large screen played college football at its entrance. On one side of the road was a row of tents that hugged the tall covered fence of the practice fields. This row of tents was all black and gold for the Vandy tailgaters. The other side of the street had a mixture of black and red tents against the edge of a few large parking lots. Georgia tents had popped up in every green space throughout the parking lots. I continued down a ways and around the corner to the Commodore Lawn.

The Commodore Lawn was full of tents from the Tailgate Guys. It was a great area for tailgating. There was plenty of room, and the kids had a nice grassy field where they could play football. Every tent was configured perfectly for a great soiree. Large screens with a satellite television package centered the spaces that had food and cocktail tables covered with white linens. Each one had large ice chests and plenty of chairs. As I would come to anticipate, they also had signs that identified each tailgate. My favorite on this day read "An Auburn Fan Paid For This UGA Tent."

After a little while, I went back over to Vandyville where the Vanderbilt faithful had arrived. Their arrangements ran the gamut from semi-swanky to downright lean - one of the spots had three people sitting on the curb under the tent eating Chick-fil-A sandwiches. They were waiting on the team to go through and then they were going to go into the stadium. Another had a chandelier hanging from the center while the tables were draped in black linen with a streamline gold stripe on its edges. The men wore black button-down shirts and khakis while the women wore black dresses. The meal was catered and served on black plates that were adorned with the "Star V" logo.

The other side of the road contained the more active tailgaters. Vanderbilt and Georgia groups seemed to alternate down the stretch of grass. Footballs and Frisbees glided through the air, as bean-bags were tossed between friends. Some party goers were boisterously rooting for teams playing on TV, while others found creative ways to consume beverages. All the while, I kept coming up empty for a ticket. Back at the entrance of Vandyville, I took a few minutes to catch up on scores and watch South Carolina on the big screen.

During a commercial, I noticed the flags at the top of Vanderbilt Stadium. There was an SEC flag and flags from other schools in the conference. I couldn't see them all from my vantage point, but I assumed that every SEC school was represented. Finally, the team came through making its way to the McGugin Center. I followed the team's path in front of the McGugin Center. I was still looking for a ticket. I talked to people everywhere. I asked guys at the letterman's tent, and I even tried talking to people as they picked up their reserved tickets. I didn't find any extras.

The Star Walk is one of Vanderbilt's favorite traditions. The players dress for the game in the McGugin Center. When it's time, they walk down the hill through the crowd and under the overhead sign stating "Star Walk." They cross over Jess Neely Drive and down the tunnel to the field. Two chosen Commodores lead the team carrying the huge gold-painted anchor. Fans line the path gyrating gold shakers. The crowd is thick and spans out in each direction. People stand on the grassy hills to get a better view of the players as they walk through the crowd. Curious Georgia fans showed up to share in the tradition. "The Spirit of Gold Marching Band" plays a loud and fun medley during and after the event.

Since it was the first home game, the freshmen got to experience going through the tunnel and running out onto the field. They call it the "Anchor Dash", and it is another long-standing Vanderbilt tradition. All first-year students get a special t-shirt made specifically for that year's Anchor Dash. They come together outside of the stadium tunnel on Jess Neely Drive where the players had walked across just a short while prior. In waves, the students get to run through the tunnel and down the length of the field with all of their classmates.

I stood outside the stadium and observed the logistics of sending 1,600 plus students running through the tunnel and onto the field. The students were excited and anxiously awaiting their moment. Their excitement grew as the distance between them and the stadium dwindled. From the outside, I could hear the crowd's appreciation. I could also see the team follow the last students onto the field. The Anchor Dash was a success, and the game was about to start. I had to find a ticket one way or another.

It was difficult finding any tickets to this game. The people that I had met didn't have any extras. I asked people throughout the week, but it seemed that many people (mostly Georgia fans) were in the same situation as I was. Everyone said "You'll find one outside the stadium once the game starts." On the street outside of the main entrance, people were asking for a minimum of 200 dollars per ticket. People, especially the Georgia fans, were starting to get antsy since the game had already started. At the intersection of Jess Neely and Natchez Trace, there was a ticket standoff.

One of the guys possessing tickets said "Two-hundred is better than missing the game!" A Georgia fan replied "No one is paying $200. One hundred dollars a ticket is better than going home with unused tickets."

About that time, I saw a Georgia fan walking my way half distracted by the controversy. I asked if he had an extra ticket that I could buy. He said "I only have this one, but you can buy mine." I offered him "everything in my wallet," which came out to fifty-nine dollars. He agreed, saying that he would watch it on TV at a tailgate. I gave him the money and headed into the stadium.

Because of the ticket fiasco, I didn't make it to my seat until Georgia was already ahead 7-0. They already had the ball again at Vandy's 33-yard line. The first play I saw was a fifteen yard completion to Demetris Robinson. Robinson was the receiver who caught the touchdown from Georgia quarterback Jake Fromm for the first score. The drive continued smoothly for the Dawgs as running back James Cook waltzed into the end zone from 18 yards out on the very next play. I had only seen two plays, and Georgia already held a 14-0 lead.

Georgia red flooded the inside of Vanderbilt Stadium. From my experience outside of the stadium, I knew that there was a strong representation of Georgia fans. It was Labor Day weekend, and many UGA supporters made the short trip to enjoy the city of Nashville. I just didn't expect it to be like a game in Athens, GA. Two slivers of the stands were black, but red covered the rest. At one point, the Georgia - Bulldogs chant was even tossed back and forth across the stadium.

Two plays into Vanderbilt's next possession, the first quarter ended. When play resumed, UGA stopped the Commodores on third down. Vanderbilt was faced with a fourth-and-two at its own 33-yard line. Sensing the need to keep the ball away from Georgia, Derek Mason (Vanderbilt's Head Coach) decided to try converting the fourth down. His gamble paid off, as the 'Dores were able to pick up a first down with a 3-yard run. VU followed it up with a long run for another first down past midfield. But after an incompletion and consecutive penalties, any momentum Vanderbilt had attained was halted.

Regaining possession of the ball, the Bulldogs' offense continued its efficient start to the season. They used seven plays to advance 80 yards and score their third touchdown in three offensive series. The Dawgs led 21-0 before anyone had barely settled into the 2019 college football season.

Vanderbilt already faced a difficult situation halfway through the second quarter. It was time for the Commodores to get their most talented players more involved in the offense.

The first play went to running back Ke'Shawn Vaughn. He only gained 4 yards, but it would have been much more if a Georgia defender hadn't tackled him via his facemask. The 15-yard penalty gave the Commodore offense life. They earned another first down at midfield. A second Georgia penalty pushed the VU offense into Dawgs territory. VU rode the momentum all the way to the UGA 8, but a holding penalty moved Vandy behind the chains. The Commodores couldn't recover and had to settle for three points. Vanderbilt was on the board, and the Vandy ROTC was cranking out "The Admiral's" roar.

The Georgia offense seemed to cool off while it was on the sideline. One first down was achieved, but then three straight incompletions gave the ball back to Vanderbilt. The Commodores looked to expand on the success it had on the previous series. It started with a powerful run from Vaughn for 16 yards. VU picked up a few more yards to cross the 50-yard line. A couple false starts wrecked Vandy's momentum, but another Georgia facemask penalty gave Vanderbilt a fresh set of downs. With time running short in the first half, Vanderbilt's Ryley Guay was given the chance to increase VU's point total. He boomed the 48-yard field goal, and the Georgia lead was cut to 21-6 at the half.

Vanderbilt started the second half with the ball. Other than an effective run from Vaughn for a first down, the 'Dores couldn't advance on the Dawgs' defense. The Georgia offense started the second half inside its own 15-yard line. They used the running game to advance to the other side of the field and then utilized the impressive leg of Rodrigo Blankenship to add a 50-yard field goal. VU's offense couldn't mount much offense and had to punt the ball back to UGA. Georgia receiver Tyler Simmons caught the punt and maneuvered 27-yards up the field.

The return set Georgia up at Vandy's 45. The Dawgs' run game moved UGA down to Vanderbilt's 17-yard line, where an incomplete pass attempt on third down left UGA with a fourth-and-one. Vandy's defense stood tall on the rush attempt, and it ended Georgia's scoring hopes. The loyal Vanderbilt supporters let their presence be known, as they showed appreciation for the defensive effort. Black-clad Vandy fans popped up around the stadium in places where they were previously unseen. The Commodores' offense wasn't able to gain ground and had to punt. Both teams repeated the act of punting over the next few series.

When the third quarter ended, Georgia continued a recently developed tradition. The band played Krypton while the fans held up four fingers and their flashlights. The people dressed in red were having a great time performing the tradition for the first time in 2019. On the field, after another Vanderbilt punt, Georgia's offense looked to produce its own form of excitement. After a couple of positive plays, Fromm completed a pass down to the 2-yard line, but then Georgia fumbled. Vanderbilt's safety Dashaun Jerkins scooped it up and ran the ball back to the 17-yard line.

However, Georgia's defense was just too much for Vanderbilt. The Dores weren't able to muster much offense in the fourth quarter, and UGA benefitted from two drives that started in Vanderbilt territory. Tyler Simmons set one of them up with a 22-yard punt return, and the other was from Georgia lineman Devonte Wyatt recovering a Commodore fumble. Georgia's Rodrigo Blankenship finished off both drives with field-goals. The final tally was Georgia 30, Vanderbilt 6.

When I left the stadium, I went back to the area of the Star Walk. The UGA equipment staff was loading the truck. I saw Vanderbilt players still in pads talking to their families there on the street. Georgia and Vanderbilt fans offered encouragement as they walked past. It was an intimate setting like one you might find after a local high school game. People showed their appreciation for the team's effort. One by one the reunions broke up as the players went inside the McGugin Center to shower.

As it thinned out, the mood of the players was evident. Every one of them had the same look in their eye. It was partly disappointment. All competitors feel that when they are not on the winning side. But there was also some resolve. They will bounce back and work even harder. There was anticipation. This was only the first game. They'll get another shot. There was appreciation. These guys are earning a degree at Vanderbilt and playing football in the SEC. There was pride. Everything is still in front of them. Anchor Down!

Vanderbilt Commodores

Linebackers

Andrew Coleman
(1978-81)

Chris Gaines
(1984-87)

Chris Marve
(2008-11)

Zach Cunningham
(2014-16)

Jonathan Goff
(2004-07)

Moses Osemwegie
(2002-05)

Jamie Winborn
(1998-2000)

Jamie Duncan
(1995-97)

Hunter Hillenmeyer
(1999-2002)

Shelton Quarles
(1990-93)

My favorite players to watch at other defensive positions:

DB - Corey Chavous (1994-97)   DB - D.J. Moore (2006-08)

DL - Jovan Haye (2002-04)   DB - Jimmy Williams (1997-2000)

Running Backs

Corey Harris
(1988-91)

Frank Mordica
(1976-79)

Ralph Webb
(2014-17)

Jermaine Johnson
(1993-95)

Jamie O'Rourke
(1971-74)

Rodney Williams
(1998-2001)

Ke'Shawn Vaughn
(2018-19)

Jared McGrath
(1997-2000)

Zac Stacy
(2009-12)

Carl Woods
(1983-86)

My favorite players to watch at other offensive positions:

WR - Jordan Matthews (2010-13)   OL - Will Wolford (1982-85)

WR - Earl Bennett (2005-07)   QB - Greg Zolman (1998-2001)

*Fan Favorites: WR - Jordan Matthews, RB - Zac Stacy, QB - Jay Cutler

3

HOTTY TODDY

Week of September 7, 2019 game against Arkansas

The second week of the season also only offered one game between SEC foes. This time it was between Western division opponents as Arkansas traveled to Oxford, Mississippi to play the Ole Miss Rebels. With their first game at Memphis a week earlier, the Rebels were hosting the Razorbacks for their home opener.

The students were also settling into their routine since school had started just a week prior. Barely removed from the dog days of August, Oxford was swirling with activity. Now that the students had returned, the town had nearly doubled in size.

Oxford, Mississippi is a classic example of a quaint Southern town. It possesses a relaxed atmosphere full of culture and diversity with coffee shops and diners whose patrons know someone just about as soon as they walk in the door. Many of the town's folks are known by their occupation. It is a town filled with an abundance of mature trees, secret fishing holes and locally owned shops and businesses which are more about taking care of people than squeezing more revenue out of them. The city also includes a centralized town square that is the epicenter of its activity.

The town square in Oxford is one of the most well known in the South. The square literally and figuratively centers around the Lafayette County courthouse. The stately white building, with tall dignified columns at its entrances, has been a part of many episodes of history through the years. It has been featured in books and movies alike. Speaking of historic, The Square is home to the South's oldest department store, the J.E. Neilson Co., which has been open since 1839. The Square offers a multitude of shopping options, including a number of boutiques.

If someone is in search of a good read, especially with a local flavor, then Square Books has it covered. It is one of the most well-known independent bookstores in the world, and there are three different entities on The Square (Square Books, Off Square Books, & Square Books, Jr.). There are also some fantastic spots to have a savory meal on The Square. City Grocery, Ajax Diner, Bouré and Oxford Grillehouse are recognized Oxford landmarks for dining. There are also gift shops, banks, business offices, and even a sporting goods store. The surrounding streets and alleys offer a variety of other choices that rival the charm and atmosphere of those directly on The Square.

Not far from The Square is the University of Mississippi, affectionately known as Ole Miss. The school was established in 1848, and it is the state's oldest and largest public university with an enrollment above 24,000. The flagship University has been designated both a sea grant and space grant institution. Its research activity has led to the "R1: Doctoral University" classification designating very high research activity. 2019 was the ninth consecutive year that *U.S. News & World Report* ranked UM in the top 100 public universities in the nation. They also declared the University of Mississippi as the 39th ranked "Best Value School" of public universities in the country, as well as rating UM's Pharmacy School as 24th best in the nation.

The Chronicle of Higher Education listed Ole Miss as one of the nation's best colleges to work for. That has paid off for its students, but it is also showing results within the faculty. Ole Miss sociology professor, Annie Cafer, was the first faculty member from any Mississippi university to be named an Andrew Carnegie Fellow. According to www.olemiss.edu, the fellowship includes a $200,000 grant for her work in the field of community resilience.

From the student perspective, UM has recorded multiple honorees of the Boren, Truman, Udall, and Fulbright Scholar awards. 2019 included two exemplary examples of these types of accomplishments by Ole Miss students. Addison Roush became the 14th UM recipient of a Goldwater Scholarship, while Arielle Hudson was awarded the illustrious Rhodes Scholarship. She is the 27th Ole Miss student to be named a Rhodes Scholar. In addition, the University of Mississippi ranks fourth among Southern schools with 24 Academic All-American football players.

The University of Mississippi is full of history and infused with tradition. As I entered the grounds of the university, I was greeted by a sign that read "Welcome to Ole Miss." The sign stood in a grassy island with its base surrounded by colorful flowers. Brick towers proudly held the sign from each end. The concrete base supported the four white columns and roof that encased the sign. Under the greeting, the sign was emblazoned with the seal of the University of Mississippi. The seal depicts an image of the evenly spaced

Mississippi, Ole Miss, UM

School Colors:

Crimson & Navy Blue

Traditions:

Tailgating at The Grove

The Walk of Champions

"Hotty Toddy" Cheer

18 mph & 10 mph Speed Limits

Locking the Vaught

Pride of the South

Fight Song - Forward Rebels

I Saw The Light

From Dixie With Love

Favorite Battle Cries:

Hotty Toddy

Go Rebs

colonnade of the Lyceum. It was then that I decided my exploration would begin at the Lyceum.

I found a parking spot on University Place next to the baseball stadium. I stepped toward University Avenue, where I took a left and proceeded west. The walk through the humid air took me past Coulter Hall (Chemistry), the Thad Cochran Research Center, Faser Hall (School of Pharmacy), and Shoemaker Hall (Biology). As I approached The Circle, I encountered a tall marble obelisk. The circumference was similar to a mature tree and it was topped with a statue of a Confederate soldier. The monument was placed to honor the "Confederate Dead 1861-1865." The commemorative display has stood in this spot since 1906.

Directly behind it was the wonderfully peaceful green space known as The Circle. It is arranged with many full-grown species of trees. You can find magnolias, oaks, elms, maples, dogwoods, pecan, and even pine and cypress trees. The criss-crossing brick-lined walkways converge into the inner circle that contains the American flag. This location is believed to be the exact center of the Ole Miss campus. The Lyceum (administration building) sits at the end of the western radius. Since the Lyceum is the front door to Ole Miss, The Circle really serves as the well-manicured front lawn of the university.

The Lyceum is the most iconic building on campus. The antebellum brick building with the white columned portico was completed in 1848. It initially served as the University of Mississippi's library. During the Civil War, the building acted as a medical facility for wounded Union and Confederate soldiers. A clock face hovering above the front columns and a wing on both the north and south sides were later added. Inside the front doors are two beautiful parlor rooms that are open for students to utilize. The building has three levels inside that all serve different purposes for the university's operations.

From the back, the Lyceum looks very similar to the front of the building. The six Greek columns are mirror images to those on the front. The only glaring difference is that the rear does not contain a clock face. There is a beautifully landscaped courtyard that sits between the Lyceum and the J.D. Williams Library. The courtyard is also the site of a Civil Rights monument, featuring James Meredith, who was the first Black student at the University of Mississippi. He enrolled in 1962 under extreme duress, endured violent protests and completed his degree in 1963.

The monument depicts a bronze statue of Meredith walking toward a columned portal that stands in a bricked plaza. The statue represents Meredith's walk into the Lyceum to register for classes. Between the top of the columns and the portal's roof, there is an inscription of a single word on each of the four sides. Each word describes what it took for James Meredith to be successful in his quest for an education. Those four words are Courage, Perseverance, Opportunity, and Knowledge.

A very short walk from there, the George Street University House sits next to the library. It is a very appealing building with a covered porch on the first level and a semi-covered patio on the second. I stood looking at it thinking that it would be a great place to live. It turns out, that it was built as a residence in 1910 for the Dean of the Law School. It was later used as housing for a number of sororities. Currently, it serves as the offices for the School of Applied Sciences.

I continued farther down to Bishop Hall and visited the Student Media Center. I was able to witness the recent upgrades to the Student Media Center before completing an interview. After exiting, I went around Bishop Hall and onto All-American Drive. I crossed the street and started east toward The Pavilion and Vaught-Hemingway Stadium. That is where I discovered a sign commemorating Poole Drive, which is a salute to the Poole family's contributions to Ole Miss.

It all stemmed from three brothers that were standout athletes for the Rebels. The trio started a family tradition of athletic excellence at Ole Miss. Jim "Buster" Poole played seven years in the NFL and was twice named a first-team All-Pro. Ray Poole played football, baseball, and basketball at Ole Miss before embarking on an eight-year professional football career (six years in the NFL and two years in the CFL). Barney played professionally for six years and was inducted into the College Football Hall of Fame in 1974. They also had cousins who played around the same time, and then there were two more generations that followed. The family has earned over 50 varsity letters from the school.

"The Pooles of Ole Miss" are legends of the SEC, a title that was officially bestowed upon Ray Poole in 2001. When his playing days were over, Ray returned to Ole Miss as a coach. Poole helped coach the "Rebs" to four SEC titles and a share of three national championships. After his retirement, Ray and his wife of 57 years (Wanda) continued their support of Ole Miss Athletics. When Ray Sr. passed away in 2008, Wanda remained an active member of the Ole Miss community. It is estimated that she has attended more Ole Miss Rebels athletic events than anyone in history. Wanda Poole is essentially the matriarch of Ole Miss.

Wanda Poole is a gracious and hospitable soul. She still sells real estate in Oxford, and she is a sociable gem. Miss Wanda recalled accounts of how the Grove has evolved from tailgating out of the trunks of cars, and how they used to attend Ole Miss/Mississippi State double headers in Jackson. I was privy to some remarkable stories of her experiences in the Southeastern

Conference. She has connections to many SEC figures past and present. Her admiration for the conference is unmistakable. "I am proud of the success of the SEC" she gushed. Mrs. Poole is grateful to be from Oxford in the middle of SEC country. "This is home, and I wouldn't want to live anywhere else...It's a wonderful place."

She has been around many legendary figures, and the pictures around her house serve as proof. We talked about some of the people that she has hosted in her home like Johnny Vaught, Bear Bryant, and Johnny Cain. She shared stories about some of her favorite people through the years. "I like a winner" she readily admitted. Her appreciation for the Manning family is evident. When talking about Peyton Manning choosing to attend Tennessee, she exuded class by proclaiming "Ole Miss is always my team ... but Peyton is one of ours, so I did root for Tennessee a little bit." More than a treasure to the Poole family and the Oxford community, Wanda Poole is truly a matriarch of the SEC.

The next morning, I started the day with breakfast at the Beacon. It is an Oxford treasure where the accents are as thick as the cheese grits and the friendliness is as delectable as the chicken biscuit. Since it would fill me up and not drain my wallet, I ordered both. While I foraged through the plastic bowl full of packets of butter, jams and creamers, I heard someone come in and ask if anyone had seen Doc Billingsly. I felt like I was serving as an extra on *The Andy Griffith Show*. When the food came, I thought that maybe "Aunt Bee" was in the kitchen. The meal was delicious. Although I declined the opportunity for pie, I did visit the other dining room that was adorned with vintage Ole Miss wallpaper.

Back on campus, I found myself on Chucky Mullins Drive in front of the regal Robert C. Khayat Law Center. I had a great view of the navy blue Ole Miss water tower just a short distance from the "Tad Pad." The Tad Smith Coliseum is a multi-use arena that has hosted Ole Miss basketball for many years. Not far from a few of the opulent fraternity houses across the street, there is a sign honoring the memory of Chucky Mullins. It tells of his story and is marked with his No. 38 and the short but powerful quote "Never Quit."

Roy Lee "Chucky" Mullins was a defensive back who critically injured himself during a 1989 football game. The collision left him paralyzed from the neck down. He worked hard in rehab for his goal of returning to Ole Miss as a student. Mullins was able to do just that in January of 1991. That May, Mullins had complications with a blood clot that lead to him passing away. His positive attitude and unflappable spirit were an inspiration to all that knew him. The Chucky Mullins Courage Award is presented each spring to the outstanding defensive player. That player receives a framed Chucky Mullins jersey and the privilege to wear the No. 38 jersey for the upcoming season.

The No. 38 is one of two numbers that the University of Mississippi football program has retired. The other is Archie Manning's No. 18. As many already know, some roads on campus have posted speed limits of 18 mph in honor of Archie Manning. There are also roadways, like the one that runs beside the football facility, that have a 10 mph posted speed limit. The No. 10 is in honor of Eli Manning. Both numbers are combined in the name of a popular dining spot on campus.

The Grill at 1810 is located in the Olivia and Archie Manning Performance Center at 1810 Manning Way. It is a nice cafeteria-style dining facility that focuses on performance nutrition. The most unique part of the eatery is the wall of windows that overlooks the indoor practice facility. The same complex contains the weight room, locker room and coaches' offices.

The lobby of the football facility is like a small Ole Miss football museum. There are a lot of displays of Ole Miss football history and a few interactive aspects as well. I was fortunate to get an exclusive view of the Manning Room which holds pictures, awards and artifacts from both Eli's and Archie's playing days. The most interesting to me were the cast and jersey Archie wore when he famously played with a broken arm.

I then went next door to Vaught-Hemingway Stadium. Some may find this weird, but the first thing I noticed was that it smelled like an SEC stadium. I somewhat find it weird myself because Ole Miss had yet to play a game in the stadium this season. It's part humid southern air with a hint of bourbon, a sprinkle of cut grass, a dash of dirty jerseys and a heaping helping of tradition. Either way, it felt like home. I was able to see the pedestal stamped with "Never Quit" (the Chucky Mullins bust is taken out of the elements during the week). I saw the "party decks" constructed for students and the field level patios where certain ticket holders can be entertained.

Outside of the north end of the stadium is a tremendous new plaza. The Jake Gibbs Letterwinners Walk contains a replica of the Walk of Champions arch at the end closest to the stadium. On the other end is the immaculate Lloyd Bell Tower. Connecting the two is a stone and brick pathway that is the culmination of the Walk of Champions. Beset on each side of the walkway are brick posts that have plaques containing the names of Ole Miss letter winners through the years. It's one of a kind, and it is a special tribute to Ole Miss athletes.

Vaught-Hemingway Stadium

Hollingsworth Field

Surface: Grass

Built in 1915

Capacity: 64,038

Record Attendance: 66,176 - 9/17/16 vs Alabama

Nickname: Rebels

Mascot:

Costumed - Tony the Landshark

*Fans' Favorite Home Games:

Won 23-17 over Alabama in 2014

Won 17-10 over Mississippi St in 1992

A few steps away, I found a statue of legendary football coach John Howard Vaught. Johnny Vaught coached the Rebels for 25 seasons and has, by far, the most coaching victories in program history with a 190-61-12 record. About that time, a group of coeds walked through and asked me to take their picture in front of the legendary leader. Around the corner is the Fed-Ex Student-Athlete Success Center which sits across from the Pavilion. The Pavilion at Ole Miss is the ultramodern arena that now hosts Ole Miss basketball. It is usually swirling with activity since it also contains an interactive lounge, multiple dining choices, a ticket office and more.

I left campus early that day to catch up with a high school classmate of mine. I wasn't aware of it until that week, but I found out that he started and runs one of the finest restaurants in Oxford. Joel and his wife have created a sophisticated dining experience at Ravine. The diverse menu relies on locally grown foods, and it regularly delights citizens and visitors alike. I really enjoyed being able to touch base with Joel, and it was a thrill to see the Oxford amenity that he has created.

On Friday, I explored more of campus. I walked by gawking at the sorority houses. They all looked like large elegant clubhouses at the most exclusive golf resorts in the world. I toured the energetic Student Union. Students flowed through there like water through a garden hose. Right outside is the original Walk of Champions arch. It is the point at which the team begins the Walk of Champions that takes them through the crowds at The Grove and ends at the stadium. The arch was given to UM by the 1962 football team that went undefeated (the only Ole Miss team to accomplish that feat).

I walked all around the tree-studded ten acre green space known as The Grove. Paths zigzag across the lush field. Each path has small street signs naming it for a legendary figure from the football program. There is Willis Way, Brewer Lane, and others named after players such as Deuce McAllister and Everett Lindsay. My stroll took me past the Grove Pavilion, which has hosted concerts, lectures, and even ESPN's *College GameDay*. Behind there sits one of the most interesting looking buildings on campus. Ventress Hall has many unique architectural features and occupies a spot on the edge of The Grove right across the street from The Circle. It has served many purposes throughout its life, but Ventress currently is the home of the College of Liberal Arts.

Before the "Great Land Grab" at The Grove (when people claim a spot for tailgating), I marched down to Oxford Square. People were everywhere enjoying the Southern hospitality of Oxford. Families went in and out of the boutiques and shops. They took pictures in front of the courthouse. It was similar to a Fourth of July festival without the fireworks. I stopped in a couple places and relished the air conditioning. One particular shop had the best display on The Square. It was a rack of gray shirts adorning a red and blue SEC logo. The small chalkboard sign read "If you're not talking SEC, we don't wanna talk."

They had me at SEC!

In the other corner of The Square, I saw a couple taking pictures near an old telephone booth. A few steps away was a statue of William Faulkner, the Nobel and Pulitzer Prize winning author from Oxford. Many of his works of Southern literature are based on his experiences and areas around the town. His statue sat there with legs crossed watching us all enjoy his hometown. I completed my loop around The Square and made a stop at The Library. I wanted to revisit the sports bar, and I was pleased to see that they have maintained the SEC paraphernalia, including an old-school pinwheel above the bar.

When I came back to The Grove on Friday afternoon, it was roped off and contained an abundance of red and blue trash barrels. The Grove was closed until 7:00 pm when an air horn would signal permission to claim a tailgate spot. People were positioned all around The Grove. As the time drew near, they assumed a running stance and prepared to dash to their desired area. When the horn sounded, it was like a herd of kids sprinting to a field of Easter eggs. Girls squealed and guys had tents bouncing off of their shoulders as they ran to the destination. One person even ran out of their shoes and left them lying lonesome in the middle of the street. In a matter of minutes, The Grove filled with tents of every shade of red, white, and blue.

Saturday figured to be an experience like no other. I arrived early and headed straight for The Grove. On the way, I encountered packs of fans coming from cars, dorm rooms, and buses at various shuttle stops. Every group had multiple people carrying or wheeling supplies for the party. It was like an enormous production crew preparing a movie set, yet this scene was much more entertaining than some Hollywood hoopla. Sure, The Grove does get a lot of notoriety, but the scene was real and authentic and it's not hard to find a good time. A favorite phrase at Ole Miss is "We never lose a party!" I don't know how someone could be disappointed at any tailgate in the SEC, and Ole Miss made a strong case as the finest from the very start.

Right away I saw a few tents that contained a chandelier and fine china. It was very nice, but you didn't have to be wearing seersucker or a bow tie to be invited in. There were others with chandeliers. Some were crafted from crystal while others were made of antlers. Every set up was different, but the vibes were all similar. People looked to get along and have a good time together. Ole Miss grads from Texas, Georgia, and Florida were all thrilled to be back as hosts to parties. Guests from Louisiana, Alabama, and

Tennessee were happy to be part of the festivities. There was even an older man dressed as the former Ole Miss mascot, Colonel Reb.

The masses all used plastic cups because you can publicly consume any drink you want as long as it's in a plastic cup. Each tent reminded me of an outdoor rehearsal dinner. Everyone was treated like the inner circle of family and close friends. People kept going around telling stories and introducing each other. Some people sat and watched football games on TV, but The Grove was mostly a field of social butterflies. Social butterflies that like to drink, dance, and pose for pictures.

My experience in The Grove was a fusion of Southern delights. A gorgeous sunlit day admired from under the cover of majestic shade trees. Enjoying a glass of sweet tea with a peaceful breeze blowing across your brow. Witnessing the shameless hospitality seeping from every stop on the trail. The scrumptious homemade morsels that satisfy your taste buds and make you feel welcome in the same bite. Feeling an appreciation for tradition and the audacity to be progressive. Taking a brief moment away from the everyday grind to celebrate the spectacle of SEC football.

The Walk of Champions is one of the biggest moments each Saturday in The Grove. There are thousands of people lined up ten to twelve people deep (sometimes more) to greet and cheer on the Ole Miss football team as the players make their way to the stadium. I watched as people yelled and chanted as the Rebels went past. After the team made it through The Grove, I kept my distance and followed to the Lettermans Walk. I observed the reception the team received at the entrance to the stadium, and I slipped over to the M-Club.

Former lettermen visit this exclusive area before games. There is plenty to eat, other ball games on televisions and old teammates visiting with each other. There is Ole Miss memorabilia on display all around. The M-Club also has a Manning Room. It is a lounge with couches and a television. There are many pictures and plaques of the Manning family, and Archie Manning's letterman's blanket is on display. It feels as if you are sitting in Archie and Olivia Manning's personal living room.

From the M-Club, I walked out onto the field to observe the teams' pregame routines. I was on the opposite end from where the Rebels entered the field, so I made my way down the sideline so I could see the Chucky Mullins memorial. It sat there peacefully gazing out toward the field where the Rebels were finishing their warm up. As the team retreated to the locker room, the crowd around me grew thicker than the early September air. I had a great spot at the end of the roped alleyway where the team would run through. I decided to stay and watch one of the most recognizable entrances in the SEC.

More and more people descended to the area. The excitement spewed over at the start of a favored tradition. A special guest on the video board always introduces the "Hotty Toddy cheer." The montage unveils a celebrity who ends up asking "Are You Ready?" The fans don't miss a beat as they proudly respond:

"Hell Yeah! Damn Right!

Hotty Toddy, Gosh Almighty,

Who The Hell Are We? Hey!

Flim Flam, Bim Bam

Ole Miss By Damn!"

Against the rope near the corner of the end zone, I retreated slightly to let kids get a better view. A few coaches came out with the captains. They respectfully ran their hands over Chucky's bronzed dome. It was as if they had a brief unspoken conversation with him. A few minutes later, the rest of the team gathered between the brick pillars. As smoke was sprayed through the air, the players began to bounce back and forth. Many in the crowd swayed in unison. Players serving as color bearers (with an American flag and an Ole Miss flag) readied to lead the charge. In an instant, the Ole Miss

Rebels burst through the corridor and onto the field. Red shakers danced in the air above the faithful in the stands.

I worked my way through the tunnel and hurried up to the press box. Although the air conditioning felt nice, I opted for the open-air camera well in front of the press box. It was a beautiful Southern evening for football as the setting sun peaked over us to shine on the stands across the field. Ole Miss prepared to receive the ball wearing one of the best uniform combinations in college football. The red jerseys with white stripes on the shoulders and white numerals above gray pants with red and blue stripes down each leg. It was topped off with a powder blue helmet that adorned one red stripe down the middle and the red script "Ole Miss" on each side.

Both teams' opening drive contained two incomplete passes as each team went three-and-out. During UM's second possession, quarterback Matt Corral began to connect with his throws. The running game contributed bits and pieces that helped the Rebels into the red zone. The drive concluded with a short touchdown pass from Corral to receiver Elijah Moore. Down 7-0, Arkansas used the talents of running back Rakeem Boyd to gain positive yards. The drive stalled just shy of the 50-yard line, and the Razorbacks had to punt back to the home team.

On the first play thereafter, running back Jerrion Ealy caught a pass for a nice gain that put UM at the 50. Ole Miss would push it down to Arkansas's 38, but they faced a fourth-and-nine from that spot. An incompletion gave the ball back to the Razorbacks.

While the first quarter bled into the second, the opponents' offenses traded punts. During the intermission between quarters, I met the state troopers assigned to protect the opposing coaches. Two of them were brothers, who played at nearby powerhouse South Panola High School. I had a nice conversation with the "trooper twins" before they returned to escort the visiting coaches down to the locker room for halftime.

As the second quarter commenced, a decent return and an Ole Miss penalty gave Arkansas advantageous field position. An effective opening run finally pushed them into Ole Miss territory. A few plays later, Hogs quarterback Ben Hicks completed a long pass to receiver Mike Woods. The momentum fizzled, but Arkansas had done enough to put itself in position to convert a field-goal attempt. The score remained 7-3 Ole Miss as both defenses stood rigid, forcing consecutive punts.

Ole Miss suddenly found itself on Arkansas' side of the field, and the Rebels found some offensive success as well. The running game produced consecutive positive results that took the Rebels inside the 10-yard line. That momentum was abruptly halted with a holding penalty that left the "Rebs" too far from the end zone to score a touchdown. They settled for three points.

The Razorbacks had a little more than two minutes to respond before halftime. Wide receiver Trey Knox subsequently escaped behind the defense for a 49-yard reception. The Hogs tried to go to Knox again, but the Ole Miss defense wouldn't let him run free a second time. The Arkansas offense couldn't penetrate past the 25-yard line. The Razorbacks tried to answer the Rebels field goal, but the attempt was off the mark. Ole Miss retained their 10-3 lead at the half.

The University of Mississippi's "Pride of the South Marching Band" performed the halftime show. The first formation they did was the letters "HYDR." This is a reference to the "Hotty Toddy cheer." Later, it looked like they formed an outline of The Grove and The Circle. Four people dressed in different colored "solo cups" started in the part representing The Grove and began to race around the area representing The Circle. The race contained everything needed for excitement, including a come-from-behind victory and a crash and burn by the red-cupped participant.

The Ole Miss kickoff team started the second half by pinning Arkansas inside their own 15-yard line. The Arkansas offense couldn't attain a first down and had to punt.

After the short punt, the Rebels again had advantageous field position. The UM offense advanced to the Razorback 30-yard line where it faced a fourth-and-one. Ole Miss attempted to convert, which it did, but a fumble gave the ball back to Arkansas.

Nick Starkel came in at quarterback to lead the offense for Arkansas, and it helped spark the Razorbacks. Arkansas began to click off first downs with regularity for the first time. Trey Knox had another big catch which appeared to be the game tying touchdown, but the play included a penalty for an illegal man downfield, so the officials wiped away the score. Arkansas ended up with a fourth-and-two at Ole Miss's 30. The one-yard gain on fourth down wasn't enough to maintain possession.

The offensive Rebels came out firing. They put together a string of successful plays to drive 71 yards into the Razorbacks' end zone. The touchdown drive put Ole Miss ahead by 14 points. During the break in action, the intro to the song "Thunderstruck" by AC/DC played over the PA system. The lighting system in Vaught-Hemingway stadium danced and flickered with the music. It caught some fans by surprise, but everyone seemed to enjoy it. The 17-3 lead and light show had the Ole Miss fans amped up.

I took the next few minutes to exit the press box area and go sit in the student section. By the time I arrived, Arkansas had moved across midfield. It was all for naught, though, as the Razorbacks fumbled on the next play. The Rebels finished the third quarter with a completion for a first down. Ole Miss began the fourth quarter with two runs that again reset the chains. That's when Arkansas made it interesting. The Hogs forced a fumble that safety Kamren Curl returned 69 yards for a touchdown. It tightened the Ole Miss lead to 17-10.

The Rebels' offense returned to finish what they had started on the previous drive. The offense progressively matriculated to around the spot in Arkansas territory where it recently fumbled. This time a pass went to Elijah Moore. His foot stabbed the ground as he veered to the right, and then again as he cut to the left. Moore then used his speed to jet into the end zone. The Rebels had indeed completed the drive, and now its lead was back to fourteen points at 24-10.

Arkansas was unable to build on an early first down, and they were forced to put their defense back on the field. The Rebels subsequently gashed them with effective running plays. Five plays and 66 yards later, the Ole Miss lead ballooned to 31-10 with six minutes to play. The students who remained were spirited and migrated down to the front of the stands. A few remained under the tents set up at the top of the end zone. The tents were positioned as a benefit to the attending students. Televisions were hooked up under each corner. I watched the televisions as they showed a replay of the final play in the Tennessee-BYU game.

I talked with a couple who were students that participate on the Ole Miss track team. They were going to stay for the whole game. The student-athletes offered their opinion about the new "party decks" meant to facilitate the students remaining throughout the whole game. They told me that it was good intentioned, but a few small things would make the difference. They would've been pleased if the area included cold water dispensers and if the televisions would have shown games from around the country. The male told me "We don't need the Ole Miss game on the TV, we have that right in front of us." Either way, he and his companion were going to stay until the game was complete.

It wouldn't be much longer. Arkansas turned it over on downs before Ole Miss went three-and-out. After receiving the Rebels' punt, the Razorbacks put together their best drive. It went for 81-yards and ended with a Nick Starkel touchdown pass. Ole Miss recovered the onside kick and expired the remaining 81 seconds to take the victory by a final score of Ole Miss 31, Arkansas 17. I watch the loyal throng of students celebrate as it exited the stadium. My new friends were thrilled with the victory. They packed up to leave and left me with a "Hotty Toddy!"

I ultimately left as well and went to an alumni tent in the shadow of the Lloyd Bell Tower. The day was designated as a "Red Day" and the Rebels had won, so the tower was aglow in red. I stood under the alumni tent and intently watched the momentous game between the LSU Tigers and Texas Longhorns. LSU's offense was unstoppable and helped solidify a huge victory in Austin, Texas. Occasionally, a migrating Ole Miss fan would inquire about the Tigers. When I notified them of the outcome, a hearty "Hotty Toddy" was uttered. After catching up on scores and knowing that LSU had won, I set off toward The Grove.

I arrived to find about half of the revelers had already left. The diehards were watching the late games while others began to clean up their area. Before long, an army of workers showed up to carry out their orders of cleaning the Grove. I was told that they wouldn't leave until everything was cleared. "This place will be back to normal by ten o'clock tomorrow morning" said a proud man who continued his experience under party lights. As the watch parties and makeshift dance halls progressively diminished, I decided to take the long walk back to my truck.

I checked out around 8:45 am on Sunday morning. I had a decent drive ahead of me and wanted to get on the road. But, before I did, I wanted to check on one thing. I filled up my fuel tank and drove over past the Grove. Sure enough, at 9:00 am, The Grove was as pristine as the calm Sunday morning. If someone had just arrived, then it would have never been known that this natural oasis held an extensive rave the previous afternoon. As I drove through, I was amazed by the cleanliness of the Grove and Circle and was once again impressed by the elegance of the Ole Miss campus. My approval could only be summed up one way. Hotty Toddy!

Ole Miss Rebels

Defensive Line

Tim Bowens
(1993)
Peria Jerry
(2005-08)
Barney Poole
(1942, 47-48)

Derrick Burgess
(1997-2000)
Bruiser Kinard
(1935-37)
Jerrell Powe
(2008-10)
Ben Williams
(1972-75)

Marquis Haynes
(2014-17)
Robert Nkemdiche
(2013-15)
Kelvin Pritchett
(1988-90)

My favorite players to watch at other defensive positions:

LB - Patrick Willis (2003-06)   LB - Tony Bennett (1986-89)
DB - Senquez Golson (2011-14)   LB - Freddie Joe Nunn (1981-84)

Quarterbacks

Kent Austin
(1981-85)
Jake Gibbs
(1958-60)
Eli Manning
(2000-03)

Charlie Conerly
(1942, 46-47)
Chad Kelly
(2015-16)
Romaro Miller
(1997-2000)
Bo Wallace
(2012-14)

John Fourcade
(1978-81)
Archie Manning
(1968-70)
Jevan Snead
(2008-09)

My favorite players to watch at other offensive positions:

RB - Deuce McAllister (1997-2000)   OL - Everett Lindsay (1989-92)
WR - A.J. Brown (2016-18)   RB - John Avery (1996-97)

Fan Favorites: QB - Archie Manning, QB - Eli Manning, RB - Deuce McAllister

4

MY OLD KENTUCKY HOME

Week of the September 14, 2019 game against Florida

The state of Kentucky provided a homecoming for me in a myriad of ways. Much of my family and a lot of my friends still live in the area, and it was nice to see so many of them. Kentucky is where I was born, and it's where I was introduced to my first love - the University of Kentucky Wildcats. I am from Louisville, but there was never a doubt that my blood ran blue. UK is also where I first experienced the Southeastern Conference. It's been a part of me since then. When I graduated from high school, the other options didn't stand a chance. I was going to be part of the SEC at the University of Kentucky.

The University of Kentucky is located in Lexington and was established as a public land grant institution in 1865. The school is the flagship university in the state with an enrollment of more than 30,000. The University of Kentucky is one of only eight institutions in the nation with the full complement of liberal arts, engineering, professional agricultural and medical colleges and disciplines on one contiguous campus. *U.S. News* ranks UK's Graduate Schools of Public Finance and Budgeting (No. 4) and Pharmacy (No. 6) in the top ten. In addition, the school is the alma mater of Nobel Prize winners William Lipscomb and Thomas Hunt Morgan (father of modern genetics).

I pulled onto campus near the Taylor Education Building. It looked similar to the time when I spent so many hours in its classrooms. I walked across the street to Administration Drive where I passed a beautiful stone wall with a sign confirming that I had arrived at the University of Kentucky. Meandering around that part of campus brought back a lot of memories. Every other building reminded me of my days at the school. There was the Patterson Office Tower and White Hall. Up around the corner were Kastle Hall and McVey Hall, which sit across from the Funkhouser Building. It somewhat felt like I was walking to class, but those days were long gone. I didn't have to rush to make it to a lecture on time. I could take my time soaking in the charming architecture that was accented with beautiful landscaping. I decided to go back west to get reacquainted with Memorial Hall.

Memorial Hall is one of the most iconic buildings on campus. The structure was completed in 1929 and dedicated to the people who died fighting in World War I. Stately white columns rising from its top step guard the front door. Overhead is a gorgeous clock tower that layers up to a steeple. The Memorial Hall clock tower has become a great symbol of the University of Kentucky. It has been prominently featured in the school's logo with the clock tower wedged between the U and the K. It's a grand landmark, and it is a terrific place to take a photo in any season.

I continued on to the Carol Gatton School of Business and Economics. This is another building that I frequented as an undergrad. Students utilized the appealing outdoor space, while I explored the updated interior. My trek took me up Administration Drive again as I went to visit the massive Bill Gatton Student Center. Although it was present while I was in school, I never spent much time there. I regretted it as soon as I walked up to the area. It's obvious that there have been many upgrades and additions since I attended UK. It is a phenomenal place. There are amenities and resources galore. It drips with school spirit, and I even saw the first wildcat statue of the visit in that building.

I popped out of the student center onto Avenue of Champions. I crossed the street and went into Memorial Coliseum. The men's basketball team played games there until Rupp Arena was constructed in downtown Lexington in 1976. Memorial continues to host women's basketball, volleyball and gymnastics events. It's remarkable how UK has maintained the 70-year-old edifice. On the backside of Memorial is the newer Joe Craft Center, which is a state-of-the-art complex for men's basketball. Across the way is the Wildcat Coal Lodge that houses the men's team. After seeing the facilities, it's no surprise that UK has consistently fielded a nationally competitive basketball team year after year.

As you may already know, basketball is huge in Kentucky. I started listening to the Wildcats' games on the hardwood with my grandfather. I can still remember listening to Cawood Ledford's eloquent portrayals of the Kentucky Wildcat games. A classy gentleman from Eastern Kentucky, Ledford was the voice of UK athletics for 39 years. Many of you might remember him doing the national radio broadcast of the Kentucky Derby or the Final Four for many years. Ledford had a capacity for telling you a genuine account of the event that

Kentucky, UK

School Colors:

Blue & White

Traditions:

Cat Walk

"C-A-T-S" Cheer

Third Down Coal Whistle

Call To The Post

"Go Big Blue" Cheer

Wildcat Marching Band

Fight Song - On, On, U of K

Kentucky Fight

My Old Kentucky Home

Favorite Battle Cries:

Go 'Cats

Go Big Blue

invariably made you appreciate the environment and the talents of athletes on either team. His final call for the Cats was the momentous 1992 East Regional Final between Duke and Kentucky in the Philadelphia Spectrum. That game also featured another SEC broadcasting legend, as Verne Lundquist handled the television coverage.

Across Avenue of Champions, from Memorial Coliseum, is where Stoll Field was located. Stoll Field was where the Wildcats played home football games until 1972. Plenty of people still tell stories of times they attended games at the site. Next to where the stadium used to sit is the Singletary Center for the Arts. The Singletary Center hosts many artistic events that promote creativity and diversity. There have been informative lectures, soulful music, artful dance and even comedy routines performed for the community there.

Crossing over Rose Street put me in position to walk through Greek Park and witness the evolution of Greek Life at UK. It has certainly changed in size and scope. Some of the organizations have even changed locations. I eventually ended up outside of the new Haggin Hall. The new dormitory replaced the old Haggin Hall in 2014. It looks fantastic, but what was inside made me even happier. A new and improved "K Lair." The K Lair was a staple among UK students for years. It was the best place to eat on campus for many of us. The new K Lair looks nothing like it did. It is now a sleek modern space that serves a variety of Kentucky Proud products. For those of you who are feeling nostalgic, you'll be happy to know that they still have the old K Lair sign.

I took the afternoon to go over to the Joe Craft Football Training Facility to watch practice. Before you even enter the building, there is a tremendously significant monument sitting out front. The monument features a stone base that holds four bronze statues, one for each of the four UK football players who pioneered integration in the Southeastern Conference. The depictions of the men stand tall, but the monument cannot fully explain the strength and courage that it took for them to conquer their colossal challenges.

Greg Page was a defensive end from Middlesboro. He enrolled at UK in 1966. His first year as a Wildcat was spent on the freshman squad. In August of 1967, while practicing for varsity action, Page suffered a neck injury that left him paralyzed. He was in intensive care for 38 days before he passed away due to complications from his injuries.

Nate "Nat" Northington was a defensive back from Louisville. He enrolled at UK in 1966 and spent that year on the freshman team. Northington first played in a varsity game on September 23, 1967. His fellow trailblazer (and good friend) Page died six days later. The day following Page's death, Northington became the first Black football player to participate in an SEC game.

Houston Hogg was a running back from Owensboro. He enrolled at UK in 1967. As a running back, he was undoubtedly subjected to cruel punishment and harsh treatment during his playing days. Despite that, Hogg persevered to earn varsity letters at UK in 1969 and 1970, setting a path for others to follow.

Wilbur Hackett was a linebacker from Louisville. He enrolled at UK in 1967. Hackett joined the football team in 1968 and proceeded to develop into Kentucky's Co-Most Valuable Player his senior year. In 1969, Hackett became the first Black athlete to be named Team Captain in any sport in SEC history.

The sports culture in the south and the SEC have forever been positively shaped because of the brave actions of these four men. It is a point of pride that these pioneers chose to make their mark at the University of Kentucky. They will be honored forevermore at the entrance to the football training center.

As you enter the inside of the training center, you'll find a large display of uniform combinations surrounded by bowl and rivalry game trophies. The lobby also contains some major individual awards that UK players have won. There are a plethora of resources for student athletes. The 100,000-square-foot building contains a cafeteria, a large open strength and conditioning area, a Gatorade bar, the plush locker room and multiple meeting rooms. A new outpost for the Center for Academic & Tutorial Services (CATS) lies on the facility's second level. This is a huge benefit to the football players because they used to have to go across campus for help with academics. The second floor also contains the coaches' offices. They are nice and spacious with many of them featuring a view overlooking the practice fields.

It was there that I caught up with my pal John Schlarman. Coach Schlarman is currently the Offensive Line Coach at UK. He is doing a terrific job developing one of the nation's best and most consistent offensive line units. Their superb performances have garnered national attention and earned them the moniker "The Big Blue Wall." John is especially proud to be part of the resurgence of the Wildcats.

"It's very rewarding to be able to see all of the hard work come to fruition." He expanded: "For us to have a level of success. It's for everyone before us who laid the foundation."

Coach Schlarman is no stranger to hard work. He had a noteworthy career as a player at Kentucky in the mid-1990s. Schlarman was a four-year starter on the offensive line for the Cats. He earned All-SEC honors and was twice named UK's Most Outstanding Lineman. Three different times, John earned the distinction of Academic All-SEC. He chose Kentucky, in part, because of former coach Bill Curry.

Schlarman on his admiration for Curry: "He was a man of integrity, and I try to emulate that in my coaching every day."

Coach Schlarman certainly does that. His combination of work ethic, character, and perseverance has earned him the nickname "The Great American" around the football complex.

Schlarman hadn't planned on a coaching career. But, not long after his playing career ended, he realized that he missed being part of a team and the competitive aspect of football. He broke into the profession as a graduate assistant at Kentucky. After living and coaching in other places, his career has come full circle. He and his family feel blessed to be at UK. Both his and his wife's families live in Kentucky.

"It's nice to be home...to be around family and friends and have the opportunity to coach at the most competitive level," he admitted. "We have received support from so many people."

John is not just a great American. He is a great Kentuckian.

I watched Coach Schlarman and the rest of the staff instruct their players at practice. Despite the heat, the team remained focused during preparation for the weekend's crucial game. When I moved around to watch an offensive team session, I ran into a friend from our days at UK. Mark Perry is now on the staff at Kentucky. I hadn't seen him earlier because I was focusing on different aspects of the practice. It was nice to spend some time with Perry.

As practice came to a close, there was an influx of young kids. It turns out that it was family night. The staff's families all came and had dinner together with the team. I met Perry's son as they tossed around a football. It was nice to see a great family environment like that. It was a perfect way to end a long hot day.

My brother had the next day off from work, so we spent it visiting quintessential Kentucky destinations in the vicinity of Lexington. The day started out at Ashford Stud in Woodford County. Ashford Stud is also known as Coolmore America because it is the American home of Coolmore Stud, which is the largest thoroughbred horse breeding operation in the world. The farm is an absolutely gorgeous place. It is a utopian playground for thoroughbred horses. Richard, who is a lifelong horseman from Ireland and runs the daily management of the horses, toured us around the facility. He is a very personable guy who has lived and worked in the Kentucky horse industry for more than three decades.

Richard showed us around the breeding operation. He was very informative, and I respected the passion and knowledge that he has for his craft. We learned that a stallion may cover (mate) up to four times a day, and that the gestation period is eleven months for a horse. I also learned that Richard is a football fan, and he was just as excited about the upcoming Kentucky-Florida game as the rest of the community. We met some of the resident stallions like Lookin at Lucky, Mendelssohn, Classic Empire and Fusaichi Pegasus. We took a picture with Uncle Mo, who is the sire (father) of 2016 Kentucky Derby winner, Nyquist. Unfortunately, Triple Crown winners Justify and American Pharoah were in Australia for the Australian breeding season.

Afterward, we traveled to Lawrenceburg to visit with Brian Sivinski. He was a college roommate of mine, and Sivinski now owns and operates Lovers Leap Vineyard & Winery. It is a facility that develops wine from the vine to the bottle. At Lovers Leap, all the wines are produced in house from grapes that were cultivated on site. There is an immense amount of labor involved in the wine making process. It was really interesting to learn about the multitude of tasks involved with making, bottling and distributing wine. I enjoyed being able to observe the lab, cold storage, and fermentation facilities on the property.

In the quaint tasting room, Colby guided us through an actual wine tasting. He was very insightful and helped me appreciate the melody of flavors in each selection. It was a very entertaining setting that offered a comfortable tasting room coupled with an inviting observation deck with gorgeous views of the vineyard. There was a stunning pavilion that hosts weddings, conferences and other special events. I was thrilled that Sivinski has created such a stunning family friendly venue with award winning wines right there in Central Kentucky. It was definitely a unique and delightful place.

It is not uncommon to find former UK athletes that have become successful entrepreneurs in the state of Kentucky. Sam Ball was a productive football player and successful businessman for many years. "Big Sam" played football at the University of Kentucky in the mid-1960s. He received over sixty scholarship offers from schools across the country, but chose to stay in

Kroger Field

C.M. Newton Field

Surface: Grass

Built in 1973

Capacity: 61,000

Record Attendance:

71,024 - 10/20/07 vs Florida

Nickname: Wildcats

Mascot:

Costumed - Wildcat and Scratch

*Fans' Favorite Home Games:

Won 43-37 over LSU in 2007

Won 40-34 over Alabama in 1997

Kentucky. He is the only native Kentuckian to earn consensus All-American honors for the Wildcats.

Ball explained "When I was a boy, I worked at a filling station. The only thing the old men there talked about were the Kentucky games."

His choice was obvious to him. "UK is the state's school. That was the only place I wanted to go."

His performance as a player led him to be named a member of UK's All-Century Team and inducted into nine Halls of Fame. Sam Ball was honored as Kentucky's SEC Legend in 2001.

In 1966, he was drafted early in both the AFL (No. 14) and NFL (No. 15) drafts. Ball played in two Super Bowls and won Super Bowl V as a member of the Baltimore Colts. Ball is confident that playing at the University of Kentucky enhanced his football career. He stated: "It opened doors for me and sent me to the pros in a big way."

After retiring from football, Ball continued to make a name for himself as an award-winning, multimillion-dollar salesman in agribusiness. He credits UK for a big part of that prosperity as well. In Ball's estimation, the support from the Agriculture Department at UK really helped farming business around the state.

Big Sam Ball's gregarious and humorous personality has led him to a successful speaking career that has endeared the legend to audiences around the world. He attributes his blessings to the opportunities he had at the University of Kentucky. He still works and lives in Kentucky. Ball is proud to have attended and played football at UK, even during the tough Bradshaw years when Ball was one of the famed "Thin Thirty." Ball loves his Wildcats, and he loves his home state. To this day, he still flies two flags; the American flag and the flag of the Commonwealth of Kentucky.

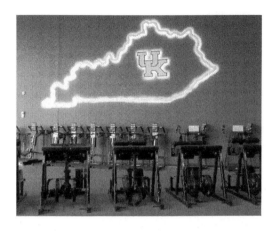

On Friday, I hung out with another one of my friends from UK. Marc took a day off and drove to Lexington with me. We parked on the southeast corner of the stadium. We entered Kroger Field (formerly Commonwealth Stadium) and found it in fantastic condition. The new blue seatbacks throughout gave it a royal look. The ribbon and video boards all sported the *SEC Nation* logo (the blue of the logo fit in perfectly). The sun glistened off of the synthetic turf while television crews constructed their wired arrangements. At the top of the east side, the breeze assisted 14 flags in waving a warm greeting to all in sight. Each flag represented a school from the SEC. Above the north end zone, there was a taller flagpole with the Kentucky state flag serving as a base for the flag of the United States of America.

We walked through the player tunnel. The walls of which contain the names of former lettermen. We noticed a lot of familiar names, but didn't take the time to find our own. The tunnel leads directly to the stadium locker room. It's actually more like a staging area since the team dresses in the training center just behind the stadium. It still has all of the essentials, but it isn't the traditional dressing room. As we walked back through the tunnel and roamed around the field, we reminisced about some of our more memorable moments in the stadium. We ran into the Florida equipment staff as they arrived to unpack the gear. They were well aware of the importance of the next day's game. Everyone understood that the game held huge implications for both teams' seasons.

Leaving the stadium, we walked past the football practice fields and up the hill toward the new baseball stadium and other athletic facilities. Until then, I had not seen the new baseball stadium or the training facilities for soccer, softball or baseball. The John Cropp Softball Stadium and Kentucky Proud Park were both impressive facilities. The baseball team was taking batting practice as we walked through the area. There were faded yellow plastic practice balls scattered beyond the outfield wall. The crack of the bat and the players' exuberant howling indicated that they were enjoying the activity.

The other thing that was scattered all around was tailgate tents. The white ones from Tailgate Guys were stacked in rows. Each tent had tables, chairs, a television screen and at least one ice chest. I am always entertained by the titles each tailgate group gives its party. With Tailgate Guys, any early passerby can get an advanced announcement of the titles. Tents for tailgating were already occupying a vast area in every direction from Kroger Field. There were people dropping off supplies at their chosen locations. We continued past the K Club house and through more groups of tents toward campus.

As we traversed past the outdoor basketball courts, we recalled times that we ran those same courts. It was kind of funny to me because it just made me feel old. What really made me feel old was seeing the Kirwan-Blanding residence complex. It was a ghost town. Doorways were boarded up and there was no one in sight. Looking in a window at Complex Commons only revealed a huge open space with a table, a couple of overturned chairs and some random tools. What used to be a hub of activity now gave an aura of an abandoned plantation. The two towers and eight accompanying low-rises now outnumbered the people within its perimeter. It was surreal.

On the other side of the complex sits Kirwan I. It was in "K-1" where most of us lived during our early years in school. It was also where we would all stay during pre-season football camp. Epic stories originate from events that occurred in that building. A tall covered chain link fence now forms a boundary to the complex. I didn't know at the time, but the complex is due to be razed in the coming year. Blanding and Kirwan Towers have been landmarks on the UK campus since they were completed in 1968, but they've run their course. Their destruction will save the university money and make way for additional modern residential buildings. The area is also going to be home to a large new green space (although I'm not sure they can replicate "Blanding Beach").

We walked down a tree-lined path alongside The 90 and Lewis Hall. Both are structures that were new to me. They sit on the grounds that used to contain the "Six Pack" (a group of six fraternity houses). As we approached University Drive, we turned right and went toward the William T. Young Library. The brick octagon building is the crown jewel of the nine libraries on campus. The W.T. Young Library sits in the middle of campus and is a popular spot for a multitude of events. On this day, the west lawn was the location for the *SEC Nation* set.

There were about fifty students who hung around the set while a live show aired and segments were being recorded. I had not seen Tim Tebow yet, but I sure heard his name a lot. There were males that I overheard asking each other if he was going to be around the set. Later, some girls were hovering to get a glimpse of him. One of their friends showed up and revealed a picture that she took earlier. They all screamed as if they were groupies of The Beatles. We found former All-American Wildcat quarterback Tim Couch waiting behind the stage to make his appearance as a guest on the show. After catching up with Couch for a few minutes, we strolled back over to University Drive.

We took University Drive all the way back to the stadium and eventually to Marc's vehicle. Different landmarks triggered more memories from those good ole college days. There is nothing like telling old stories to make it feel like a homecoming.

We hadn't had lunch so we went down on Broadway to KSBar & Grille. The eatery is a derivative of the popular Kentucky Sports Radio (KSR) blog. It is filled with Kentucky decor. Most of it is based around UK sports. It was crowded and getting more packed as the Friday afternoon wore on. UK fans were getting an early start for the pivotal game against the Gators.

Saturday was another early start. I rolled into Lexington around 10:00 a.m. Even nine hours before kickoff, I had to park down Nicholasville Road close to a mile from the stadium. Groups of people were walking toward their tailgate spots as they passed by others who had begun partying in front yards. Around the stadium, the festivities were already well underway. All of the tents that I had seen the day before were now neighbors to lines of cars. Smoke billowed from pits and plowed through a throng of dancing flags. The sun illuminated asphalt dance floors while makeshift DJs continued the musical inspiration. Corn hole boards, mini footballs and even horseshoes kept the guests occupied as the cuisine was still being prepared.

It was a delightfully warm sunlit afternoon. The assembly celebrated the South's biggest holiday - a college football Saturday in the SEC. Both teams were looking for signature wins early in the year, and they each were going to have to do it without key players. Florida was going to play without wide receiver Kadarius Toney and corner CJ Henderson while the Kentucky offense would be void of starting quarterback Terry Wilson. There was true anticipation for each 2-0 team's first conference game. An undeniable zeal bounced around the masses of both fan bases outside of Kroger Field. They knew that they were about to witness a great game and felt confident that they would be elated with the outcome.

The Nissan Heisman House made an appearance in Lexington, and it blended right in with the activity around the stadium. Plenty of people took advantage of the presence of the Heisman House. There was a long line for people to have their picture taken with the Heisman Trophy. It was in front of a green screen, so you could choose your favorite winner to be included in the picture. There were other activities including a stage where past UK greats would interact with fans. Wildcat quarterbacks Andre' Woodson and Tim Couch were scheduled to make appearances later in the day.

Just around the corner from there was a convergence of blue tents shading revelers. Kentucky-themed balloons filled with helium spun around each other on the corners. The tables were covered in blue cloth. The longer table suggested that a few of the guests had recently completed Kentucky's famed Bourbon Trail. There was a five-foot alligator laid out on the lower level of a large barbeque pit. The guys had it brought in specifically for this week's game. The cooking instructions had already produced a nice char that promised a tasty main course. The biggest news at this tailgate was that it also served as an engagement party (Paul & Lauren). The popular young couple was in the planning stage for their May 2021 wedding.

I continued to work my way around the stadium, and was able to talk with many people that I had not seen in years. I ran into a lot of former players, managers and classmates that all had their own party groups. I even saw an old college friend's parents. It was great to see all of them and be updated on their families. It's somewhat strange when you run into people that you know from college, who now have kids going into high school or college themselves. They were each in different stages of parenthood, but they all wanted to provide the opportunity for their kids to experience Kentucky Football. There was some retelling of stories, but it was mostly what they had been doing and how their goals had evolved. It was a homecoming indeed.

It was getting closer to game time, and I needed to hurry over to experience the Cat Walk. It was already packed with fans. I found an open spot on top of a hill between the stadium and the Nutter Field House. More people showed up and I was surprised how many people were there to support the team as they arrived for the game. The coaches and team marched through, while the cheerleaders and the band provided further entertainment. There was also something new that I was proud to witness. It was Kentucky Football's newest tradition.

Leading the way at the Cat Walk was the "Lift Them Up" pushcart. The specially designed pushcart carries a child from UK's Children's Hospital and leads the Cat Walk. A different pediatric patient is chosen the week of each home game. Offensive Tackle Luke Fortner, a mechanical engineering major, joined a team from Toyota Motor Manufacturing of Kentucky to help the project become a reality. It gives a child the life-changing experience of sitting in the "driver's seat" and leading the Wildcats into the stadium. Those children and their families are dealing with some tough issues, and it is heartwarming to see them have the opportunity to experience some of the same joy that many of us fans get to have every week. It's an awesome feeling to know that my alma mater is doing such a noble deed.

After the Cat Walk, I went to some tailgates on the other side of the stadium. Next to the practice fields was an area filled with tents and covered trailers. I spent some time with a host that I had met setting up a day earlier. It was a great arrangement that had a television for the kids to play video games and another for the adults to watch college football. I was able to catch up on the scores of the day next to a tent proudly displaying both Kentucky and LSU flags. As I was leaving the area, I ran into my older brother and his friends. We hung out a little bit and made calls to find an extra ticket. The game had been sold out for weeks, and tickets were hard to find.

My brother found a friend who had an extra ticket for him. He was on the other end of the stadium. We went on the hunt to find the ticket bearer. The former defensive lineman would normally be easy to spot, but the outside of the stadium was jammed with people. When we did find him, the exchange was coupled with a few celebratory toasts. I had another stop to make before I went into the game, so I said goodbye and set off toward the RV lot. While sorting through the festivities, I crossed paths with other long lost acquaintances on their way into the game. It wouldn't be much longer before I headed the same way.

The stadium was filling up quickly, and the atmosphere was lively. There was a small section sprinkled with orange, but blue largely flooded the stands at Kroger Field. The band was shaped in the outline of the state of Kentucky. When they played "My Old Kentucky Home", tears involuntarily streamed down my face. I hadn't stopped to process it all, so I guess that it was spontaneously released during the heartfelt song. It was all that I have been through outside of this state. My mind filled with memories of my mother who had recently passed and my grandfather, who introduced me to UK sports. I also thought of the effort that I had put into this program, and all of the others who had sacrificed to improve Kentucky football. It was the pride we have for the program and this state. UK pride and an appreciation of SEC football swelled inside of me.

I was grateful to be in that moment. I was home. In My Old Kentucky Home!

At the time the teams entered the field, white shakers convulsed all over the stadium. The energy was tangible. Florida received the opening kickoff, and the crowd was ready for football. The Gators put together a few first downs before Kentucky ended the drive with an interception. The place went crazy. It was like when a coffee pot whistles as it lets off steam. The UK fans were releasing their excitement for the Cats to get the ball and attempt to score. They would have to wait to liberate that excitement as Kentucky fumbled the possession back to the Gators.

Florida used the field position to establish its offensive attack. The 31-yard drive ended with a touchdown pass to receiver Freddie Swain. Kentucky's offense retaliated with a 12-play drive that ate up 79 yards and the rest of the first quarter. Two plays into the second quarter, the Big Blue faithful were allowed to unleash a tremendous roar. Massive wide receiver Ahmad Wagner made an unbelievable catch in the end zone to tie the score at 7-7. The Florida offense again advanced into Kentucky's territory, but the Gators also repeated turning it over to the Cats. After regaining possession of the ball, the Wildcats used another double-digit play drive to reach the end zone again. The fans cheered exuberantly. They were feeling more confident that this was the UK team that they thought it could be.

The Gators got the ball back and set out to prove that they were worthy of their No. 8 ranking. UF drove down to the Kentucky 10, but would eventually have to settle for a field-goal attempt. The 27-yard field goal did not split the uprights and the fans were ecstatic with UK maintaining a 14-7 lead. The Wildcats' offense gained a few first downs and put itself in position to earn its own field-goal shot. After a couple incompletions, that hope was lost. The halftime lead would stay at seven.

The Cats opened the second half with a beautiful drive to advance inside Florida's 20-yard line. A penalty set UK back, but the drive was still promising. That was until an interception and 72-yard return flipped the script. Florida wasn't able to do much in the red zone against Kentucky's young defense and settled for three points. With its lead at 14-10, UK's offense was determined to correct the previous failure. The drive was much like the preceding one, but this time they would pierce the end zone. Florida was going to have to answer. The Gators marched inside UK's 40, where they faced a fourth-and-one. The failed attempt on fourth down gave the ball back to Kentucky. Unfortunately, Florida quarterback Feleipe Franks suffered a season-ending injury on the play.

Kentucky fans were feeling good about their chances. A 21-10 lead late in the third, with Florida relying on a backup quarterback who didn't have much experience. UK also had the ball. The Cats had crossed midfield as the third quarter ended. The flashlight and fireworks show between quarters stoked the crowd, as they hungered for a decisive score. Kentucky eventually faced a fourth down, and decided to test the Gators defense. Florida's defenders conquered the challenge. After the stop, Florida unleashed Kyle Trask at quarterback. He came out firing, completing multiple passes before running back Lamical Perine finished the scoring drive with a rushing touchdown. The failed two-point conversion attempt kept Kentucky's lead at 21-16.

Kentucky punter Max Duffy bombed a punt on the next possession that left Florida inside their 5-yard line. UF acquired some real estate through the air but eventually had to punt. Tommy Townsend's long punt left Kentucky starting at its own 8. It seemed like Kentucky's running game was primed to take over and exhaust the clock. That wasn't what unfolded. Florida picked off a long Kentucky throw to give them a chance to take the lead. Kentucky's defense attacked the challenge, but was a bit too aggressive, as two penalties put the Gators within striking distance. That strike came from Trask and went to tight end Kyle Pitts inside the 10. Florida scored two plays later to take the lead. Another thwarted two-point conversion left the Gators leading 22-21.

With just over four minutes to play, UK's offense set its sights on a scoring drive that would win the game. The running game was primed after all. The Cats used it with a few passes to move inside Florida's 20. The Gators defense made a huge stop on third-and-two to force a fourth down. With 58 seconds remaining, Kentucky used fourth down for a field-goal attempt. The kick couldn't find its way between the uprights, and Florida retained the lead. Kentucky tried to create a turnover, but Florida's Josh Hammond exploited that on third down. He raced 76 yards for a Gator touchdown. UK wasn't able to muster a score in the last 30 seconds, and the final score was Florida 29, Kentucky 21.

The Kentucky faithful was deflated. People quietly exited while the Gator fans triumphantly cheered. Some of the home fans tried to make sense of what just happened. It was a tough loss for sure, but that's the way it goes in the SEC. Only one team can win. It is the best thing in the world when you win, but equally as dejecting when you fall short. I stood in silence and observed the opposite demeanors of both teams' players. As other fans filed out, I waited for the UK Band to close the ceremony. My devotion was affirmed and my resolve restored as I affectionately consumed the band playing My Old Kentucky Home!

Kentucky Wildcats

Linebackers

Jerry Blanton
(1974-77)

Randy Holleran
(1987-88, 90)

Danny Trevathan
(2008-11)

Chris Chenault
(1985-88)

Jim Kovach
(1974-76, 78)

Dean Wells
(1989-92)

Wesley Woodyard
(2004-07)

Joe Federspiel
(1969-71)

Marty Moore
(1990-93)

Avery Williamson
(2010-13)

My favorite players to watch at other defensive positions:

DL - Josh Allen (2015-18)

DL - Oliver Barnett (1986-89)

DB - Melvin Johnson (1991-94)

DB - Ron Robinson (1986-89)

Quarterbacks

Tim Couch
(1996-98)

Pookie Jones
(1991-93)

Babe Parilli
(1949-51)

Billy Jack Haskins
(1995-96)

Jared Lorenzen
(2000-03)

Derrick Ramsey
(1975-77)

Andre' Woodson
(2004-07)

Stephen Johnson
(2016-17)

Rick Norton
(1963-65)

Bill Ransdell
(1983-86)

My favorite players to watch at other offensive positions:

RB - Moe Williams (1993-95)

WR - Randal Cobb (2008-10)

OL - Mike Pfeifer (1986-89)

TE - Jacob Tamme (2004-07)

*Fan Favorites: QB - Jared Lorenzen, QB - Tim Couch, RB - Benny Snell

5

IT'S GREAT TO BE A FLORIDA GATOR

Week of the September 21, 2019 game against Tennessee

The University of the State of Florida is what the school used to be named. That is appropriate because the University of Florida is the flagship institution in the state. The school was established in 1853 and began classes in Gainesville in 1906. Three years later, in 1909, the school officially became known as the University of Florida. The institute of higher learning has experienced growth ever since. It boasts an enrollment of over 56,000, and *U.S. News and World Report* currently ranks it the seventh best public university in the country. It is a top research university and one of the few schools nationally to hold the designation as a land grant, sea grant, and space grant university. There are many features and accomplishments to appreciate at the southernmost school in the Southeastern Conference.

The University of Florida served an undeniable role in the development of Gatorade. Florida football coach Ray Graves had asked for a solution to the heat and dehydration problems that his players faced. Robert Cade and Dana Shires led a team of scientists from the university in developing the first version of the formula. The early tests were done in 1965, when ten players were selected to consume the fluid during practices and games. During the subsequent seasons, Florida earned a reputation of being a second half team. Many people attributed it to the Florida team's use of the "Gator-Aid." Of course, its popularity grew from that point. The Gatorade formula was the pioneer of the sports drink industry. Stemming from a settlement almost 50 years ago, the University of Florida is reportedly still paid a portion of the royalties from the product.

Gatorade is definitely not the only contribution the university has had on college athletics. John J. Tigert, had an instrumental role in many things that changed the landscape of college sports. Tigert served as the U.S. Commissioner of Education under Presidents William Harding and Calvin Coolidge. During which, he was a vocal leader for national education reform. He left that post to assume the role of president of the University of Florida in 1928. Tigert was the third, and longest standing, president of the University of Florida. He had previously served as the president of Kentucky Wesleyan College at the age of 27. While at Florida, he helped guide the academic and athletic future of the university.

Tigert graduated from Vanderbilt University, playing football and becoming a Rhodes Scholar along the way. Tigert was later a professor at the University of Kentucky, where he also served as athletic director. During his time in Lexington, he also had stints as the head coach for the football team along with the men's and women's basketball teams. When he was the president at the University of Florida, he continued his enthusiasm for amateur sports. He spearheaded efforts to build Florida Field in 1930. To help oversee construction, he instituted the University Athletic Association. He was also an influential factor in founding the Southeastern Conference. In fact, it was Tigert who delivered the address announcing the schools defecting from the Southern Conference to form the new Southeastern Conference.

John J. Tigert served as the president of the SEC on two separate occasions. It was under his influence that the conference was moved to form a determined set of rules (mostly in regard to eligibility) that would govern the member institutions. Tigert was disgusted by the "under-the-table payments" to amateur athletes that seemed to be universal at that time. He led efforts to develop a method of granting scholarships to athletes, which is now mandated for today's NCAA members. Tigert made a huge impact on how athletics operate at Florida, in the Southeastern Conference and throughout the NCAA. John J. Tigert was inducted into the University of Florida Athletic Hall of Fame, and for his play at Vanderbilt, he was elected into the College Football Hall of Fame in 1970.

The University of Florida's Athletics Department has seen its share of success over the years. The Gators have finished seventh or higher in the Director's Cup standings every year since its inception during the 1993-94 school year. They are the only Division I program to finish in the top 10 of the national all-sports standings in each of the past 36 years. Florida owns 41 national team titles and sits 11th for the most among NCAA Division I programs. Gators claimed 315 national individual titles and is No. 5 nationally for NCAA individual titles. According to CoSIDA, Florida has the ninth most Academic All-Americans in Division 1 since 2000 and the seventh most all time in Division I college athletics. The University of Florida has proven that they have a commitment toward its student-athletes.

Who wouldn't want to go to class on that campus? It is a marvelous setting. The sun smiles on the campus practically every day. There are placid parks and peaceful

Florida, UF

School Colors:

Blue & Orange

Traditions:

Two Bits

Swaying to "We Are The Boys"

Singing "I Won't Back Down"

The Swamp

Gator Chomp

The Pride of the Sunshine

Fight Song - Orange and Blue

Jaws, Go Gators

Let's Go Gators

Favorite Battle Cries:

Go Gators

Gator Bait

green spaces filled with courtly trees of all kinds. Many of the trees have Spanish moss hanging off of them like strands of party lights dangling from the roof of a palapa. Brick-lined pathways lead you to some of the campus's more popular destinations. There are lakes, ponds and fountains that spring up throughout the grounds. It is southern, but in its own way. With the mix of various palm trees, I would call it "Tropical Southern." Overlooking all of it is the most iconic of landmarks on campus - the Century Tower.

The Century Tower reaches 157 feet into the air. The university built it in 1953 to commemorate the school's centennial year. The Century Tower serves as a memorial to the students and alumni that died during World War I and World War II. Century Tower casts a welcoming shadow over the many gabled roofs as its 61 bronze carillon bells sing to mark each quarter-hour. There is a great view of the tower in almost every direction, and its melody can be heard all through campus. Some of the students have the fortune of taking carillon lessons. They climb the 11 floors to the small room twice a day to play the piano-like setup. It is evident that the students have an affinity for the magnificent structure. The Century Tower has become a great symbol for the university. Many of the brochures and pamphlets for prospective students appropriately feature the Century Tower.

The Century Tower is just one part of the historic north campus. There is the beautiful dormitory complex adjacent to Ben Hill Griffin Stadium. Murphree Hall, Thomas Hall, Sledd Hall, Fletcher Hall and Buckman Hall all have fantastic views to wake to each day. There is the Plaza of the Americas surrounded by Griffin-Floyd Hall, Keene-Flint Hall, Anderson Hall, Smathers Library East and Peabody Hall. It is a wonderful area with plenty of mature trees and unbelievable architecture. Continuing east, the campus reveals more history with Matherly Hall and Bryan Hall. Just south of there one will find a great doorstep to the university. Tigert Hall is an eye-catching building in a picturesque area of campus. It really looks like a courthouse. Tigert Hall (named after UF's third president) serves as the institution's administration building.

These buildings are paired with many others to form this historic area of the 2,000 acre campus. Most of the buildings share many of the same traits--red brick with stone lintels and sills, gable roofs with clay tiles, and stone arch entrances. Not all do, and some of the newer buildings are unique, but this section of campus maintains a fairly uniform look. Walking through this part of campus feels like being in a small All-American community where everyone knows each other. One could leave Tigert Hall (the courthouse), walk down to the Plaza of the Americas (the town square) and talk to multiple people that will relay all the community happenings. From there, students and visitors could find anything they would need by just stepping into Smathers Library East (the general store).

Some are probably wondering why the library has a funny name with east on the end of it. That's because the University of Florida has nine libraries that I know about (maybe others that I don't know of). This particular one lies just east of Smathers Library West, which is newer and a very nice library. While on campus, I had an interview set up in a room in Smathers West. We almost missed the scheduled start time. The person was from out of town and had trouble finding which library to go to (his gps showed many libraries on campus). When he finally asked someone for Smathers West, they were able to direct him right to it. He found the correct floor and meeting room, and we were able to start the visit on time. The next problem was exiting the building. We left at different times, but met up again in the basement trying to find the way out. That's how many books are at UF. We had trouble getting out of just one library.

The next morning, I spent a good amount of time exploring the buildings around the Reitz Union Lawn. Naturally, the Reitz Union is the hub of activity around campus. One of the main attractions is the game room. They offer bowling, foosball, ping pong and pool tables. There always seemed to be students taking advantage of the amenities. The Reitz Union has an arts and crafts center, shopping, an art gallery, eateries, meeting rooms and a very cool amphitheatre. The bookstore and welcome center are attached to the southern end. There is even a hotel on the north end.

I wasn't about to inquire about the cost of a room on game weekends. I still had 11 more weeks on the road, so I needed to be as frugal as possible. The place was great though, and it would definitely be a convenient stay for athletic contests.

For the record, I did not see any live alligators, but there are definitely some around campus. Everyone that I asked nonchalantly confirmed the rumors. There are sightings all of the time. My "sources" told me that there is a gator in Reitz Pond, and that they have seen small gators walking across roads. Those sources also continually mentioned the west side of campus around Lake Alice and just south of there on Mowry Road. I didn't see any live gators, but I did see plenty of gator statues. They are on pedestals in courtyards, in the libraries and around Ben Hill Griffin Stadium. My favorite gator statue was the one dedicated to the 1996 national championship team. It sits at the end of the Gator Walk, and I think it looks the most menacing.

A lot of people prefer the "Bull Gator" that sits on the corner of Gale Lemerand Drive and Stadium Road, just outside of the football facility. Admittedly, it is a lot bigger, and I do have to come clean about my first sighting of that statue. I came up from the west side of the stadium past the Heisman Plaza. As I passed the player plaques and All-American stones, I was on the phone confirming an appointment. I kept walking past the bushes that shield the bull gator from the back. I didn't expect to see it, and it stopped me in my tracks. I don't know if anyone saw it, but I was startled. It was just a momentary pause, but it was enough to get me laughing at myself. Bull gators are the big ones, and this one was on its toes and ready to pounce. I'll have to admit that this gator statue is a good one, but I'll stay loyal to my first choice.

There is a lot to see in and around the stadium. The football facilities are located behind the Bull Gator, and the Stephen O'Connell Center (the O-

Dome) is across the street. A little ways east down Stadium Road, I walked up a large ramp to the backside of the stadium. The Florida Gymnasium and Rec Center is next to the stadium below that ramp. The stadium is open to joggers, stairs runners and walkers. I went on in to check it out.

It is a very nice stadium, but it was strange to see the field logos only have a white painted outline since it was still early in the week. There were blue seatbacks already in place all around the stadium. The blue seats under the press box had two separate sections of them painted orange to spell out "Florida". A level lower in the north end zone, the seats were orange with certain ones painted blue spelling out "Gators". The famed orange walls were fun to see again in person. Painted in blue was each corner's message:

➢ Northwest Corner - "SEC Champions" ...with the years listed underneath

➢ Northeast Corner - "This Is... GATOR COUNTRY"

➢ Southeast Corner - "National Champions" ...with the years listed underneath

➢ Southwest Corner - "This Is... THE SWAMP"

The press box is two levels and runs the length of the west sideline. I was pleased to see the giant letters at the top of the press box declare "Steve Spurrier - Florida Field."

Steve Spurrier is the most important single person to the history of success that the Gators have enjoyed. Hands down. Case closed. There is no argument. He won the Heisman Trophy as a player in 1966, and he coached the football team to its first national championship in 1996. That in itself would put him in the conversation. But, Steve Spurrier did much more than that for the Florida program. When he arrived as the head coach in 1990, the University of Florida football program was in turmoil. The two previous regimes had some wins, but both head coaches had been fired for rules violations. There was a feeling that Florida may not get over the hump to be a consistent winner. "The Head Ball Coach" was dead set on changing that. He was going to change the culture. No more dirty tactics. No more just decent seasons. And there was definitely not going to be anymore of the "three yards and a cloud of dust" offensive approach.

Coach Spurrier had just come from guiding Duke to an ACC title by putting the ball in the air. His teams were throwing more passes than about anyone in the country at that time. Spurrier told people that he was going to continue to do that at Florida. Many people, especially in the SEC, had doubts that it would work. He didn't care because he was confident in what the offense could do. Not only did they win, they posted huge numbers along the way. Florida was successful right away under Spurrier. He led the Gators to six SEC Championships in his 12 seasons. Prior to that, the Gators had won only one SEC crown (1984-which was later vacated). Coach Spurrier had Florida believing that they could not only win SEC titles every year, but also compete for national championships.

Steve Spurrier accomplished some things that few, if any, have ever achieved. He became the only person in history to win a Heisman Trophy and also coach a Heisman winner (Danny Wuerffel -1996). Coach Spurrier's 208 victories (at Florida and South Carolina) still rank him second all time for SEC coaching victories. Steve Spurrier is one of two people (Paul Bryant) to be the winningest coach in program history at multiple SEC schools. He is also only the fourth major college person to be inducted into the College Hall of Fame as a player (1986) and a coach (2017).

Coach Spurrier won games at Florida, but he did more than that. He proved to Gator fans that Florida could be a winner. He made the SEC and the rest of the country believe in the power of the Gators.

I came back out of the stadium at the point I entered because I didn't want to miss anything. On the north side of the stadium is where the Gator Walk converges with my favorite gator statue. It is right in front of the Letterman's Association. There is the Gator SportShop to the left at Gate 9. Walking toward the west side of the stadium, the Lee Chira Family Heisman Plaza features statues of all three of Florida's Heisman Trophy winners (Steve Spurrier-1966, Danny Wuerrfel-1996, and Tim Tebow-2007). Continuing on, there are plaques dedicated to some of Florida football's best players that are adhered to the brick facade. Some notable players are Jack Youngblood, Wilbur Marshal, and Emmitt Smith.

I continued past entrances to the Athletic Administration offices and reached the area with the Bull Gator. There are stones placed in the bricks to recognize every Florida player that has been awarded All-American honors. The entrance to the football facility is behind there, with a plaque containing the words of "The Promise" adorning the wall. The promise was what Tim

Tebow made after an upset loss to Ole Miss in 2008. The Gators were the overwhelming favorite to win the national championship. They fell to Ole Miss 31-30 on September 27, 2008. In the post game press conference, Tebow made this statement that is displayed on the plaque:

THE PROMISE

"To the fans and everybody in Gator Nation, I'm sorry.

I'm extremely sorry. We were hoping for an undefeated season. That was my goal, something that Florida has never been done here.

I promise you one thing, a lot of good will come out of this. You will never see any player in the entire country play as hard as I will play the rest of the season. You will never see someone push the rest of the team as hard as I will push everybody the rest of the season.

You will never see a team play harder than we will the rest of the season.

God Bless."

Tebow made good on the promise as Florida won the rest of their games by double-digits. They won the SEC Championship over No. 1 Alabama and the national championship over Oklahoma (24-14), who featured the highest-scoring offense in the history of college football at the time. It is an entertaining place for any football fan, as the places around the stadium are filled with college football history.

From that area, I walked across the street, past the O-Dome, and down to Perry Field, which is the baseball facility. I noticed the team taking batting practice as I perused McKethan Stadium. A new football training facility will replace the stadium when it is razed after the 2020 baseball season. The baseball team will play in a new stadium being built on the southwest part of campus (scheduled to begin play there in 2021). The football training facility will finally be adjacent to the practice fields that are just north of the current baseball stadium. When I exited the baseball stadium, I was in a corridor that separated the baseball facilities from the football practice location. I watched some of football practice from a perch under the shadow of McKethan Stadium.

On Friday morning, I was on University Avenue across from the stadium. I was in front of Emerson Alumni Hall, where they gave away "Beat Tennessee" t-shirts. It has become a tradition for the University Alumni Association to give out the "beat t-shirts" for the biggest games of the year. Apparently this was the first game to do this in 2019. It was only for students with an ID, so I didn't wait in line for one. I went back across University Avenue and talked with a lady preparing tailgate spots.

Setting up tailgate spots for groups has become a big business. This lady secured the spots from UF and leased them to groups looking for a celebration point before the game. She took care of it all from the decorations to the catering. It has become a booming business in the last few years. The Tailgate Guys are one of the biggest and most well-known tailgating companies in the Southeast. They already

Ben Hill Griffin Stadium

Steve Spurrier - Florida Field

AKA – "The Swamp"

Surface: Grass

Built in 1930

Capacity: 88,548

Record Attendance: 90,916 - 11/28/15 vs Florida State

Nickname: Gators

Mascot: Costumed - Albert and Alberta Gator

*Fans' Favorite Home Games:

Won 32-29 over Florida St in 1997

Won 62-37 over Tennessee in 1995

had tents and chairs in place just about 50 yards away. Up and down Gator Walk were the familiar white tents that the Tailgate Guys use to reserve the party locations. The durable tents and unique signs announcing the tailgate title were easily recognizable.

I continued down University Drive into downtown Gainesville. There are restaurants, shops and bars lining University Avenue all the way into downtown. It was obvious that game day was nearing because there were people everywhere. These areas were buzzing during the week, but now it was like a festival was underway. After milling around for a while, I made my way back to campus. I went south at 34th Street and cut across campus near Gator Pond. I went past the Aquatic Science Building and onto the Reitz Union lawn to discover more construction for pre-game festivities. I continued across to Fraternity Drive where I noticed that the partying had already begun.

I completed the roundabout and joined a friend (who does work for UF) down on Stadium Drive. After the team left for the hotel, we met up with the equipment guys (Tyler and Jake) to get a tour of the football facility. In the equipment room, I saw something that I didn't expect. There were a couple Gator helmets that were burned and had been encased in a display. The equipment truck had caught fire coming back from a road game against Mississippi State (coach Dan Mullen's return to Starkville) in 2018. The fire burned a lot of the gear and melted much of the rest. Those helmets were scarred, but they were about the only things left (the uniforms went on the plane and avoided the fire). The equipment staff had to work around the clock to re-outfit the team for a nationally televised home game less than seven days from having all of its equipment destroyed. They were able to get it done, and the team did too. The Gators beat LSU 27-19 in the next game while using new and borrowed equipment.

We saw the weight room, meeting rooms and the locker room (complete with the new LED lighting system). We also witnessed the different displays commemorating acclaimed Gator players and teams. I saw championship rings from the three national championship years (1996, 2006, & 2008). We gathered around the same gator head that the team does before it enters the "Swamp." I was able to walk through the tunnel to see the logos on the playing surface completed with orange and blue paint. I thanked Tyler and Jake for their hospitality and wished them luck.

On Friday night, I went all around SW Archer and SW 34th Street. There were plenty of activities and a lot of people in town for the game. It took over an hour to be seated at the Bonefish Grill. It was worth the wait. I joined a few couples that had met up from different cities across the state of Florida. These trips have become the few times that they see each other all year. It's good for them to hang out together, but they were also excited to come watch the Gators play in the Swamp. After dinner was over, it was time to find a place to celebrate their fandom. The revelry that took place rivaled anything the college kids had going on.

Saturday morning came early. I regularly show up way before game time, but this time was tough. Not because of the night before, but because it was a noon kickoff. I woke up, showered, and was on my way at 5:30 am. I felt like I would be pushing it because, at best, I would be parked a mere six hours before game time. It turned out that I parked at 5:53 am, mostly because the roads were fairly clear. Most people had not shown up yet.

Would six hours be enough to do everything that I needed to? The good news was that I didn't have to find a ticket. Either way, it was still a pretty early morning whether the kickoff was at noon or not.

During my journey, I learned that many of the fan bases are pretty set on the times that they want their team's games to be scheduled. While I was in Gainesville, it was obvious that no one liked having the game at noon. At the time, it seemed like everyone hoped for the 3:30 pm time slot on CBS. People even explained how it allowed them ample time to tailgate. They could go watch the Gators play, and then they could catch the night games when they made it home. It sounded like a solid plan to me. Maybe they were just used to the Gators playing Tennessee on CBS. The result was that no one was thrilled with it starting at noon.

Since that week, many of the Gator fans I talked to said that they don't mind the 3:30 pm CBS game (especially considering the stakes that would be involved), but their ultimate preference would be a night game at Steve Spurrier-Florida Field. Their reason for demoting the 3:30 ET window was because the swamp can be very hot and humid during the day (especially early in the season). It's not as bad after the sun goes down, but they also like the late game best because the Swamp comes alive at night. In their recollections, the loudest games at Ben Hill Griffin Stadium have been at night.

As darkness gave way to twilight, I was helping my hosts setup the tailgate area. They had a Florida Gators tent and a great converted trailer to carry all of the supplies. It was white with pledges of gator fandom plastered all around it. There was an orange and blue SEC logo along with the "Pell Logo" that split the front surface area. One side had a huge Florida Gator emblem. The door on that side had the state of Florida in blue with an orange outline. Underneath the state outline were the words "WE'LL all stick together ... FOR FLORIDA". The window on the other side was open for the TV, so I didn't see what was painted on it. The back doors had a blue and orange striped tie on one side, while the other said "ALL for the GATORS stand up and HOLLER"

The graphics on the back doors alluded to "Mr. Two Bits." George Edmondson Jr. was Florida's Mr. Two Bits. It all started when he attended a home football game in 1949. The Florida team was having a rough patch, and the fans began to boo. Mr. Edmonson wasn't fond of booing, and he wanted to help boost the crowd's morale. From his seat, he led a cheer about bits (two bits is a quarter of a dollar). The infamous cheer says "Two bits, four bits, six bits, a dollar; all for the Gators, stand up and holler!" Florida won the game, and the cheer caught on with the fans. Edmondson returned the next week, and it started to become a tradition.

Edmondson soon started leaving his seat and leading the cheer at spots around the stadium. The fans enjoy it so much that, at one point in the 1970's, the university asked Edmondson to start leading the cheer from the field. He continued to do supplemental performances in sections around the stadium, and he always wore his "uniform." His attire was a yellow long-sleeved, button-down shirt, with a blue and orange striped tie, atop blue and white seersucker pants and saddle shoes. It was what he wore that day, and he continued wearing throughout the years. He performed the duty until he retired from it following the 1998 season. Mr. Two Bits would lead the cheer from his seat until he was persuaded to once again do it from the field.

Mr. Two Bits' finale came at the end of the last game in 2008 after 60 seasons! Since 2013, the University Athletic Association has invited special guests to come back to the Swamp to lead the beloved cheer. Edmondson was thrilled to see famous people want to emulate him. In July of 2019, Edmondson passed away. His family was dignified with the honor of leading "Two-bits" before the first home game in 2019, as well as running out with the team. Many people in the stadium wore yellow t-shirts adorned with an orange and blue tie. My friend hosting the tailgate (Travis) told me stories of how he would randomly hear a certain section start going wild. "We'd all look at each other and say, it has to be Mr. Two Bits," he fondly recalled.

Most everything was now in place, and the cooking began. I had a small window before game time, so I had to head toward the stadium. There was already a collection of people tailgating. I had a short early interview and went exploring. I found an old school bus with loads of Gator spirit. I saw the Tennessee band followed by Smokey. People were walking around observing things like they were on a boardwalk in Destin. Kids ran around tossing the pigskin. I made my way back over to the tailgate, had a quick bite to eat and something to wash it down. I spent some time talking with Travis and some other guests. I had to get rolling, so Travis and I made plans to meet back up in the stadium.

I made it over to Gator Walk just in time to see the spectacle as the players turned off University Avenue. Remember, it was between 9:45-10:00 am, so it was still mid-morning. Yet, there was a substantial and lively crowd. After the Gator Walk, there was the "Parade of Champions." It was "Champions Weekend" where UF honors past championship teams that are having reunions. Those teams are honored during the game, but now they are also part of the Parade of Champions, which follows the Gator Walk. I went across the street to the parking lot next to the indoor facility and stopped by a few more entertaining gatherings. I migrated up to the O'Connell Center (where they were hosting a volleyball tournament) and then made my way across the street and into the stadium.

I was pleased to learn that my seat would be the first row above one of the famed orange walls. Appropriately, it was the one stating SEC Champions. I couldn't help but notice that the group of flags around the top of the stadium contained representation of all the schools in the Southeastern Conference. The University of Florida Fightin' Gator Marching Band (The Pride of the Sunshine) was already in full swing. The crowd was already into it as well. When the time came to yell "Go Gators," I was impressed with the ferocity of the crowd's responses. I was also impressed by the precision of "The Pride of the Sunshine" as they formed into the shape of Florida and then the script Gators. It was a moving moment when everyone stood to proudly state the Pledge of Allegiance before singing the National Anthem.

Travis was finally able to make it in after cleaning up the tailgate area. He introduced me to the people we sat beside in our row. Mr. Charles and his daughter were to our right. Charles Hollingsworth has been going to Gator football games for almost 70 years! He is 90 years old and works in agriculture. He started working a little less when he hurt his back ... a whopping three years ago when he was a spry 87-year- old. His daughter loves being at the games too, and she is pleased to be able to help her father attend. As the big screen shows the Gator players converge around the gator head in the locker room area, the band and cheerleaders are followed by nearly 90,000 in doing "The Chomp." The crowd is whipped into a frenzy with the help of a video, and the Florida Gators take the field through a tunnel of white twirling flags emblazoned with the Florida Gator logo.

The Gators started out strong when they received the opening kickoff and proceeded to go 75 yards in five plays for the game's first touchdown. Tennessee converted its first third down of the day with a long completion to receiver Jauan Jennings. After a penalty, UT didn't do enough for another first down and had to punt. The teams traded turnovers before Florida put together another decent drive. The drive ended when UF failed to convert a fourth down at Tennessee's 30. The first quarter finished with the Gators leading 7-0, but UT had the ball.

A few plays into the second quarter, Tennessee quarterback Jarrett Guarantano threw his second interception of the game. Florida drove inside the 10-yard line, but had to settle for a field goal. Each team's defense picked up the pace, forcing punts on the next couple of possessions. When the Gators received the ball back with about five minutes to play in the half, they were determined not to give it back to Tennessee. They did not. Florida's possession moved down to the 1-yard line. Facing a fourth down at the 1, with only two seconds on the clock, Dan Mullen decide to go for the touchdown. The next play saw the Gators reach the end zone, expire the clock and take a 17-0 halftime lead into the locker room.

I sat and talked to Mr. Charles during halftime and most of the third quarter. He is an inspiring guy with great stories. I heard about him and a friend climbing the fence to watch Gator games when they "were just kids." He explained how the tops of the orange walls used to be the top of the stadium. Mr. Charles is a fabulous example of a long-standing loyal SEC fan. As we talked, Tennessee put a drive together that resulted in a field goal. Florida abruptly answered with a touchdown drive. That meant that I wasn't bad luck, and Mr. Charles didn't have to send me back to my seat just yet. The rest of the third quarter was turnover after turnover for both teams. It became comical to our section, as people wondered aloud if anyone wanted possession of the ball. I finally made it back to my seat, as the third quarter was about to end.

One of Florida's most cherished traditions is when the band plays "We Are the Boys" at the end of the third quarter. Everyone in the stands throws their arms around each other and sways back and forth as they sing the old tune. It isn't an intense sway. It is more like a "blowing in the wind" sway. It's a good time, party-like environment that continues with the very next song.

Playing Tom Petty's "I Won't Back Down" is UF's newest tradition. People sing along as they continue the party. It's like being at a concert without the lighters. Tom Petty is a favorite son of Gainesville, and UF has embraced his legacy since his death in 2017.

Midway through the fourth quarter, they play "Free-Fallin'" and the party continues. People sing loudly to it ... oh, wait. Is there a game still going on? Yes, there is, but it's not as entertaining as the fans (and definitely not as interesting as Mr. Charles). It was a good fourth quarter for the Gators. Florida's offense was pretty consistent with a couple of nice scoring drives.

Meanwhile, Tennessee was never able to gain much traction against a very good Florida defense. The final Score was Florida 34, Tennessee 3.

I like to hang around the stadium for a little bit after the games. The Florida fans vacated the area quicker than most on this day. There were people cleaning up around the stadium almost immediately. I walked around the concourse taking in the different scenes. I would periodically step out to the stands to soak in the views from a distinct location. At one point, I found myself directly across the field from where I sat during the game.

The stadium was quiet and close to being empty. It looked nearly identical to when I walked in at the beginning of the week. But, it felt different. The sunbeams shot through the clouds and over the top of the press box. I thought about the week that I had. I thought about the gorgeous campus and all of the success in this stadium. I thought about the convincing win just minutes earlier and the number of people who soaked it into their souls. My thoughts settled on one repetitive theme: "It's Great to be a Florida Gator!"

Florida Gators

Defensive Backs

Matt Elam
(2010-12)

Joe Haden
(2007-09)

Vernon Hargreaves III
(2013-15)

Reggie Nelson
(2005-06)

Louis Oliver
(1985-88)

Keiwan Ratliff
(2000-03)

Lito Sheppard
(1999-2001)

Fred Weary
(1994-97)

Will White
(1989-92)

Jarvis Williams
(1984-87)

My favorite players to watch at other defensive positions:

LB - Wilbur Marshall (1980-83)   DL - Jevon Kearse (1996-98)

LB - Brandon Spikes (2006-09)   DL - Huey Richardson (1987-90)

Wide Receivers

Reidel Anthony
(1994-96)

Wes Chandler
(1974-77)

Cris Collinsworth
(1977-80)

Jabar Gaffney
(2000-01)

Jacquez Green
(1995-97)

Percy Harvin
(2006-08)

Ike Hilliard
(1994-96)

Jack Jackson
(1992-94)

Willie Jackson
(1991-93)

Ricky Nattiel
(1983-86)

My favorite players to watch at other offensive positions:

RB - Neal Anderson (1982-85)   OL - Lomas Brown (1981-84)

RB - Emmitt Smith (1987-89)   QB - Rex Grossman (2000-02)

*Fan Favorites: QB - Tim Tebow, QB - Danny Wuerffel, RB - Emmitt Smith

6

HERE'S A HEALTH, CAROLINA

Week of September 28, 2019 game against Kentucky

As I traveled north from Gainesville on Sunday, I stopped by Jacksonville International Airport to pick up my wife. Nora had taken vacation to accompany me during a week of my journey. Our plan was for her to join me for the Florida-Tennessee game as well, but weather disrupted the flight schedule. We spent time in Savannah, Georgia before heading to Charleston, South Carolina. We had a mini-vacation in Charleston and left for Columbia on Tuesday morning.

Charleston is a charming southern city. Nora and I enjoyed exploring the Lowcountry. We discovered the Cathedral of Saint John the Baptist, visited The Citadel and Charleston Southern University and walked around the Charleston Harbor Marina. On Sullivan's Island, we witnessed some fantastic and eccentric homes. I parked near the lighthouse, and we walked to the beach. For some reason, it reminded me of the beach scene in the movie *Wedding Crashers*, although there were a few more people. It was a very peaceful and serene setting.

On our way back into Charleston, we stopped in Mount Pleasant and had an early dinner at Saltwater Cowboys. It was a great choice that provided us with a delectable meal and a terrific waterfront view. The timing was perfect because we had plenty of daylight to tour the unique neighborhood of Rainbow Row. From there, we traversed a cobblestone road down to

Waterfront Park. As the sun was setting, we had our picture taken in front of the Pineapple Fountain.

We arrived at the University of South Carolina to find a great deal of activity. USC is a public research university with an on-campus enrollment exceeding 35,000. The school boasts 56 nationally ranked programs. Nineteen of those ranked programs are in health sciences, including a No. 1 ranking for the Ph.D. program in Exercise Science. There is a top ten ranked hotel, restaurant and tourism management program, and a social psychology graduate program that is ranked fourth nationally. *Public University Press* declared the South Carolina Honors College as the nation's best public university honors program.

USC is a sea grant institution that is known to have very high levels of research activity. In fact, the Carnegie Foundation recognized the University of South Carolina with its top-tier designation for both Research and Community Engagement. South Carolina is ranked in the top-five percent of U.S. public universities in the number of national awards its faculty has received. The University of South Carolina has had at least one Fulbright Scholar in each of the last 18 years and one or more Goldwater Scholars for 27 consecutive years. *Kiplinger, Forbes,* and *U.S. News* all consider South Carolina a best value public university.

The university was founded in 1801. The Rutledge Building, completed in 1805, was the first structure on campus. Rutledge sits next to the president's house on the Horseshoe, which is the quad where the original campus was built. It oozes with history and drips with charm. The Horseshoe is a peaceful locale that lies beneath a range of towering elm and oak trees. The u-shaped brick path escorts you through the history of USC's original campus. Ten of its 11 buildings were built in the 19th century, and all ten of those are listed on the National Register of Historic Places. Many of the buildings on the Horseshoe exhibit federal-style architecture.

That style of architecture was because of South Carolina native Robert Mills, who was the nation's first federal architect. Mills designed the original campus and many of its buildings. His designs can be found all around east coast states. The majority of his most well-known projects are in Washington D.C. He developed the designs for the U.S. Patent Office Building, General Post Office, The Smithsonian American Art Museum and the Department of Treasury Building. Although it wasn't his first use of an obelisk, Mills' most famous work is the Washington Monument.

The first known instance of Mills using the pylon-type design is the Maxcy Monument, which sits in the center of the Horseshoe in honor of the school's first president. Another of Mills' creations is the South Caroliniana Library; that sits on the western corner of the Horseshoe. Its second floor reading room is an exact replica of the original reading room of the Library of Congress. The South Caroliniana Library is the oldest freestanding academic library in the United States. Unfortunately, we weren't able to enter the building because it was under renovation.

We walked through the gates of the Horseshoe and headed southeast on Sumter Street. After you pass the

South Carolina, Carolina, USC

School Colors:

Garnet & Black

Traditions:

Cockaboose Railroad

The Entrance to "2001"

Sandstorm

Rooster Crow After a Touchdown

"Game" and "Cocks" Chant

Mighty Sound of the Southeast

Fight Song - The Fighting Gamecocks Lead The Way

Step To The Rear

We Hail Thee Carolina

Favorite Battle Cries:

Go Cocks

Get Cocky

Journalism School, you come upon Longstreet Theatre. The building was completed in 1855 and looks like a Roman temple. It was intended to be a chapel although it was never used for that purpose. During the Civil War, it was used as a hospital and a morgue. Longstreet Theatre is now the nucleus of the Arts Department at the University of South Carolina. When we went inside, we found the theater in-the-round being situated for the next performance.

The history of Columbia was forever shaped by the Civil War. It seems like everywhere you go there is a surviving structure, replacement, or monument stemming from the conflict. U.S. General William Sherman was not the kindest to the region. During our first day in Columbia, we came across three major references to the Civil War attacks and fires ordered by Sherman. One was at the Horseshoe itself. The story goes that the Horseshoe was spared because it served as medical facilities for both the Union and Confederate sides. It is thought that since Sherman didn't know which side each one served, he refrained from burning any of them. It is also theorized that the stone wall surrounding the Horseshoe is the only thing that kept the fires from penetrating.

A second mention was downtown at the Basilica of Saint Peter on Assembly Street. The original building of the Catholic church was designed by Robert Mills and completed in 1824. The Parish housed an order of nuns on the premises during the Civil War. Legend has it that Sherman had a sister who was a nun. He wasn't sure if she was stationed there or not, so he left the church unharmed. That building remained until 1906 when a new church replaced it. The new Saint Peter's is 113 years old (2019), and it was included on the National Register of Historic Places in 1989.

That evening, we went to the South Carolina Statehouse. The capitol building is a mighty and dignified structure. There are sporadic bronze stars at odd points around the outside of the building. I was informed that the stars mark the places where Sherman ordered cannon fire against the statehouse. A handed-down account says that he and his troops couldn't cross the Congaree River because weeks of rain had washed out the bridge. His men went to work rebuilding the bridge, but Sherman ran out of patience. He ordered a cannon assault from across the river, and the spots that were hit are where the stars are today.

The South Carolina Statehouse grounds is really a great place to visit. There is a ton of history, but it's also a gorgeous setting. There is a wooded area that lies next to Assembly Street and the statehouse faces Gervais Street. Many statues and monuments grace the entire area. There is the exquisite plaza honoring law enforcement officers who were killed in the line of duty. The significant African American History Monument depicts the journeys of the enslaved. The artistic Palmetto Regiment Memorial venerates South Carolinians who fought in the Mexican-American War. There are statues of George Washington, Strom Thurmond and James F. Byrnes. All types of people were jogging, taking pictures and just hanging out around the capital building. It encompassed many efficacious aspects that represent South Carolina.

The next morning, we parked in the parking garage at Cregger Athletic Village. We walked down a path that took us to the track facility that borders Rosewood Drive. On the way back, we were afforded a second look at the softball stadium, the tennis center, and the rare beach volleyball facility. The raised walkway runs between those fields and the Roost Athletic Training Center. It continues back toward the courtyard where two impressive buildings welcome you to the Athletic Village.

The Rice Athletic Center is an impressive building with plenty of windows that was built in 2012. It is the home of many Gamecock sports, and it also houses the athletic administration. There are displays throughout the building that characterize USC sports. The building contains the grand Gamecock gallery that chronicles the history and passion of USC Athletics. A good portion of the Gamecock gallery is visible from the courtyard, and there is also a good view of the similarly impressive Dodie Anderson Academic Enrichment Center. The Dodie opened in 2010 and has been a boon to the academic success of the student-athletes at South Carolina. With computer labs, tutor rooms, study lounges and a full-service kitchen, everything is in place for academic achievement.

We walked northwest between Stone Stadium (soccer) and the fieldhouse, continuing past the band's practice field and the challenge course. Our path took us alongside the Blatt P.E. Center on Wheat Street where we saw a food truck titled "The Coop" with USC's mascot (Cocky) painted on the side. We angled through the South and East Quads, admiring the aesthetic quality of both residential complexes.

Crossing over Blossom Street, we navigated the wooded incline behind Patterson Hall. It brought us back around to Bull Street, which led us to the Melton Observatory. The astronomical observatory was built in 1928 and is available for both students and public use. Just around the corner, you will find a statue of Cocky sitting on a bench. It's a popular place, right outside of Davis College, where students like to take pictures. We upheld the tradition before resuming our self-guided tour.

The stroll through Gibbes Green was refreshing. The thick foliage is a continuation of the wooded area in the Horseshoe that sits just around the corner. It was nice having cover from the intense sun. What was even nicer was walking into the heavenly air-conditioned McKissick Museum. Sitting at the head of the Horseshoe, McKissick serves many purposes. Along with being a gem of a museum, it also works as a research facility and a welcome center for visitors.

Going down the left side of the Horseshoe, the breeze and the trees helped us gradually re-acclimate to the heat. We passed by the president's house. It is really neat to see a building with so much history look so well-maintained. There was a huge tent going up on the lawn of the Horseshoe that would eventually be the site of the president's tailgate for the week's Family Weekend celebration.

We stopped briefly for lunch and then joined the human traffic on the way down the incline on College Street. Following it past the School of Music, we eventually ran into Lincoln Street. That is where we found Colonial Life Arena, where the basketball teams play. It has a gorgeous front plaza and lobby. We weren't able to see much more of it because they were preparing the arena for a concert. We had to settle for feeling the cool mist from the outdoor fountain and headed up Greene Street toward the Darla Moore School of Business.

The Moore School is the crown jewel of academic centers on campus. The business program was celebrating its centennial year (started in 1919), and there is no better place to do it than the innovative new home that was completed in 2014. We were fortunate to get a tour of the remarkable facility. The building contains many sustainable features like the over 23,000-square-foot green roof that includes two stunning glass roof-top pavilions. All of the green features assisted the building in being awarded the LEED Platinum certification.

It contains resources like the W.W. Hootie Johnson Performance Hall, which is centered around a number of classrooms and lecture halls. It also contains the

Williams-Brice Stadium

AKA – "the Cockpit"

Surface: Grass

Built in 1934

Capacity: 80,250

Record Attendance: 85,199 - 10/6/12 vs Georgia

Nickname: Gamecocks

Mascot:

Costumed - Cocky

Live - Sir Big Spur

*Fans' Favorite Home Games:

Won 35-21 over Alabama in 2010

Won 30-22 over Florida in 2005

Sonoco Pavilion and a full-service cafe. My favorite aspect of the Darla Moore was the Dr. Olin S Pugh Trading Room. The study room has a live stock ticker ribbon board running around the top of it. After seeing the resources in the building, it was no surprise to learn that USC's undergraduate and graduate international business programs rank tops in the country. *U.S. News and World Report* has ranked the International MBA program in the top three of graduate international business programs in the United States for 30 consecutive years.

The clear sky let the sun reign down on us again Thursday. The Torch Bearer statue in front of Wardlaw was a popular gathering spot for students. At the Journalism school across the street, students were focused on their tasks at hand. I was amazed at the concentration of students in classrooms with glass walls. We went over to the old parade grounds that are now an oasis with a large pool and fountain leading to the Thomas Cooper Library. We walked to the rear and through a corridor to the Hollings Special Collections Library. Inside were special exhibits that displayed old comic strips and the history of South Carolina politics.

We saw a bigger presence of families who had arrived early for the Family Weekend festivities. They walked up and down Greene Street, which had the atmosphere of a town festival. The street featured a gigantic Gamecock logo painted on the asphalt. We stood next to the Tree of Knowledge while a steady stream of families popped in and out of the university bookstore. It was a joyous scene as families treasured the quality time together.

During our journey that afternoon, we learned about a popular entertainment district called The Vista. For a long time, Columbia entertainment has been associated with the Five Points area. That area is still around. Some of the students and locals that we talked to said that Five Points has turned mainly into a college party scene. We were advised to visit The Vista and Motor Supply Company Bistro on Gervais Street.

When we finally did make it down there, it supplied us with a variety of establishments for dining and entertainment. Many museums call the district home, highlighted by the South Carolina State Museum. There was live music, art galleries, clothing stores, and lodging choices. There was also no shortage of places to have a great meal or a refreshing drink. I didn't recognize anyone in particular, but it felt as if many of the families from earlier joined us down at The Vista. It was very lively from the time we arrived until we left a few hours later.

Friday was a full day of touring the football facilities. We were fortunate to find parking on Berea Road just southeast of the stadium. We crossed over to Gamecock Park. This area used to be the Farmer's Market, and it has been transformed into a park-like setting that is a premier tailgate spot for Gamecock football games. The tree-lined 50-acre green space can accommodate over three thousand vehicles on game days. The area offers shaded tent zones, cable TV hookups, electrical outlets and four permanent restroom buildings. It's also where the cheerleaders, football team and marching band parade though on their way to the stadium.

The Jerri and Steve Spurrier Indoor Practice Facility caps the western end of Gamecock Park. It contains a full synthetic football field that bears the same markings as those on the field at Williams-Brice Stadium. At 111,000-square-feet, it is one of the largest indoor football facilities in the nation, as well as one of the very few that are air conditioned. It opened in 2015 and butts up to the southern edge of the outdoor practice fields. The Spurrier Indoor Practice Facility is impressive inside and out. Game days deliver multitudes of fans that want to tour the inside and take pictures in front of its entrance.

Right next door is the Cyndi and Kenneth Long Family Football Operations Center. The new home of Gamecock football opened in January of 2019. It is a spacious state-of-the-art facility with many mentions of the history and accomplishments of South Carolina football. The weight room, equipment room and training room are all massive and functional. The players also have the benefit of having a barber shop, players lounge, hydro pools and even the Darius Rucker Gamecock Studio (music studio). It also contains an impressive recruiting area and coaches' offices that overlook the practice field.

From the front of the Football Operations Center, there is a fantastic view of Williams-Brice Stadium. The stadium has been home to the Gamecocks since 1934 and has made appearances in multiple movies. The unique configuration of the overhead lights makes it one of the most recognizable stadiums in college football. The inside of the stadium is full of distinctive markings of USC. Most notably is the view of the ramps in all four corners. From inside the stadium, the ramps announce the names and accolades of the best players and coaches in USC history.

The natural grass playing surface is very well kept, and the emblems were receiving a final coat of paint before the game. The outer edge of the field had a thick block of color that alternated from garnet to white. On the south end was the locker room. The automatic sliding glass doors open up to an elegant lobby area. The space is filled with pictures of past Gamecock greats. A lighted dome shines down on a very well crafted statue of a fighting gamecock. Jerseys were being hung in spacious lockers as the dressing room was being prepped for the next day's big event.

Saturday was going to be a long, hot, all-day affair, so it was key to find a good parking spot. I went early to try and find a spot on Berea Road. Even though it was only 10:00 am, there wasn't one spot to be had. I did a loop around Williams-Brice Stadium and drove down Key Road. Across a fenced field, I spotted a UK tent. I figured that it wasn't permit parking if the visiting fans were there. It was worth a try to see what was available. I made it back out to Bluff Road, went toward the stadium and took a right on Eden Street.

Thankfully, it was the correct road. Eden Street wrapped around to where the Kentucky fans were set up. We pulled up and asked them about the location. It was an area that offered free parking, and the couple suggested parking on the other side of their tent. It was perfect. I could see the stadium, which was about a half a mile away. I felt comfortable having my vehicle parked next to an active tailgate that would watch out for its security.

Sherman and Olivia are actually residents of Charleston, South Carolina. The UK grads moved to Rock Hill for work and eventually settled in Charleston. It has become a tradition for them to travel up to Columbia when the Wildcats visit. They host the temporary tailgate and invite a circle of friends. Sherman presented his infamous concoction that would be served throughout the day. As the sun beat down on us, we continued introductions over the refreshing beverage.

Nora and I grabbed a couple bottles of frozen water and set off toward the stadium. South Carolina fans were arriving all around us. Across George Rogers Boulevard, the State Fairgrounds were filling up quickly. There were already cars and tents all over the long-time tailgate destination. Flags flew throughout the lot, including some SEC flags. We kept walking around the stadium until we were across from Gamecock Park. After finally making it across Bluff Road, we felt the buzz of activity as we reached the plaza entrance.

It was a great family atmosphere. Sponsor booths and tents were on either side of the entrance to the promenade. There were inflatable castles and obstacle courses for the kids to play. Thick block letters spelled out "Game" and "Cocks" so people could stand between them for a memorable picture. In the middle of the plaza sat a mobile bar where adults could get a drink and watch football games on televisions hanging from the ceiling. We walked down to the Spurrier Indoor Facility. A vast field of tailgaters lined the horizon. Many of the tailgates around the walkway were getting into the college football games being televised. Guests from other parts of the country had their Gamecock hosts rooting for other teams to attain victory. Everyone treated each other like teammates where the team's only objective was to conquer a good time. They seemed to be making significant progress toward that goal.

We came back up toward the stadium and decided to make a trip back to my truck for more water. When we arrived, we found that Sherman and Olivia had been joined by a number of new friends. It was a fun scene filled with all of the quintessential tailgate activities. Nora and I were even recruited to join a co-ed cornhole tournament. Sadly, neither one of us did very well. It was probably good we hung around a little while because we needed a break from the sun. It was a hot day and the sun was intense. It felt like there wasn't a single cloud that dared to block the stare of the sun that went right through you.

I had a cool moment at that tailgate. I personally met a fan of one of my books. She is an avid reader, and she had received a recommendation for my publication. I was able to personally sign a copy for her. She doesn't pay attention to football and was just there to visit her friends. What a small world. Of all places, we ran into a fan on a side street tailgate party, in South Carolina, for an event that she doesn't even follow. I appreciated the moment. I was more excited about that than if they would've put my book title on the screen in front of 80,000 people at Williams-Brice. Well, maybe. I guess that I would have to see it up there to know for sure.

I made certain that I had the tickets when we left because we weren't planning on coming back before the game. We went over to the northwest corner of the stadium to talk with George Rogers. He sets up a tent and meets with Gamecock fans in front of his statue on game days. He has been doing that outside the stadium for years. Now, he meets fans in conjunction with USC to provide a better game day experience for the fans. When the statue was unveiled in 2015, it was the natural place to continue giving back. George Rogers is a lovable guy who appreciates the South Carolina fans, and they love and appreciate him too.

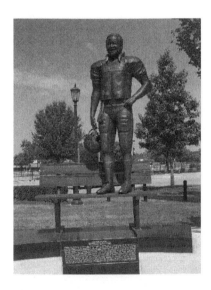

George Rogers played running back for the South Carolina Gamecocks between 1977-80. He won the 1980 Heisman Trophy after a stellar senior season. That year he tallied a nation-leading 1,781 rushing yards. Rogers was the first overall pick (New Orleans Saints) in the 1981 NFL draft. He led the NFL in rushing and earned Rookie of the Year honors in 1981. He was traded to the Washington Redskins in 1985, earned Pro-Bowl status in 1986 and won Super Bowl XXII with the team in January 1988. Rogers is a member of the Saints Hall of Fame, and he was inducted into the College Football Hall of Fame in 1997.

We had some laughs and took some pictures with George Rogers before we went back out to the State Fairgrounds. That's where we met up with long-time USC football fan Matt Fletcher. He has been attending games at Williams-Brice Stadium since he was a student. I don't want to age him too much, so I'll just say that it was before South Carolina joined the SEC. Now, his daughter attends their tailgate as a USC student herself. Their spot had a remarkable view of Williams-Brice Stadium, as the stadium sat nobly watching the surrounding celebrations.

We had good conversations about the state of South Carolina's history and memories of USC football. Fletcher recounted some of the ways they used to tailgate and how those procedures have changed. He and a friend reminisced about some of the more memorable games they've witnessed in the stadium. More offspring came and went with their companions. As is usually the case at many southern tailgates, one of the guests was a fan of another SEC team. They'll always graciously cheer for the home team, but constantly wonder about their favorite squad. Auburn was represented here, and she was anxious about her team's game with Mississippi State later that night.

We said farewell to Fletcher's crew and set our coordinates southeast of the stadium. That's where the famed Cockaboose Railroad resides in its tailgating lore. Twenty-two cabooses neatly painted with a uniform design sit permanently attached to an inactive railroad spur. The outsides may look virtually the same, but each one has a custom interior. Not only are the decorations different, but the inside configurations are unique. Some have the feel of a school cafeteria while others are more like an intimate living room. Many of them have an outdoor space constructed on the roof. Either way, they are convenient to the stadium and have been a whole lot of fun since 1990.

As we approached from the west side of the stadium, the team was finishing their trek into the stadium. The "Mighty Sound of the Southeast" followed in a spirited fashion. The high energy band was playing, singing, chanting and dancing. A large portion of the crowd, including revelers on tops of the cockabooses, stuck around to watch the spectacle. Perched outside one of the railcars was Sir Big Spur. The Old-English, black-breasted red gamecock is the official live mascot of South Carolina Athletics.

We met many of the party hosts on the Cockaboose Railroad. They were popular people. There was a steady flow of well-wishers that climbed the stairs to greet the masters of ceremonies. I thought that this is what it must have been like when politicians would take trains on the campaign trail. Yet, the party hosts didn't have to give any speeches to the on-lookers down below. There was a fantastic view from atop of the party headquarters. Festivities could be seen on both sides.

Behind one end of the severed spur of railcars, was a large parking lot in front of an apartment building. A pavilion sat in the middle for gatherings such as this. Running parallel behind the rest of the stagnant line of cabooses were high-end condominiums. On top of a cockaboose, it almost seems as if you can reach out and give a high-five to someone on the upper deck of a condo. The condos are in as high demand as one of the cockabooses. There was constantly someone who liked to point out that Darius Rucker owns one of those condos.

We happened to be in one of the cabooses when North Carolina attempted a two-point conversion to take a late lead on Clemson. South Carolina fans almost want Clemson (the hated in-state rival) to lose more than they want South Carolina to win. Everything stopped when the Tar Heels lined up for the play. Not long after the ball was snapped, profanities filled the air, as it was obvious that North Carolina wasn't going to be successful. The Tigers had escaped and so did an opportunity for an epic bash before our game even started. There wasn't a detonation of unadulterated joy, but the celebration of Gamecock football continued.

A magnificent purple and orange sunset hung over us as we entered the stadium. "The Mighty Sound of the Southeast" serenaded us as we searched for our seats. It was still warm as the dark of the night set in, but it was a welcome relief from the blistering sun that drained us earlier. The band had a special tribute for Family Weekend. They channeled animated families and formed the characters as they played the theme songs. Among the shows that they honored were *The Flintstones*, *The Jetsons*, *Family Guy* and *The Simpsons*. Then a gaggle of tiny young cheerleaders came on the field to perform in front of the crowd.

Everyone paused for an invocation before the performance of the national anthem. When the anthem was finished, the stadium reverently sang the "Alma Mater." The last line to the *Alma Mater* is "Here's a health, Carolina, forever to thee!" As this part is sung, the fans raise their right hands like holding a cup during a toast. It symbolizes the unity in saluting their home state and toasting to the good health of its citizens and state affairs. It all precluded the climax that would occur in just a few minutes.

The band was in place and a platform sat on the field surrounded by a black curtain. The Opening Fanfare (2001) played while white towels were furiously twirled all around the stadium. At a crescendo, the black curtain around the platform, is pulled down to reveal Cocky (the costumed mascot). He elicits cheers from the crowd as pyrotechnics spray from the top of the platform. The song continues to build. People are going wild. As the song's opening hits the finale, flames shoot from columns placed in the end zone. Flag bearers take off in a sprint with their banners in tow as the football team erupts onto the field.

The "2001" entrance has been called the best in the nation. There is some debate about which one is the best just in the SEC. I have to give Carolina credit, it certainly gets the crowd pumped before the game. I had not personally witnessed it in over 20 years, but it was just as special as it was back then. Those 60 seconds alone warrant putting a South Carolina game on the bucket list.

The excitement of the crowd carried over to the team. South Carolina had the ball first, and they surely utilized the first possession. Carolina running back Rico Dowdle set the tone early with a 15-yard scamper on the first play from scrimmage. Quarterback Ryan Hilinski later converted a key third down with a 12-yard completion to running back Tavien Feaster. The Gamecocks had a healthy mixture of run and pass plays on that first drive. The 75-yard drive was later completed by a 2-yard Feaster run into the end zone. South Carolina led 7-0 before Kentucky even had the ball.

When Kentucky did get possession, it didn't last long. After earning a first down with a completion to wide receiver Lynn Bowden Jr., the Kentucky passing game delivered one to South Carolina's defense. The interception gave the Gamecocks a terrific opportunity to build on the early lead, but Kentucky's defense joined the party and forced a South Carolina punt.

The punt pinned Kentucky inside its own 5-yard line. Without being able to convert a first down, the Wildcats were left no choice but to punt it back to the Gamecocks. But the punt careened off the foot of the return man and the Cats recovered.

South Carolina's defense was up to the challenge on all four plays of the Kentucky possession. Yes, Kentucky attempted to convert a fourth down. With six yards to go, they completed a pass for five yards and gave the ball back to USC.

The teams shared three-and-outs before the Gamecocks received another opportunity. The drive started during the last seconds of the first quarter. As the second quarter started, the Carolina offense also got going. A balanced mix of passes and running plays helped the Gamecocks advance inside of the UK 10-yard line. Kentucky held there, and USC decided to add three points to the lead. The teams practiced punting the rest of the half, and South Carolina lead 10-0 at the break.

The Kentucky offense came out throwing in the second half. That approach didn't produce much during the first two plays, and then it led to a big turnover for South Carolina on the third play. As UK's quarterback stood in the pocket, South Carolina edge rusher D.J. Wonnum delivered a blow that knocked the ball free. Defensive end Aaron Sterling recovered the fumble for the Gamecocks. Dowdle made the rooster crow on the very first play. He scampered 30 yards to the end zone to put South Carolina ahead 17-0.

The next several possessions produced three-and-outs for both team's offenses the way fast food joints pump out hamburgers. Kentucky's offense finally gained some traction with the help of a couple Gamecock penalties, and two key third-down receptions from receiver Ahmad Wagner. The Cats faced another third down at the South Carolina 35-yard line. This time, UK quarterback Sawyer Smith couldn't connect with Wagner. Down 17-0, Kentucky went for it on fourth-and-eight. On fourth down, Wonnum had another impactful collision with the quarterback that ended any chance of Kentucky scoring on the drive.

It was back to the drive-thru mode, as each team kept producing punt after punt. During the woeful stretch of drives, the third quarter ended. The break between quarters produced more excitement than the two offenses. First, it was "2001." The flashlights from cell phones looked like thousands of lighthouse beacons as towels circled in front of their paths. It was followed by a hype video on the big screen and fireworks that originated from outside the stadium. "Sandstorm" was the exclamation point. The place was rocking. People bounced up and down while white towels whipped feverishly in the air all around the stadium.

Each offense continued its campaign for the punter at the beginning of the fourth quarter. South Carolina decided to continue its efforts with the running game, and it developed into a sustained drive. Kentucky tried to steal the possession away by forcing a fumble. The ball did pop out, but South Carolina receiver Bryan Edwards recovered. The near failure sparked Carolina's offense to finish the drive. Feaster had a touchdown run of 19 yards, and the Gamecocks led 24-0.

Kentucky substituted Lynn Bowden Jr. at quarterback, and it seemed to inject life into the UK offense. The Cats went 84 yards in five plays to put points on the board. UK running back Christopher Rodriguez Jr. completed the march with a two-yard touchdown run with 2:27 remaining in the game. South Carolina successfully handled the onside kick attempt, and USC burned off the time remaining on the clock. The game ended with a final score of South Carolina 24, Kentucky 7.

Most of the people who were still in the stadium started their descent down the ramps to the exits. A few, privy to the custom, stuck around to listen to the "Mighty Sound of the Southeast" deliver the closing ceremony.

First up was "We Hail Thee Carolina," the school's *Alma Mater*. It was a final salute to the team's conquest that included the toasting motion at "Here's a Health, Carolina, forever to thee!" The night ended with a stirring performance of "Amazing Grace." A single trumpeter performed the first verse, and then the entire band joined in to complete the rest of the song.

We exited the stadium from the north end. Cars jockeyed for position as they tried to get out of the State Fairgrounds lot. There were still a lot of people walking around enjoying the victory. Going around the east side of the stadium allowed us to make another stop at the Cockaboose Railroad, where the festivities continued for some. On the other side of Key Road, there were other railcars that kept the party going. We saw chandeliers hanging from the covered modification on the roof. There was laughter and dancing. As we rounded the corner of Eden and Market Streets, the notes of "We Hail Thee Carolina" floated through the darkness. We reached the truck and I turned toward the stadium. Raising my right hand in a toasting motion, I said "Here's a Health, Carolina!"

South Carolina Gamecocks

Defensive Linemen

John Abraham
(1996-99)

Jadeveon Clowney
(2011-13)

Kalimba Edwards
(1998-2001)

Dominic Fusci
(1942-43, 1946)

Melvin Ingram
(2007, 2009-11)

Javon Kinlaw
(2017-19)

John LeHeup
(1970-72)

Cliff Matthews
(2007-10)

Eric Norwood
(2006-09)

Andrew Provence
(1980-82)

My favorite players to watch at other defensive positions:

DB - Sheldon Brown (1998-2001)   DB - Stephon Gilmore (2009-11)

LB - Jasper Brinkley (2006, 2008)   LB - Skai Moore (2013-15, 2017)

Wide Receivers

Robert Brooks
(1988-91)

Pharoh Cooper
(2013-15)

Bryan Edwards
(2016-19)

Bruce Ellington
(2011-13)

Alshon Jeffery
(2009-11)

Kenny McKinley
(2005-08)

Sydney Rice
(2005-06)

Deebo Samuel
(2015-16, 2018)

Sterling Sharpe
(1983, 1985-87)

Fred Zeigler
(1967-69)

My favorite players to watch at other offensive positions:

RB - Marcus Lattimore (2010-12)   QB - Steve Taneyhill (1992-95)

RB - Duce Staley (1995-96)   OL - A.J. Cann (2011-14)

*Fan Favorites: RB - Marcus Lattimore, QB - Connor Shaw, DL - Jadeveon Clowney

7

GOOD OL' ROCKY TOP

Week of the October 5, 2019 game against Georgia

I entered the campus's perimeter from the west side. The first place to go was the Visitor's Center. From the parking lot, there were sweeping views down to the Tennessee River. The first thing that I saw in the building was a painted overhead message that read "Welcome to Rocky Top." There were others in the building that said things like "Go Vols!" I didn't find anyone in the building, and it became obvious that this was not the visitor's center. Outside, there was a sign explaining that the visitor's center had been relocated. This building is now the UT Culinary Institute and Creamery, but the beautiful scenery remained. As I set off to find the new location for the visitor's center, I took a moment to admire the panorama of the river bend.

The University of Tennessee was established in 1794. It is one of the oldest public universities in the nation, and it's actually two years older than the state itself. The state of Tennessee was admitted into the Union in 1796. It's no surprise that UT-Knoxville is the flagship university of the state's University of Tennessee system. The school has an enrollment that exceeds 29,000. Many UT graduates have gone on to have successful careers. There are founders of major businesses, astronauts, Pulitzer Prize winners and many politicians who have earned a degree from the University of Tennessee. UT is an esteemed research university and recognized as a "Green Campus" by *The Princeton Review*. The University of Tennessee has the distinct honor of having been named a Purple Heart University.

I eventually found the welcome center, but not before I saw another "Welcome to Rocky Top" greeting. The welcome center is housed in the newly completed student union. I walked into the welcome center suite under an arch of orange balloons. It was a modern space with odes to Tennessee consistent throughout the building. The second stanza of "On a Hallowed Hill" (UT's *Alma Mater*) was stamped on an acrylic plaque with an orange outline of the state, and it hung proudly in the foyer. The people were as welcoming and friendly as you would expect. They provided me with a campus map, and we talked about the upcoming events and best sites to visit on campus.

I didn't need a map to find one of the best places on campus. I was already there. Although, I could have used a map to navigate the humongous 395,088-square-foot structure. It took over nine years to finish the student union that occupies the heart of campus. The building offers homes to student government organizations, an auditorium, recreation area, post office, many restaurants, a credit union and more. There are also centers for leadership and service, student engagement and career development contained within the Student Union. My favorite feature was the windowed bridge connecting two of the buildings. The words of the song "Rocky Top" were sequentially displayed down the hallway on horizontal banners hanging from the ceiling.

When I left through the southeast corner of the student union, I was cattycorner to Neyland Stadium. I had plenty of time to explore it later, so I went north under a crosswalk proudly marked with "The UNIVERSITY of TENNESSEE." I ventured back up Phillip Fulmer Way toward "The Hill." This is a collection of the oldest and most historic buildings on the UT campus. Ayres Hall serves as the epicenter of the area. It has reigned over the rest of campus since it was built in 1921. I climbed up the mountain of stairs to reach the entrance to Ayres and looked down from the summit to Cumberland Avenue. It is a grand building that reaches even higher with its impressive clock tower. The checkerboard markings sprinkled around the clock tower are apparently what inspired the design commonly associated with the university's branding.

Tennessee's iconic football coach, General Robert Neyland, noticed the unique pattern on Ayres Hall and thought it looked like a checkerboard. Legend has it that once during fall camp, when he didn't think his players were practicing hard enough, Neyland told them to "run to the checkerboard." He sent them sprinting up the hill to Ayres Hall and back down before resuming practice. General Neyland later

Tennessee, UT

School Colors:

Orange & White

Traditions:

The Power T

The Vol Navy

Running Through the T

Checkerboard End Zones

Vol Walk

Pride of the Southland Band

Fight Song - Down The Field

Rocky Top

Spirit of The Hill

Favorite Battle Cries:

Go Vols

Go Big Orange

revised the tactic during the season. When the offense was facing Ayres during practice, Coach Neyland would direct them "Don't stop until time runs out or until you reach the checkerboard and once you get there...get there again!" Other times he commanded "Charge the checkerboard!"

To be clear, the end zones were never painted with the checkerboard motif until Doug Dickey was the coach in 1964. It has been reported that Dickey got the idea after seeing an ad in a magazine. The "run to the checkerboards" mantra became popular in Knoxville. The end zone design was subsequently lost in 1968 when artificial turf was installed in Neyland Stadium. The checkerboards did not return until the design was sewn into that same turf in 1989. It hasn't left since. When the surface went back to natural grass, the checkerboards had to be painted, but they continue to grace the end zones still to this day. The checkerboard pattern can be seen on the ends of the basketball court, uniforms and game day apparel like hats and even overalls.

After circling Ayres, I waded through the Science and Engineering complex of buildings and classrooms. I found myself at the northeastern edge of campus in front of a statue of Smokey. Smokey is the Bluetick Coonhound that is the official live mascot of the University of Tennessee's athletic teams. I came to find out that there are 10 Smokey statues around campus--one for every Smokey that has served as mascot for UT. So, naturally the current mascot is Smokey X. The particular statue that I was standing next to had a fantastic view of the Knoxville skyline, including the Sunsphere, which was built as a tribute to Knoxville for the 1982 World's Fair.

I continued my exploration around campus the rest of the day. I realized just how hilly the campus really is. At times, it seemed like there was an upward climb no matter what direction I was going. I feel like we must all be descendants of a UT student. Didn't everyone's parents say something like "When we were younger, we had to walk to school, uphill both ways ... barefoot ... in the snow?" In any event, UT students do get their exercise and it's walking uphill to class in most cases. There weren't nearly as many students who used scooters or skateboards like at other campuses. There are buses that run through campus, but many of the students preferred to walk.

Why wouldn't they walk? With the youthful energy of a college student and great weather like on this day, the UT campus is a lovely place. The main drag at UT is Cumberland Avenue. That's where most of the action is for the college students. Cumberland's path cuts through north campus and runs right on through to downtown Knoxville. There are shops, restaurants, nightclubs, and about everything else a student would need. Going from west to east on Cumberland, after negotiating yet another hill, I wound up on campus where there is a cluster of classroom buildings and an additional pedestrian bridge declaring the University of Tennessee. The path then goes past The Hill and into downtown.

I took that route to discover more of Knoxville. Market Square is a really neat place that hosts festivals, farmers' markets and even outdoor concerts. There is something going on there practically every night. I also went past the Knoxville Convention Center. The shape made it look like a long barn or church house. I don't know if it uses solar power or not, but the top of it looked to be all glass. I walked through the area where they hosted the 1982 World's Fair and saw the Sunsphere. The sphere is covered in gold-colored glass to represent the sun. The Sunsphere stands over 260 feet tall and has been a landmark associated with Knoxville since the 1982 expo.

Knoxville also has a lot of trails for its citizens to access the wonders of the city's outdoors. I found my way onto the Neyland Greenway, and it took me down to the river and past numerous sites. The Three Rivers Rambler was wrapped around a portion of the riverbank. The Rambler is a tourist train that parks alongside the Tennessee River in the area where the Vol Navy docks. It has railcars from a different era and different railway companies. The most interesting one this week had to be the red one with "Georgia Railroad" painted near its exterior ladder.

There are some great bridges to see soaring over the river while walking through Volunteer Landing Park. There are splash pads, a fountain and benches at Volunteer Landing. Then you get to the infamous Calhoun's on the River. They have their own dock, an outdoor area, the inside restaurant and a long parking lot along the river. The Star of Knoxville is an authentic paddlewheel boat that is tied off just past Calhoun's parking lot. The riverboat does cruises on the river for special events and at scheduled times.

I had been walking for a while, so I turned back and went to Calhoun's for an early supper. Finding a seat at the inside bar, I grabbed a menu, ordered a water and was alerted of the happy hour deals. The bartender (Amy) offered bread, which I accepted. Amy told me about how busy they are on game weekends. She explained the tailgating environment in Calhoun's parking lot on game days. She also told me about the schools who travel best (Georgia, Alabama, Florida, and ... Middle Tennessee). While I waited for my food, I took a self-guided tour of Calhoun's. On my return, I found the "bread" waiting for me. It was a basket with a parmesan roll, a biscuit, and a slice of cornbread.

A biscuit and cornbread. Now that's southern hospitality y'all.

After the meal, I made my way from the river to the more undulating terrain of campus. My journey took me past Neyland Stadium to Circle Park. The lawn is a beautiful area with trees and benches surrounded by a lighted walking path. University buildings, including the McClung Museum of Natural History and Culture, line its borders. There is another Smokey statue and the Torchbearer statue at the opening to the plaza. The Torchbearer represents education, success, and security. It takes form in a specific part of the Volunteer Creed:

"One that beareth a torch shadoweth oneself to give light to others."

I continued west on Volunteer Boulevard and had my first sighting of The Rock. The Rock is a gigantic stone that was found during excavation efforts for construction in the 1960s. The huge mass was moved to a new site where it sits today. Some students painted graffiti on its face and a tradition was started. Today, students paint symbols and messages, craft pictures and cartoons and tell their stories and emotions all by the artwork on The Rock. It has two sides and most times you can see a masterpiece present on each side. The pictures only last until someone paints over it. While I was there, I never witnessed anyone painting, but I did observe seven unique displays on either side of The Rock.

After exploring throughout the next morning, I ended up at Fieldhouse Social for lunch. I couldn't have picked a better place. The flags of every SEC school lined the front edge of the roof on the building. I walked in and saw UT and SEC memorabilia scattered throughout the restaurant. This was the place for me. It only got better. I was able to sit in peaceful anonymity in a bank of recliners facing big-screen televisions. It was a welcome rest in a nicely air-conditioned clubhouse. The food was really good, and it was great to put my feet up and watch the SEC Network replay classic football games. I eventually forced myself to go back out into the heat and pound the pavement again.

My trek took me through some residence halls, to the Aquatics Center and

Neyland Stadium

Surface: Grass

Built in 1921

Capacity: 102,455

Record Attendance:

109,061 - 9/18/04 vs Florida

Nickname: Volunteers

Mascot:

Costumed - Smokey & Davy Crockett

Live - Smokey X

*Fans' Favorite Home Games:

Won 31-14 over Florida in 1992

Won 28-24 over Arkansas in 1998

down to the Tennessee Recreation Center for Students (TRECS). The TRECS always had students going in and out of it. Even when I passed it on game day, there were students utilizing the facility. It's across the street from Fraternity Row, which is a beautiful section of Fraternity houses. The frat houses were all very nice and featured unmistakable Southern architecture. A stream of students continually swept through to either maintain the grounds, make their way to TRECS or to attend classes.

Back across Volunteer Blvd was the turf fields of TRECS, where the band had gathered for practice. That was obvious by the sound of students testing their instruments with their interpretations of various tunes. A steady flow of students, with instruments in hand, arrived at the spot where they prepared for the weekend's performance. The Tom Black Track and LaPorte Stadium sat vacant next door. I continued the climb to Stokely Hall at the corner of Volunteer and Lake Loudoun Boulevard. A quick right turn presented an uncommon decline that led me down to a couple of desirable locations.

The first was the Doug Dickey Hall of Fame Plaza. It is located outside of the Neyland-Thompson Sports Center where many of the athletes go for training. People were setting up and testing the PA systems for the dedication that would occur the following afternoon. Further south is the entrance to the football training facility. To the right are monuments honoring all of the UT representatives in the National Football Foundation and College Football Hall of Fame. Across the street from there is an area that is special to every University of Tennessee Athletics fan.

Under the shadow of Thompson-Boling Arena, lies the Pat Summitt Plaza. The tribute is to Pat Head Summitt who served as the head coach of the women's basketball team at Tennessee from 1974-2012. Coach Summitt brought attention to the women's game that it had never experienced previously. She was an extraordinary coach, who had success throughout her career. Not once in her tenure did she fail to have a winning season or make the post season tournament. Her Lady Vols made the NCAA Final Four 18 times and her squads won eight national championships.

Summitt earned countless awards and held virtually every coaching record at the time of her retirement. Every player that completed their eligibility under Coach Summitt played in at least one Elite Eight and also graduated with a degree. In 2009, *Sporting News* ranked Summitt No. 11 on a list of the greatest coaches of all time in any sport (professional and collegiate). In 2011, Pat Summitt was honored with the Presidential Medal of Freedom by President Barack Obama.

Coach Summitt was a trailblazer and champion for the University of Tennessee, women's sports and all of us in the South.

That afternoon, I was able to scout out Neyland Stadium. The stadium on the banks of the Tennessee River has been renowned for being one of the biggest in the nation for a long time. The capacity topped the 100,000 mark in 1996 and has remained above that number since then.

Along with being full of seats, it is also full of history. I passed a doorway with "East Stadium Hall" painted above it. This was one of the dormitories in the stadium. Yes, students used to live there, and they continued to do so until 1985. Now the spaces are used for classrooms, offices and storage.

From underneath the stadium, about all you can see are steel beams and ramps that go in every direction. Stadium renovations seem to be as constant as the flow of the river outside its gates. As you get to the concourses, it begins to warm up with orange and white decorations and pictures of great teams and players. I thought of Reggie White flashing up the middle for a sack, and Dale Carter breaking up a pass in the end zone. I remembered Chuck Webb scooting around defenders, and Joey Kent running under deep passes for touchdowns. This place has seen plenty of exciting action.

Neyland Stadium has two full bowls (upper and lower) that rise from the field into the sky. On both the west and east sides, massive structures sit atop the upper bowl. It looks like gigantic air-conditioning window units were plunked down on each side of the stadium. That is where the press boxes, coaches' booths, and suites are located. Above the south end zone is the large video screen that replaced the giant letters (spelling V-O-L-S) for the 1999 season. A canopy covers the very top rows in the north end zone.

Later, as I walked down the tunnel that is the stadium portion of the Vol Walk, I saw banners telling the storied history of Volunteer football. As you progress to the field, overhead banners display the 13 SEC Championships, 8 retired numbers, 6 national championships and numerous Hall of Famers. I veered left toward the Peyton Manning Locker Complex. The wooden lockers have a beautiful wood finish and were marked with players' names and numbers. As you leave the locker room, the exit is protected with a sign in the shape of the state that declares "I will give my all for Tennessee today!" Across the hall is the tunnel where so many Vols players waited to run through the "T."

Leaving the stadium, I walked across Neyland Drive and went over to where the boats congregate to forge the Vol Navy. This is one of the most unique traditions in the Southeastern Conference. People bring their boats in from as far as 50 miles away. They come in and tie off to one another forming a floating tailgate community. Most of the boat owners have grown to know each other over the years, and many of them have conceived creative names for their boats that usually allude to something about their Tennessee Volunteers.

There are boats of all shapes and sizes, but they all display support for the Vols. The rows can get as long as 13 boats deep, depending on how far each row reaches out into the water. If a row gets too long, then authorities simply have the boats start a new row. Everyone is there for the same purpose - to have a good time and eventually go to the game. Because of that, the crews in the Vol Navy are helpful and respectful to each other. It is a tailgating scene like no other, and it begins early in the week.

On Friday morning, I was able to go out on the water myself. I joined Dr. Brian Alford and his crew of researchers as we tracked lake sturgeon. It was a gorgeous early morning on the water. There were a total of six of us on the vessel. Dr. Alford's crew worked in unison to make sure that everything went smoothly. To everyone's excitement, we did pull up a lake sturgeon. It was very interesting to watch the crew go to work recording data and tagging the prehistoric creature. As the sun started to wake the region, and waves rocked the boat, we talked a lot about SEC and UT football. On the trip, I learned the term VFL (Vol for Life). The football memories and opinions continued even after we pulled the boat out of the water. I can't think of a much better way to start a football weekend in the SEC.

When I got back to campus, orange shirts were everywhere. Eventually, I discovered that it was "Big Orange Friday," where everyone wears orange to celebrate the University of Tennessee. Throughout the week, the temperatures had been in the mid-90s, but it was cooler on Friday and Saturday. The highs were only supposed to be around 89 degrees. It doesn't seem like much, but the difference is noticeable when walking around campus with an elevated climb around every corner.

The campus was rejuvenated on Friday. I don't know if it was from the new painting on The Rock, the refreshing drop in temperature or the approaching end of the long hot week. It was probably all of it and that UT had a big game against Georgia on Saturday. Whatever it was, UT's campus had a different energy beginning on Friday.

As I was walking around the corner of the stadium, I saw the Georgia equipment truck arriving. I assisted them in backing down the long narrow hill towards the visitor's locker room. I could not imagine trying to navigate that hill and its subtle turns as the operator of an 18-wheeler. It is a very tight spot with trees, fence posts, and medal beams daring a driver to kiss them with the side of the truck. The driver maneuvered the truck into a spot that seemed to leave only six inches of space on each side.

His partner was driving the bus holding the support staff. When he came down to the area, we started to converse. I couldn't help but notice that he was wearing an enormous ring. I asked him about the ring, and he immediately took it off and handed it to me. I expected to see an SEC Championship ring or some bowl ring, and I definitely didn't think that he was going to hand it to me. It turned out to be the last thing that I thought I would see that day. It was a Chicago Cubs World Series ring from 2016!

I'm a Cubs fan, so this was very cool. Plus, if you think about it, how many people in the world have seen a legitimate ring from the Cubs winning the World Series?

I went over to the Anderson Training Center for a tour of the football facility. I sauntered through the indoor facility, as the ESPN crew was finishing up its pre-game prep work. I walked through the doors to the football area and met up with Hawk, UT's Assistant Director of Equipment & Apparel. He showed me around the equipment room, the locker room, weight room and indoor practice field. I saw areas exhibiting all of UT's All-Americans and major award-winners. There were bowl trophies and honors of all types for the Tennessee program.

The most exclusive thing I was able to experience was the Peyton Manning Room. It is a very secure location. It's like getting access into a vault with a treasure trove of artifacts from Manning's career. Peyton Manning has been very generous to the University of Tennessee. Things that are highly sought after items were personally donated to UT by Peyton himself. The game-worn uniforms from both his Super Bowl victories were in the Manning Room. One of his cleats even had confetti still caked on the bottom of it. There are game balls, pictures and trophies on display around the room, and there is a great view out onto the practice field. I would describe it as a really awesome man cave, only it's at a football facility overlooking the practice field. I am sure that Manning enjoys it when he comes in town for practices and games.

The day was flying by. I had already seen a lake sturgeon, a Cubs World Series ring and the jerseys Peyton Manning wore while winning Super Bowl titles. I walked around the south end of Anderson Training Center and over to Lindsey Nelson Stadium. I watched a little bit of an intrasquad scrimmage and continued up the hill to the Student Health Center. I noticed that The Rock (across the street) had been painted again. I continued straight down Volunteer Boulevard past the Torchbearer statue and onto Peyton Manning Pass.

That is the road where the Vol Walk starts on Saturdays. I walked past the "Power T" and checkerboard painted on the street and over to the west entrance of the stadium. That is where the statue of General Robert R. Neyland sits. The monument depicts Neyland kneeling. It is nine feet tall and has Neyland's famous game maxims carved into the base. General Neyland actually had 38 maxims that he developed, but the 7 chiseled into the base were his favorites to use.

After first attending Texas A&M, Robert Neyland received an appointment to West Point. While there, he was a star football and baseball player as well as a champion boxer. After serving in the Corps of Engineers during WWI, Neyland worked as an assistant coach at West Point. He moved to UT as an assistant in 1925 before being named head coach and athletic director in 1926. Tennessee was the only school which Neyland served as head coach. He started in 1926 and retired after the 1952 season. His tenure was interrupted twice (1935 & 1941-1945) to serve our country as a member of the United States Army, where he earned the rank of brigadier general for his exemplary service.

Robert Neyland was one of the greatest coaches in the history of college football. His record of 173-31-12 only tells part of the story. The Vols kept the opponent from scoring in over half of the games he coached (109 shutouts in 216 games). Under Neyland, Tennessee won seven conference championships (5 SEC) and four national championships. Coach Bear Bryant, the beacon of modern college coaching, never defeated a Neyland coached team in seven tries (0-5-2). Coach Neyland retired from coaching in 1952 and was inducted into the College Football Hall of Fame in 1956. He continued as Tennessee's athletic director until his death in 1962. General Robert R. Neyland was a gifted athlete, an incredible coach and a great American.

Saturday started early. I went to watch my good friend's son compete in a cross-country meet off campus. When it finished, I rushed over to find parking on campus. I had an early interview to do with Colin Castleberry for 90.3 The Rock. I was fortunate to have made it on time, but we had fun talking about the UT Vols and SEC football. From there, I walked back across campus to join a tailgate party with Dr. Alford. There were already a bunch of people occupying spots. Most of the hilly park was filled with tents and families having a good time. It was good to see Dr. Alford and most of his crew again, and it turned out to be very productive.

It was certainly a fun time. I enjoyed seeing and talking to fans from both Tennessee and Georgia. There was music playing and televisions showing football games. The aromas floating into the tented areas made everyone hungry. Finding something to eat wasn't a problem, but I also still needed to find a ticket. My host asked the group if there were any available tickets that I could buy.

A man named Tom (the father of one of the students) jump up to confirm that I needed a ticket. He told me to wait just a minute, and he took off. The melodies of Rocky Top sprung up to a loud cheer from the people on the hill. Dr. Alford explained the popularity of the song; "Whenever Rocky Top is played, UT fans tend to gather around it." All of a sudden, Tom is handing me a ticket. I tried to pay him for the ticket, but he fabricated a story about how someone around the way just gave it to him. I made my rounds to say goodbye, and then I returned to attempt to compensate him for my admission. He still refused and said, "Just enjoy the game!"

I know that you paid for the ticket, Tom T. I wish you would've let me pay you for it, but I am very appreciative of your generosity.

I maneuvered the roller coaster of terrain back across campus, hearing versions of Rocky Top on the way. There is a tailgate party in about every nook and cranny of the campus. I made it just in time for Vol Walk. I didn't see much except for a sea of orange and white. There were people everywhere, and they wore anything orange that they could find. There were striped pants, Dr. Seuss hats, overalls and full suits in orange and white. After the "Pride of the Southland" went through playing Rocky Top, people started to disperse from that area. There was plenty of activity around the stadium, and the energy was contagious. I rushed down to visit with the friends I made in the Vol Navy.

When I arrived, everything was in full swing. The docks, landing and all of the boats were jammed with people. Folks walked back and forth across the sterns of boats to get drinks and say hello to friends. Different music choices clashed in mid-air like two boxers coming out for the final round of a close fight. Orange and white gonfalons danced in the wind. Carousers danced in an inebriated state. Everyone was happy for another day to party and watch the Vols with their friends. The loudest speaker played Rocky Top and revelers started to sense that the party was moving to Neyland Stadium. The enthusiasm continued to build as game time neared.

I started making my way to the stadium, and a feeling came over me as I crossed the street. It was a feeling of immense pride and appreciation. These are the moments that I dearly miss--the times that I yearn for every autumn. There were all of these Georgia and Tennessee fans running around; they were fired up and having fun. They were cordial and good-spirited. There was Neyland Stadium. It stood sturdy and strong over the Tennessee River. It was a Southern coliseum ready to host a monumental clash. It was football time in Tennessee! This was the South that I know and love. This is the SEC!

Arriving at my seat, I discovered the community that I would keep during the game. There were a few couples to my right, a couple older gentlemen in front of me and a rowdy group of middle-aged men to the left and behind me. They were all good people and good fun. One of the friends in front of me had been watching UT Football since 1951. He informed me that Billy Cannon (1959 Heisman winner from LSU) is the only UT grad to win the Heisman. Cannon did attend graduate school at the University of Tennessee. The raucous group beside me was ready for the game. Many of them were loud and opinionated. They were neither polite or rude with their comments. They were just real, and I appreciated that. When the first notes of Rocky Top rang out, exuberant passion exploded out of people. There were orange and whites shakers jerking back and forth over the heads of most of the fans.

The Pride of the Southland Marching Band was phenomenal. They are one of the best bands that I have ever seen in person. This is the 150th year of the band, and the Volunteers fans appreciate their contribution to the experience. As we approached game time, there was an invocation before the Anthem. I was impressed that they said a prayer before the game and proud that they continue to express their beliefs. I was thankful to share a "homecoming" with strangers in the best region of the best country on earth.

I saw the band form a single lined "T," and I knew what was about to occur right below where I was sitting. There was a stirring video narrated by John Ward that whipped everyone into a frenzy. The cheerleaders were bunched up at the mouth of the tunnel. The Pride of the Southland dynamically marched outwardly to open up the Power T. The fans were hysterically cheering. Smokey and the cheerleaders led the way for the players to "run through the T." The fans went crazy watching it. A few minutes later, the place went berserk when the first kickoff was preceded with the announcement of "It's Football Time In Tennessee!"

The big news for the Tennessee offense was that Brian Maurer was starting at quarterback. Although the first possession ended with a punt, fans could sense that the freshman was ready for the moment. Georgia took advantage of its first possession by driving it 84 yards for a touchdown. It was a nice mix of run and pass that continued to yield first downs and ultimately a 7-0 lead. The next time Maurer threw a pass, cheers from Vols fans detonated throughout the stadium. It was a 73-yard touchdown pass to receiver Marquez Callaway. With the score tied 7-7, Georgia followed with a decent drive that stalled after a penalty. Rodrigo Blankenship crushed a 50-yard go-ahead field goal.

The Vols once again started from their 25-yard line. And, once again, they took it 75 yards for a touchdown, this time with a longer, more methodical drive. Nine plays into the drive, the first quarter ended with Tennessee on Georgia's 12. When play resumed, Maurer threw to wide receiver Jauan Jennings for the touchdown and a 14-10 Tennessee lead. Georgia started driving again, but the offense once again stalled. A field goal brought the Bulldogs within one point. There were a few punts back and forth before Georgia started moving again. Only, this time UGA didn't stall out and pushed into the end zone to take the lead.

The next two possessions told the story of the game. Tennessee put together back-to-back big passing plays to get into Georgia territory. Once there, the Vols put together back-to-back incompletions to force a field-goal attempt. Unfortunately for Tennessee, the field goal was no good. Georgia took possession with just under a minute left in the half. Five plays and 50 seconds later, the Dawgs were in the end zone. The two-point conversion failed, but Georgia led 26-14 at halftime.

The Pride of the Southland Marching Band is so good that people don't leave their seats at halftime. I usually don't leave my seat at halftime, but I was thoroughly entertained this time around. Tennessee also shows pretty awesome videos at halftime and throughout the game. The videos feature great moments and legendary players from the storied history of Tennessee Football. I admired the fans of Tennessee. Their team was having a difficult season so far, but they stayed loyal and supported their Vols. The people loved their team no matter what, and I loved that about them.

The third quarter was a tough one for the Volunteers' offense. They never could get a rhythm established, and they also had a turnover. The Bulldogs didn't do much better, but they did manage another field goal. One UT fan was prompted to stand and yell "We're still here Georgia!" It sounds somewhat funny, but the Tennessee team and their fans are resilient. They've stuck by their team, and the team has continued fighting and improving. As the fourth quarter began, the Dawgs were on their way to showing they were the best team that night. A long scoring drive took plenty of time off of the clock and gave them a comfortable lead.

People stayed and cheered on the team. The most entertaining thing was to watch people taking photos around the stadium. It seemed as if every photo included both a UT and UGA fan together. I was surprised at how many people wanted to capture the moment together as rival fans. Then, lightening struck in the form of a fumble return for a touchdown. Georgia defensive back Eric Stokes created the fumble that linebacker Tae Crowder returned 60 yards into the end zone. The place was abuzz after that. The Georgia fans were happy about the score, and the Tennessee fans were happy that an official was trampled by the players in hot pursuit of Crowder. UT's offense did put together a long drive, but they were stopped on downs at the Georgia 5. The final score was Georgia 43, Tennessee 14.

After leaving Neyland Stadium, I walked over to Calhoun's. It was crowded, but didn't seem like anything more than a typical football Saturday night. The gangs of Georgia fans were enjoying the hospitality of the Tennessee folks. I continued past Volunteer Landing Park toward the Vol Navy. All of the boats were still there. About every other one still showed significant activity. The game result didn't deter them from having a good time. Neon lights reflected off of the water. Some people sang karaoke while others were dancing to their own tunes. The colors and music made it resemble a floating interpretation of the strip on South Beach in Miami. As I climbed back on to the mainland and started to walk to my truck, a familiar sound bid me farewell. It was Rocky Top. Win or lose. Rain or shine. Alumni or guest. There will always be "Good ol' Rocky Top.....Rocky Top, Tennessee."

Tennessee Volunteers

Linebackers

Kevin Burnett
(2000-01, 2003-04)

Leonard Little
(1995-97)

Jamie Rotella
(1970-72)

Keith DeLong
(1985-88)

Curt Maggitt
(2011-12, 2014)

Raynoch Thompson
(1997-99)

Al Wilson
(1995-98)

Steve Kiner
(1967-69)

Paul Naumoff
(1964-66)

Jackie Walker
(1969-71)

My favorite players to watch at other defensive positions:

DB - Dale Carter (1990-91)   DB - Eric Berry (2007-09)

DL - John Henderson (1999-2001)   DL - Reggie White (1980-83)

Offensive Linemen

Cosey Coleman
(1997-99)

Cody Douglas
(2002-05)

Bill Mayo
(1981-84)

Antone Davis
(1987-90)

Bob Johnson
(1965-67)

Michael Munoz
(2000, 2002-04)

Eric Still
(1986-89)

Steve DeLong
(1962-64)

Chip Kell
(1968-70)

Aaron Sears
(2003-06)

My favorite players to watch at other offensive positions:

WR - Carl Pickens (1989-91)   QB - Peyton Manning (1994-97)

WR - Tim McGee (1983-85)   RB - Jay Graham (1993-96)

*Fan Favorites: QB - Peyton Manning, TE - Jason Witten, WR - Peerless Price

8

M-I-Z, Z-O-U

Week of the October 12, 2019 game against Ole Miss

The University of Missouri is one of the newest members of the Southeastern Conference. They are fairly new to the SEC, but success and excellence is certainly nothing new to them. Founded in 1839, the University of Missouri is considered the first public university west of the Mississippi River. "Mizzou" resides in Columbia, Missouri. It shares the town with other colleges and universities, but the University of Missouri is the flagship university for the entire state. It is a land grant and space grant institution that currently boasts more than 30,000 students. The prolific research university is consistently ranked as one of the best programs for undergraduate research in the country. The University of Missouri has a great history of academic achievements as well.

The location is virtually the same distance from Kansas City to the west as it is from St. Louis to the east. That creates different allegiances visible in stores throughout the town. Some carry an abundance of Kansas City Chiefs gear while others have a bigger selection of St. Louis Blues items. I did see much more loyalty toward the St. Louis Cardinals, but there was still some Kansas City Royals representation as well. One thing that everyone can agree on is that Columbia is a Mizzou Tigers town. Black and gold can be found without a problem in any apparel store.

The campus is decent sized, and it's packed full of history and tradition. On its grounds lies Thomas Jefferson's original tombstone. Jefferson's final resting place, Monticello (in Virginia), is actually marked with a replica. The original tombstone was donated to the University of Missouri by Thomas Jefferson's own descendants. It sits along the walk to the east side of Francis Quadrangle, although the marble epitaph is displayed a few steps away in Jesse Hall.

Some people have wondered why it was donated to the University of Missouri. Many assume that it had a lot to do with Missouri being the first university founded within the borders of the Louisiana Purchase. Whether for that or some other reason, there was a special connection between the University of Missouri and Thomas Jefferson. Many still believe that Missouri's campus was modeled after Jefferson's ideas for his beloved University of Virginia, which he founded in 1819.

The University of Missouri's campus has always been centered around the Francis Quadrangle. That is where Academic Hall stood for the first 53 years of the school's existence. In 1892, there was a massive fire that took Academic Hall to the ground. The fire was devastating. The only things left standing were six stone columns. The tragic event eventually led to the expansion of Francis Quadrangle and the construction of Jesse Hall on the south end of the quad. Jesse Hall was built in 1895 and served as the replacement for Academic Hall.

With the expansion of the quad, there was also construction of new buildings to utilize the existing space. Those buildings were mainly constructed with red brick. The choice of building material led many people to refer to the area around Francis Quadrangle as "the red campus." A few years later, when more buildings were constructed (to handle the demand of additional academic programs), the buildings were mainly made from limestone. That led people to refer to the area, east of the quad, as "the white campus." Those monikers aren't used as often today as the campus continues to grow in scope and size.

As for the columns that were left, the city of Columbia successfully lobbied for the school to keep them as a symbol for the campus - a symbol of the collective strength of the University of Missouri. The Columns sit almost directly in the center of the quad, and it is the most recognizable landmark on the campus. Many times, it is the location of special events. The Columns will routinely anchor banners in between them throughout the year.

There were three banners hanging when I was there. A black homecoming banner in the middle with gold banners set to both sides. The banner to the left vertically spelled "MIZ" while the one on the right displayed "ZOU." Many students enjoy the serenity of the area. I witnessed students sitting on the large stone bases studying or playing on their phones, and it was even a backdrop for some photo shoots.

Another popular location for a photo shoot was Traditions Plaza. The words Traditions Plaza (along with the dedication year of 2014) is predominantly displayed on the face of the brick wall at its entrance. Behind that wall, rises a line of flagpoles carrying University of Missouri flags. There are four brick columns, on stone bases, that displayed each of the four values

Missouri, Mizzou, MU

School Colors:

Black & Gold

Traditions:

"Miz" – "Zou" Chant

The Rock "M"

Big Mo

Truman's Taxi

Missouri Waltz

Marching Mizzou

Fight Song - Every True Son

Fight Tigers (2nd Fight Song)

Tiger Rag

Favorite Battle Cries:

MIZ - ZOU

Go Tigers

of the university. Those four values are respect, responsibility, discovery, and excellence. Within the plaza, there are a few powerful messages engraved in the stone. They state "Wise shall be the bearers of light" and "Let these columns stand. Let them stand a thousand years." Traditions Plaza is a popular gathering spot for people at the university. The area hosts concerts, movies (during the summer), pep rallies and sometimes even classes.

Traditions Plaza is at one end of Carnahan Quad, and it's a continuation of the red brick motif that is "the red campus." Continuing south through Carnahan Quad, the path leads into Tiger Plaza. It features an impressive tiger statue surrounded by an array of beautiful flowers. The life-size sculpture is standing over a waterfall that flows in front of the words of "Old Missouri," the school's *Alma Mater*. Of all of the places on campus, this might be the best for a photo opportunity. It is fairly easy to get everyone and the tiger in the shot and still have room for the dome from Jesse Hall in the background. The students have been known to take pictures while they "ride the tiger."

The students all seem to enjoy studying at MU. Yes, the University of Missouri is called MU. It used to be known as Missouri State University, and people abbreviated it as MSU. When the name changed, the MU stuck. It was a reflection of the idea that it was still Missouri's university. Proponents of it even went as far to say that quickly verbalizing MU sounds a lot like Mizzou. In any case, it is known as MU, and the people love the place. The students were very polite and helpful. They were excited to talk about the school and its traditions. I was told about the annual tradition of painting the "Rock M" at Faurot Field. Students do it at the beginning of the semester before the first football game. They use mops and buckets of white paint to coat the large rocks that form the "M" on the hill in the north end zone.

I was also privy to hear about the seven "hidden" traditions. They aren't necessarily a secret or hidden. Everyone knows about them, although some of them do require covert ops to complete. They range from silly harmless fun to risking legal troubles or even severe injury. In no particular order, the seven "hidden traditions" are:

- ➤ "Ride the Tiger" - Get on and "ride" the tiger at Tiger Plaza by yourself or with a friend.
- ➤ "Kiss the 50" - Kiss the 50-yard line at Faurot Field. Normally it is easy because a student can do it after painting the "M," but it was roped off this year.
- ➤ "Swim in Brady Fountain" - Jump in Brady Fountain, which is in a very busy part of campus.
- ➤ "Explore the Tunnels" - Apparently, there is a series of tunnels underneath the campus. It isn't a place that anyone is supposed to be, so there would be consequences if caught.
- ➤ "Speaker Circle" - Yell "I love Mizzou!" while in a crowd at Speaker Circle.
- ➤ "Climb Jesse Hall" - This isn't the safest thing to do, so it is definitely frowned upon by the administration. There is security personnel and video surveillance constantly monitoring the area.
- ➤ "Streak the Quad" - Run the length of Francis Quadrangle in your birthday suit. I heard theories about how to successfully do it while avoiding law enforcement. That's the one secret that I won't reveal at this time.

None of the people that I talked to admitted to accomplishing the feat, but they did boast about the people that they know who have completed all seven. They have all heard stories of the ones who have supposedly conquered them all and the crazy ways they did it. Many of the students had their doubts as to the validity of some of the tales. They did, however, have their own individual plans for somehow accomplishing all seven before they graduate.

This was the first week that I experienced a severe shift in the weather. It wasn't necessarily because Missouri is the northernmost school in the conference, but because a cold front was blowing through at the time. The front brought rain and wind that really dropped the temperature from what I had grown accustomed to the first month of the season. The week before had been fairly warm in Columbia, so it was just as dramatic of a change for the citizens of the town as it was for me. I was hoping for some fall weather, but it skipped right past that with the temperature dipping under 30 degrees at times. The leaves had started to change color a little, but they really only fell because of the weight of the raindrops. I just had to make it through the week, because the weekend was supposed to be nice. Despite the conditions, it still felt like home walking around an SEC campus.

I spent the majority of the following day around the athletic facilities. The facilities are grouped together on the south end and separated from campus by Stadium Drive. I was parked behind Missouri Arena and the rain was fairly constant. There were some breaks at times, but there were also times when it came down pretty hard. From Memorial Stadium, I took the overhead crosswalk (above South Providence Road) over to the practice fields. There wasn't much activity since practice had been moved to the indoor facility. Since I was already over there, I walked through the track facility and Taylor Stadium (baseball). On my return, I noticed that practice was over and the players and coaches were headed back across Providence Road to their new facility.

I hung around and explored the Daniel J. Devine indoor practice field. Even though most people think of Dan Devine winning a national championship at Notre Dame, he had a very successful career at Missouri. As the head coach of the Tigers from 1958-70, he led Missouri to a 93-37-7 record, including an 11-0 tally in 1960. He guided the program to six bowl games and won four of them. Devine also served as athletics director on two different occasions. It was fitting to see him being honored at MU. The indoor is a nice facility that undoubtedly helps the team get its work in on inclement weather days. The end zones had the familiar diamond pattern spelling out Mizzou, and there were banners representing MU's post-season accomplishments. There were also SEC logos in black and gold on banners and on the field.

I walked out, noticed the absence of rain and walked back over Providence Road via the crosswalk. My path took me down the hill and past the new tiger statue in front of the football center. I continued up the Tiger Walk to the other side of the stadium, and then the skies opened again. This was the hardest that it had rained to this point, so I quickly made my way to Mizzou Arena. It is a very nice basketball venue. There were tributes to basketball coach Norm Stewart and many of the different Missouri sports. I even saw an SEC "pinwheel." It was definitely nice to see the tributes while drying out, but there was a bonus. Inside Mizzou Arena, there is also the University of Missouri Hall of Fame. There was one specific grouping that included Brad Smith, Ben Askren, Ian Kinsler, and Max Scherzer. It was fun to go through the list of athletes and coaches who have been inducted into MU's athletic HOF.

Not only was it fun, but it also reminded me that Missouri is the only SEC school to have wrestling as a sport. So, when the precipitation ended, I sauntered over to the Hearnes Center. That is the former basketball arena, which now houses indoor track and field, gymnastics, volleyball and wrestling. Some great athletes have performed in that arena. First-rounders such as Anthony Peeler and World Champions like J'den Cox.

During this particular week, Hearnes was also the home of the blood drive held every year during Homecoming Week. After some exploring, I exited through a side door that dumped me close to the softball stadium. Missouri has a competitive softball team that is consistently improving. They have made the NCAA tournament 15 of the last 16 years. It was good to witness all of it, but it had been a long day, and I needed to change into some dry socks.

I noticed the SEC logo displayed all over the athletic buildings. They certainly take pride in being a member of the conference. Their conference history has evolved over the years. In the early 1900s, the Tigers competed in the Missouri Valley Intercollegiate Athletic Association (MVIAA). In 1928, the conference split, leaving six of the original state schools to form the Big Six Conference. The conference eventually decided to keep the MVIAA name, but most fans and media continued to use the Big Six name.

When Colorado joined in 1947, it was known as the Big Seven. Oklahoma A&M (Oklahoma State) rejoined in 1957 making the conference eight teams deep. The conference was officially titled the Big Eight Conference in 1964. That affiliation continued until the conference dissolved in 1996. That's when they joined four schools from Texas to form the Big 12 Conference, complete with divisions and a championship game. In 2011, it was announced that Missouri (along with Texas A&M) would leave the Big 12 to join the Southeastern Conference. They began SEC play in 2012.

One of the things that MU has always been associated with is its outstanding journalism program. It is one of the oldest in the world and is credited with being the first "J school" in the country. It was established in 1908 and has continued to evolve over the years. The school's home base is Neff Hall, which sits on the north end of the Francis Quad. It's one of eight buildings that make up the journalism complex.

The next most recognized facility is the Donald W. Reynolds Journalism Institute. This massive facility is a leader in researching ways that traditional journalism can use today's ever-evolving technology. In addition to Mr. Reynolds, there have been many recognizable personalities educated at Mizzou's innovative journalism school. Some of the most popular are *Sportscenter* anchors John Anderson and Michael Kim, along with ESPN writer Wright Thompson. There are many others as well. Many of them are well known, and they can all credit a portion of it to the knowledge that they gained at the Missouri School of Journalism.

Something else that the University of Missouri can claim as being the first to establish is the tradition of Homecoming. There are a handful of schools that will challenge the validity that Missouri was first, but Mizzou fans are quick to point out that even the trivia show, *Jeopardy*, acknowledges that the tradition began at the University of Missouri. It all started in 1911 when the alumni were encouraged to come back to campus for the annual game against Kansas. Illinois claims to have begun the tradition when they invited alumni back to campus in the spring of 1910, but Missouri is widely regarded as the

Memorial Stadium

Faurot Field

Surface: Fieldturf

Built in 1926

Capacity: 62,621

Record Attendance:

75,298 - 10/4/80 vs Penn State

Nickname: Tigers

Mascot:

Costumed - Truman the Tiger

*Fans' Favorite Home Games:

Won 36-27 over Oklahoma in 2010

Won 41-26 over Georgia in 2013

first school to do it in conjunction with a regular season athletic event. The annual gathering continued, and it soon became a tradition at Missouri - and at most colleges and high schools around the country too. This was Homecoming Week, and it was the perfect time for *A Season of Homecomings* to visit the origin of the actual tradition.

Homecoming is a special and much anticipated time at the University of Missouri. Even the theme of "Traditions Stand Forever" was appropriate for my visit. The Greek organizations on campus are very involved with the Homecoming activities. They set up activities for local children, construct house decorations and build floats for the parade. The "house decs" are a big deal in the Greek community. On the Friday of Homecoming Week, the "Campus Decs" are put on display for the local community.

It is a major source of pride to be awarded "the best house decs" on campus. Sororities and fraternities team together and work for weeks on constructing their best versions. There are limitations to the percentage of "pomps" that can be used, and there always seems to be some controversy surrounding certain groups' efforts to extend the parameters. Either way, it is the biggest family event in Columbia all year, and the students love being part of it.

I enjoyed touring Greek Town and seeing all of the progress being made on their decorations. I made it around to the other parts of campus, and I was really impressed with care that MU takes to maintain the grounds. Every area seemed full of attractive landscaping. The campus was heavily populated with manicured areas that are perfect to sit and relax, reflect or read. It is home to a great number of plaques, monuments and statues. One that surprised and entertained me was the Beetle Bailey sculpture. Throughout campus, there is a myriad of donated benches. Each one is dedicated to someone and invites people to share its scenic environment.

I woke up Friday morning to a cold and wet Columbia, Missouri. For the first time on the trip, I had to scrape the ice off my windshield. It wasn't necessarily how I wanted to spend turning a year older. After making it to campus and completing an interview, I ventured over to The Mizzou Store. The outside of the university bookstore showed its spirit with a giant tiger tail flowing from the top of the building. I was pleased to find SEC gear available in the store. I was even more pleased to find that the store offers 25% off everything on Fridays before home games. I took the opportunity to splurge and buy myself a birthday gift. It was an SEC cap that I had seen at many of the other bookstores.

Friday afternoon was a great time to be out walking. The rain had stopped, the sun was out, and a cool crisp breeze was blowing through Columbia. It was well after noon, and I hadn't eaten, so I decided to meander to downtown Columbia for a late lunch. Before deciding where to eat, I explored the area. There were a lot of people out basking in the semi-warm rays of sunshine. Families, who were reunited for Homecoming, were enjoying the time they had together. There was a lot of activity, and the shops were brimming with visitors. People were all over the place preparing for the weekend. Whether they were fueling up with adult beverages or purchasing Tiger apparel, it was their way of preparing to enjoy the weekend's festivities.

I had a late lunch at a place called Booches. It is a long-standing Columbia establishment with pool tables occupying its back half. The place was half pool hall and half modern day saloon. It was filled with people. Many people were there to watch the St. Louis Cardinals play in the postseason, while others just came for an afternoon drink. Students brought their Homecoming visitors for a sampling of the fare. The place was packed. When a patron vacated a small table near the front door, I quickly snatched a seat. I searched for a menu only to find it posted on the wall. I placed my order for a hamburger, and the waitress asked "Just one?" I confirmed the order and thought to myself "Man, they must eat good here in Missouri." When the order came, I understood why she asked the question. It was a small sandwich (just bigger than a slider) served on wax paper. It wasn't very big, but it sure was tasty.

After a little more exploring, I made my way back onto campus. Walking through Greek Town, I was able to get a sneak peek of the finished designs before Campus Decs officially started at 6:00 pm. The students were thrilled to show off their work, and they were all very gracious in giving me access. I migrated to Tiger Ave, turned south, and walked past Stankowski Field toward Memorial Stadium. I was on my way to the south end zone open house. The south end zone is the new home of the University of Missouri football training center. The state-of-the-art facility opened in January 2019, and the university was hosting the open house so fans could witness the upgrades in person. I arrived a little before the starting time of 7:00 pm, and the lobby was crowded. As more people arrived, they stood outside in the dropping temperatures because there wasn't any space left indoors.

Finally, a representative came out to thank everyone for coming and explain the procedures of the event, which was created to show appreciation for the fans' support. The only "rules" were to respect any boundaries that were set up and to have fun. I sat back and let most people go through before me. I did that to avoid the crowd, but I also wanted to take a clear photo of the "golden" SEC logo that donned the lobby wall. After doing so, I also took a picture of the Battle Line Trophy, which is awarded to the winner of the Missouri-Arkansas rivalry game. It is a nice trophy that is much bigger than I expected it to be. It was pretty cool to see the excitement of the kids that walked through the facility.

It really was a nice functional place. I was impressed with the number of televisions, especially in the area with the hot and cold pools. The weight room had a lot of space and was a favorite of the fans in attendance. After leaving the weight room, the tour led out to the field. People could walk into the south end zone and take pictures. The video boards and ribbon boards displayed the word "HOME." The shape of the state of Missouri, with a Missouri Tiger logo in the center, formed the "O" in home. From the field, people walked right into an area that was set up like a sports bar. It was a premium area for fans to watch the team warm up from the field level before games. There was access to the locker room, Bunker Club, Show Me Club and meeting rooms. It was an impressive facility and a great event that many fans really enjoyed.

The Homecoming Parade was scheduled to start at 9:00 a.m. on Saturday morning. I was advised to be in place no later than 8:30 am. I watched the parade from a spot near the tower of Memorial Union. There is a sign there that designates the University of Missouri as a Purple Heart University. The designation is to recognize the university's support of men and women who were injured or killed while serving in the U.S. military. The names of 117 MU men, who were killed while serving during WWI, are inscribed inside the archway of the tower. A plaque commemorating the tradition of "Tipping of the Hats" is affixed to the stone on the other side of the archway. The tradition is that you tip your cap while going through the archway as a sign of respect to those who were lost.

The crowd for the parade was thick on both sides of the street. It was a chilly morning, but it did not stop throngs of people from enjoying the long-standing tradition. I recognized plenty of students as their floats eased by. I marveled at how much better their creations looked as a finished product. The parade was larger than some of the corporate parades that I had seen previously. The exhibits just continued to turn and work their way up Hitt Street. At one point, I even thought that the organizers may have sent them around the loop one more time. When the event ended, I left the area and felt the excitement inside of me starting to build as it was another football Saturday in the SEC!

It was still eight hours before kickoff, so I needed to pace myself. A quick stopover at my truck revealed a much fuller Turner Avenue parking structure. At the very top, where I was parked, people had already started partying. Across the street from there, I stopped by the campus' Newman Center to buy breakfast and support their efforts. As I progressed toward the stadium, I saw more and more people arriving. I also noticed more and more students attempting to "hydrate" themselves for the game. There were people set up on a grass stretch near another parking structure. They showed support for two sets of Tigers (Missouri and LSU). There were many people set up in a parking lot across the street from the stadium. I saw Alabama and Vanderbilt declarations there. A few more schools were represented too, but nothing trumped the support for Mizzou.

As I emerged from the tunnel under Stadium Drive, I found myself in an intimate parking lot right outside the north end zone. When I turned to my left, I saw the first SEC flag of the day. That's where I was headed next. That's also where I met Jeff and his gang. It was a great little tailgate. It was decked out in Missouri paraphernalia, and had football showing on TV, interesting stories, a good variety of drinks and plenty of good people hanging around. It even had a chandelier hanging inside the tent.

Jeff told me that he was proud to fly the SEC flag since the day Missouri was admitted into the conference. I was proud of him, too. Yes, because he flew the SEC flag, but more because he did something that I've never seen. He had baskets of small stuffed tigers. When kids go by, they are offered a chance to choose a tiger to take home. It was a fantastic gesture and the reactions of the kids are priceless.

For the record, as I was talking to Jeff, I saw an SEC flag over his shoulder. It was in the lot across the street that I had just walked through. I missed it going by, so I still declared Jeff as the first that day. Besides, he is a great ambassador for Missouri and the SEC.

Southeast of the stadium, behind the Hearnes Center, there was a huge parking lot with plenty of tailgaters. There were big stuffed tigers everywhere. Most of them just sat on the roof of cars or tailgates of trucks, but some people did get creative with them. I didn't see many signs of allegiance to other schools. I did get people proclaiming that they were from Nashville or Fayetteville or Athens. One lady had both as she wore an Ole Miss button (on her Mizzou shirt) and told me how she was from Oxford. Most of the people I met (from other states) had dual allegiances, but were strictly for Missouri that day.

It was a gorgeous day for tailgating - clear and sunny with a light breeze. The leaves were beginning to change as autumn continued to migrate onto campus. Kids tossed footballs around the parking lot. School spirit and colors emitted from all directions. Norman Rockwell would have loved this scene for a college football tailgate version of one of his masterpieces. There were tailgates under big awnings, small tents, outside of motor homes, out of the trunks of cars and some just had a blanket on the ground. No one was there to judge. They were all there to have a good time and root for their Tigers.

I went by other tailgates flying SEC flags. One group had multiple SEC flags, which suited me just fine. There was a contingent there that was happy to see Georgia lose to South Carolina. That would place Missouri in first place in the east with a victory against Ole Miss. I reminded them about Florida also being undefeated, but they felt that UF would lose enough with its schedule. Plus, they liked their chances against them in the November cold in Columbia. They were excited about the upcoming trip to Kentucky so they could go to a few distilleries and possibly the horse races. I enjoyed talking about the conference with them. They had thoughts about everything ranging from basketball to Missouri's football prowess under former coach Gary Pinkel. It is always interesting to hear different people's perspective.

However, when the televisions were changed to the St. Louis Cardinals' baseball game, it was my cue to move on. It was a football Saturday, and I wanted to see Alabama play at Texas A&M.

There were some people near the Tiger Walk that had the SEC games on TV. I stopped to catch the scores, and they invited me in to the tailgate. After a few series of game action, I stepped over and watched the band serenade the fans as they cheered on the players and coaches walking down to the stadium. When they all had gone through, everyone returned to their parties. I went down to the gates outside of the stadium so that I could score a ticket. It didn't take long, but I had to part with $30. I walked around to Jeff's tailgate to check scores again and say thanks for his hospitality. He was having a great time, but he ran out of tigers when I was there. I started seeing groups of Ole Miss fans as I made my way into Memorial Stadium. It was a very orderly and helpful crowd even around large cardboard boxes of free stuff.

The treasured boxes contained plush tiger tails. They were all individually wrapped in a clear package. The University of Missouri had put them out for its fans to take. Fans wave the tiger tails while they cheer, and they are mostly donned when it's third down. Third down used to be the "key" down at Missouri. When the opponents faced a third down, the fans would shake their keys. That tradition has changed to the tiger tails and the fans seem to like it. I commend the University of Missouri for providing the tails and not monetizing the tradition.

Much of the game day experience is centered around making it inclusive and interesting for the fans. As I made it around the stadium, I found a newspaper stand containing the 2019 Mizzou Football Yearbook (with an insert for that night's game) that was free for the fans. The fans are also welcome to sit on the hill or even on the Rock M. Masses of kids were running up and sliding down the hill until it became too crowded to continue. There were many more people on the hill than I expected. And, of course, there was BIG MO, the massive MU drum set up at the top of the hill next to the band. Before the game, a celebrity guest hits the drum six times as the fans spell out M-I-Z-Z-O-U!

There was a cool flyover at the end of Marching Mizzou's rendition of the National Anthem. Truman the Tiger was riding on an old fire truck around the asphalt perimeter as the Tigers entered the field. They had a race between a fan (100 yards) and the Missouri helmet cart (60 yards). The cart took a while to get going and the fan won. When Missouri got a first down, the PA announcer would say "Another first down M-I-Z" and the fans responded "Z-O-U." The video boards showed the word "Home" with the "O" made from the shape of the Missouri (with the Tiger logo in the middle of it). It was all done in an effort to enhance the experience of their loyal fans.

The crowd was into the game from the start. Missouri started off slowly, and Ole Miss quarterback John Rhys Plumlee looked like a baby Manziel. The first quarter ended with Ole Miss on top 7-3. After the first quarter, the Missouri fans waved their arms to the Missouri Waltz (the Missouri State Song). It pepped up the fans and the Missouri offense. Quarterback Kelly Bryant began to do some good things, and Missouri took a 12-7 lead. Despite having an earlier touchdown called back for holding, Ole Miss looked to take back the lead right before halftime. They had the ball inside the 10 right in front of where I sat. The Rebels worked down to the 1, but the Missouri defense was ready for the test. I watched closely as the Tigers stopped Ole Miss on third and fourth down, from the 1-yard line, to preserve the halftime lead.

The third quarter was a completely different story. The Missouri offense, led by Bryant, continued to improve its efficiency. They consistently had big plays while Mizzou's rushing attack turned up the heat with running backs Larry Rountree III and Dawson Downing. The touchdown Ole Miss had called back (in the first half) would have put them up 14-3. Instead, the momentum shifted and by the middle of the third quarter, Missouri led 28-7. Mizzou's Jonathon Johnson added to his stellar receiving numbers with eight catches for 110 yards. The third quarter ended with Missouri holding a 35-14 lead.

Ole Miss tried to mount a rally. Down 35-21, the Ole Miss defense intercepted a pass to give the offense another chance, but when the Missouri defense stepped up again, the outcome was inevitable. Final score - Missouri 38, Ole Miss 27.

When the game ended, I walked out of my section and onto the hill. I went around its base to just behind the goal post. There were kids running up and down the hill and families taking photos in front of the Rock M. The video board in the background displayed a graphic that triumphantly stated "Tigers Win!" As I walked up the hill, I realized two things about the area. The hill is steep and the rocks of the Rock M are larger than I'd anticipated. The rocks are all different sizes, but they are bigger around than the circumference of a football. When I reached the top, I was able to exit the stadium and search for someone watching the LSU-Florida game.

My search proved to be futile. It was difficult to find anyone that hadn't already left or wasn't packing up to leave. I decided to go north toward my truck. As I went, the same story played out. No one in the area was sticking around. After maneuvering through the campus, I found myself at the top of the parking garage. Very few cars were left, and there wasn't a person in sight. I opened the doors to my truck and found the game on the radio. With the doors open and the radio up, I grabbed a bottle of water and had my own makeshift tailgate. The radio call carried through the cold, night air as I explored the campus from a different vantage point. I could see the top of Jesse Hall lit up, and I wondered if tonight was the night that someone attempted to "streak the quad." After a long day and realizing that LSU was going to beat Florida, I decided to pull out of the parking garage. As I drove down Tiger Avenue one last time, a chant kept running through my head. M-I-Z, Z-O-U!

Missouri Tigers

Defensive Linemen

Harold Burnine
(1953-55)

Kony Ealy
(2011-13)

Jeff Gaylord
(1978, 1980-81)

Markus Golden
(2012-14)

Charles Harris
(2014-16)

Danny LaRose
(1958-60)

Shane Ray
(2012-14)

Michael Sam
(2010-13)

Justin Smith
(1998-2000)

Lorenzo Williams
(2004-07)

My favorite players to watch at other defensive positions:

LB - Sean Weatherspoon (2006-09)   DB - Aarion Penton (2013-16)
LB - Kentrell Brothers (2012-15)   LB - Cale Garrett (2016-19)

Tight Ends

Dwayne Blakley
(1998-2001)

Chase Coffman
(2005-08)

Michael Egnew
(2008-11)

Andy Gibler
(1979-82)

Conrad Hitchler
(1960-62)

J.D. McCoy
(2000-03)

A.J. Ofodile
(1991-93)

Albert Okwuegbunam
(2017-19)

Martin Rucker
(2004-07)

Kellen Winslow
(1976-78)

My favorite players to watch at other offensive positions:

QB - Brad Smith (2002-05)   WR - Jeremy Maclin (2007-08)
OL - Evan Boehm (2012-15)   RB - Henry Josey (2010-11, 2013)

Fan Favorites: QB -Chase Daniel, WR - Jeremy Maclin, QB - Brad Smith

9

HAIL STATE!

Week of the October 19, 2019 game against LSU

Mississippi State University is located in the town of Starkville. For years, people around the South have called it "Stark Vegas." Rival schools didn't mean it as a compliment. The moniker was used as a way of saying that there isn't much to do in Starkville. Like most rival-given nicknames or tales, there is a little bit of truth and a whole lot of embellishment. The town and the university have embraced the moniker and used it to accentuate the uniqueness of the place. Starkville is a special community that is proud to host a fantastic school like Mississippi State University and its more than 22,000 students that call Stark Vegas home.

The school was established as Mississippi A&M in 1878 and began classes in 1880. Its roots come from the Morrill Act of 1862. In addition to its land grant status, Mississippi State is one of the few schools nationally to also have the distinction of being a sea grant and space grant institution. MSU is also classified as an R1 doctoral university, which is attributed to being at the highest level of research activity. Mississippi State University has earned a top 10 national ranking in agriculture-related research for a number of years. MSU has been named the FAA's Unmanned Aircraft Systems Center of Excellence.

MSU's campus is large (4,200 acres) and spread out. The campus originates and is centered around the area known as the Drill Field. This is the quadrangle that used to be utilized by the ROTC to do marching drills. Today, the southern end is occupied by the Dave C. Swalm College of Chemical Engineering. The grandiose building mirrors the building that sits on the north end of the quad.

Walking north through the Drill Field, there is a massive American flag and then a bust of Stephen D. Lee (the school's first president). Past his memorial, sits Lee Hall, which is located on the north end and is an enantiomorph of Swalm Hall. There are beautiful, historic buildings all around the quad such as Colvard Student Union, McCool Hall, McCain Hall and Carpenter Hall. The Mitchell Memorial Library sits on the southeast corner of the Drill Field, and it contains the Ulysses S. Grant Presidential Library.

Northeast of the Drill Field is the Chapel of Memories. It is a wonderfully peaceful place with a classic brick finish. When it was built, they used bricks that were salvaged from the Old Main dormitory, which was an enormous residence hall that was destroyed by a fire in 1959. The Chapel of Memories had three wooden doors in the front, all of which have the same pattern of colored glass inserts. Gorgeous landscaping encompasses the whole complex. There was a meditation plaza next to it that has a fountain and a tall clock tower. The clock tower and exterior of the plaza are all made with the same red brick as the Chapel of Memories.

Continuing west down Barr Avenue, it passes Davis Wade Stadium. The recently renovated north end of the stadium was magnificent. It was unrecognizable compared to the last time I was here. The north end was completely closed in after the renovations. I walked down the west side of the stadium and went to the Cullis Wade Depot. This serves as the Welcome Center for the university. There was a beautiful clock featuring the Mississippi State logo on its face. The building also housed the Cullis & Gladys Wade Clock Museum. It was a really interesting museum, but be ready to hear ticking from all directions. There was also an eye-catching display of different variations and designs of the cowbell.

This is basically the center of campus. Traveling south revealed the University Greenhouse, Agrictulture & Biological Engineering buildings and further to Thompson Hall (Wildlife, Fisheries, & Aquaculture). Going east on Bully Blvd was Allen Hall (Math & Statistics). The road eventually went past Eckie's Pond and toward the president's house on Morrill Road.

Going north from the Cullis Wade Depot will take people around all of the Athletic facilities. There was the soccer

Mississippi State, State, MSU

School Colors:

Maroon & White

Traditions:

Cowbells

Tailgating at The Junction

Dawg Walk

"Don't Stop Believing"

Cowbell Yell

Famous Maroon Band

Fight Song - Hail State

Go State

Battle Hymn of The Republic

Favorite Battle Cries:

Hail State

Go Dawgs

complex, Humphrey Coliseum, Palmeiro Center, the Seal Football Complex along with the track, tennis, and softball complexes. There was the Bryan Building (Athletics Administration) and the fabulous Templeton Athletic Academic Center too. This area of campus also includes the crown jewel of collegiate baseball stadiums. Complete with its unique Left Field Lounge, Dudy Noble Field is considered the best place to watch college baseball in the country.

I also spent some time in the town of Starkville. Starkville was known as Boardtown when it was established in 1831. It was renamed Starkville, in honor of Revolutionary War general John Stark, in 1837. I walked through the Cotton District with its colorful array of old southern inspired architecture. There are some cool buildings to see, and I liked how it all seemed like a close-knit community. The Overstreet District was another fascinating area that drips with historic tones. I eventually made it over to Casa Bravo to order the starkvegas quesadilla for lunch.

Back on campus, I decided to get reacquainted with Davis Wade Stadium. I hadn't been there in years, and it certainly didn't look like the place that I recalled. It used to only have east and west stands for the fans, and the north end was open with a freestanding Jumbotron. The locker rooms were in a building behind the south end zone. To get to the visitor's locker room, you had to walk up a concrete ramp. Players had to hold on to the rails because it was so slippery in cleats. Paradise sure didn't await them when they arrived either, as it was a long cramped room with narrow lockers, and it was usually sweltering hot.

Everything has improved dramatically since the renovations in 2014. The north end is very modern and connects the two sides. It houses suites and loges above a new student section, and there is a huge video board above it all. The field level seating is a great feature, and those folks can even go inside to a fantastic lounge area. The entire north end is filled with modern comforts that make it a treat to watch a game from there. There are ribbon boards that run the length of both the east and west sides.

The south end has also been improved, and includes its own massive video board. It has been dressed up with some landscaping and premium seating. That concrete ramp still exists behind some of the landscaping, but they are now covered with neoprene foam, and it isn't for the opposing team any longer. The visitors are housed downstairs in the former home locker room. The old coaches locker room is now the officials' locker room while the old team locker room is now a reception room. Of course, it looks a whole lot nicer than it did prior to the renovations.

On the home sideline at the 50-yard line, there was a monument for Bully, the live bulldog mascot for Mississippi State. The first Bully (Ptolemy) was actually buried under the home bench area when he died in 1939. He is the only Bully buried on the grounds, but the ashes of others have been spread at the stadium. The monument had a small plaque for each one of the bulldogs that have served as the mascot. "Jak" is the reigning mascot, and he is Bully XXI. Bully is beloved as an important part of the treasured traditions at Mississippi State.

Another tradition that State fans hold dear is the cowbell. Legend has it that a dairy cow wandered onto the field during the week of a game against Ole Miss back in the 1930s. The Bulldogs beat the Rebels soundly that week, and the students took the cow incident as a sign of good luck. They started bringing cows to the game, but soon figured out that the bell was much easier.

The fans used to have to sneak them into stadiums because they were banned from 1974-2010 as part of the SEC's rule against artificial noise makers. The "Cowbell Compromise" (an adjustment to the rule) in 2011, made it permissible to again bring the cowbells into the stadium. The cowbells cannot be rung between the time the teams line up and the snap. After the snap, it's fair game and MSU fans take full advantage.

The cowbells have been a staple at Mississippi State for more than 80 years. Every cowbell is unique. Upon acquisition of a cowbell, each fan has it personalized in some way. It might be by a special design or even the memories made with each cowbell. Many of them have been passed from generation to generation, and they are considered a cherished artifact. On game days, cowbells are more essential to a Bulldog fan than even a wallet.

On Thursday afternoon, I made it downtown to an event called Pumpkinpalooza, held on Main Street in Starkville. I was there early, but the street was already blocked off, and the storefronts were readying for a crowd. I walked the length of the street all the way down to City Hall and worked my way back on the other side. It was a family event with music, candy, picture opportunities and the MSU Spirit Squads. Everyone seemed to know one another, and they all had a good time together. Honestly, it felt like the movie *Sweet Home Alabama* in the scene downtown at the city festival.

I spent some of Friday morning around The Junction, which is a large grassy area south of the stadium and is a hotspot for tailgating. There were groups of students who camped all night to save a tailgate spot. One kid was still zipped all the way up in his sleeping bag when I walked past. He looked like a giant caterpillar as all of his buddies were making plans for breakfast. People can unload tents and supplies on the outside of the area in The Junction, but they can't set anything up until 4:00 pm on Friday. It was going to be a while before people were allowed to set up, so I went next door to Davis Wade Stadium.

After walking through the stadium and viewing the final touches on the field, I decided to go attempt to verify parking. The University Parking Office informed me that the athletic department handled parking for game days. I hiked north up to the Bryan Athletic Building, but once there, I couldn't find anything marked with parking. I also didn't see anyone to ask except a lady in the Bulldog Club office. As I walked in to ask for directions, I held the door open for a gentleman walking out. The lady was extremely nice and pointed me toward the ticket office (they also handle parking for games). When I walked out, the gentleman was still there and introduced himself to me.

His name was Brad, and he is a retired Mississippi cotton farmer. He is also a long-time supporter of Mississippi State Athletics. He inquired about what I needed, and we talked for a good while. After seeing and talking to some other folks, Brad asked if I'd had lunch. I hadn't, but I needed to take care of the parking situation first. He instructed me to not worry about that. We went to his vehicle and conversed during a trip to his house. He introduced me to his wife, Mary, as he went inside. He came back out with a parking pass that he gifted me. We switched vehicles and went to lunch.

I saw parts of Starkville that I never would have known about without meeting him. There were neighborhoods being built all over the place. Gorgeous communities that looked catered to families. I learned a lot about Brad's background and some history of Starkville. We had a nice lunch with the conversation mostly centered on Bulldog Athletics. I thought that I was going to be able to pay him back by taking care of lunch. I was able to snag the check first and give the waitress my debit card. That plan was foiled when there was a mix-up with the check. When she returned with the news, Brad gave her his card and instructed her to put the tab all on his card. I was very appreciative, but I didn't want to abuse his generosity either.

On the drive back to my truck, we discussed what makes Mississippi State special. Brad explained it like this: "We are one big family around here. Wherever you go, we go with you."

He gave me a tangible example: "When Dak (Prescott) and KJ (Wright) were drafted, we put up billboards in those towns." When you go to Mississippi State, it is a big family and they are going to take care of you. Brad takes pride in that. He pointed out where their tailgate would be on Saturday and asked me to drop by. He made sure that I was clear on where to park and dropped me off at my truck.

I went to The Junction on Friday afternoon to witness MSU's version of the land grab. The perimeter of the squares was marked off with white spray paint and there were people standing right at the painted border. They waited for the notice to take their spots. People were getting antsy as the time neared. A few people started setting up right at 3:59 pm. Others began to dispute it until they figured that they had better join them. All of a sudden, there were tents going up all around The Junction. Some people rushed to get their tents opened while others just methodically put everything in place. In five minutes, the grassy field had turned into a metroplex of pop up tents.

I drove onto the campus at 7:30 am Saturday morning. There were a number of people already out jogging at that brisk dawn hour. I pulled in to the reserved lot right next to the stadium. The attendant was caught off guard when she noticed me turning in. There wasn't a problem with the parking pass, as I was in the right place; I was just there so early. The only other car in the lot was operated by her supervisor, who was there to deliver breakfast. I was instructed to choose any spot in the parking lot that I wanted. I backed my truck in next to the bus shelter that shielded the CBS command station from the rest of the parking lot. I figured that the CBS trucks would provide a pretty secure area and there weren't going to be any buses coming through there. I made sure that I had enough room on each side and then I took off for The Junction.

Tailgate tents of all colors populated the lawn at The Junction. Tunes pumping through loud speakers entertained the condensed crowd of people who already occupied the front rows for *SEC Nation*. The gray skies reminded me of the day's threat of rain. The wagons full of supplies and the trash-can lined sidewalks left no doubt that a party was about to commence. I went down just a little further to see all of the *SEC Nation* corporate sponsor's layouts.

Velveeta gave samples and passed out t-shirts. Samples of different flavors of Dr. Pepper were available and so was the opportunity to choose a custom design for a "Fansville" t-shirt. Regions Bank took pictures of people with a gigantic green bike, and they also gave out retractable banners. Aflac had a little wind tunnel where kids could go in and grab tickets. Belk had a huge mobile slot machine, where one inserted an SEC token, pushed the button (twice), and waited for it to land on a prize. Academy Sports & Outdoors had a ski-ball game where fans could accumulate points to win different prizes. It was somewhat like a mini-state fair next to the stage on a college football morning. There was plenty of "swag" to go around for everyone. I was just observing until one of the students representing Academy got my attention.

They had a platform shaped as an enormous Academy Sports & Outdoors

Davis Wade Stadium

Scott Field

Surface: Grass

Built in 1914

Capacity: 61,337

Record Attendance: 62,945 - 10/11/14 vs Auburn

Nickname: Bulldogs

Mascot:

Costumed - Bully

Live - Bully XXI (Jak)

*Fans' Favorite Home Games:

Won 38-23 over Auburn in 2014

Won 23-20 over Ole Miss in 1999

camping chair. The purpose was for people to be able to sit on the platform and take a picture holding the logo of their favorite school. As I walked by, he was offering everyone within earshot an opportunity to take a picture with "....any SEC team of your choice." Wait, did he say any SEC team? I asked him if it meant that there was a cut-out for each school. He said "Yeah, every team is in there. Which one do you want?" In the most involuntary manner, I blurted out "I want all of 'em!" He had never heard that before, but he graciously helped me stack twelve of the schools' logos around the base. I held the logos of the teams playing that day (MSU & LSU) in each hand, while the SEC logo stood in my lap. He snapped some photos for me and my new personal tradition began.

By now, the show was about to begin. The fans in the pit were loud and rowdy. They were going to "show out" for Stark Vegas. As the camera drifted south over the Bully statue and up toward the stage for the show opening, *SEC Nation* viewers witnessed a crazed pack of Bulldogs fans. There was a nice level of energy while I was there for the first few segments of the show. The entire area started getting congested pretty quickly. The crowd at the stage grew and started to flood some of the surrounding tailgates. The once lonely tents were now electrified. Televisions, speakers, crock pots and lights all sucked juice from generators. All of the tables and chairs were standing and supporting food or those consuming it.

As I meandered through the criss-crossing pathways of The Junction, the smell of juicy grilled burgers tracked my every step. Somebody was going to do some good eatin'. Different genres of music (mostly country) accompanied the sounds of joyous families enjoying the cooler weather. Footballs, Frisbees, bean bags and washers were being tossed with regularity. The Junction was jammed with people from the *SEC Nation* set all the way to the edge of the stadium. It had filled with people and parties quicker than a clapper jumps from side to side in a ringing cowbell.

I headed west and crossed Stone Blvd. On that side of the street were more formal events for alumni and distinguished guests. As I went by, I noticed an additional huge patch of tents. I followed its path to Fraternity Row and then north all the way to the soccer complex. It was the same story. Rows and rows of fans coming together to celebrate another fall Saturday in Stark Vegas. It continued on both sides of Humphrey Coliseum and out past the east side of Dudy Noble Field. Most of them were State fans, but there were pockets of LSU fans scattered throughout as well.

The menus at these tailgates were as eclectic as the people preparing them. There was everything from steak and crab legs to hotdogs and cheese dip. Traditional Louisiana fare like jambalaya and gumbo graced the plates of each fan base. There was a similar variety of beverages, but brown liquid seemed to be the most popular. Bulldogs and Tigers fans alike were more interested in having a good time than giving each other grief. That was until I made my way back toward the Amphitheater. That's when a charter bus full of Tigers fans drove down Stone Blvd. The driver was blasting his horn the whole way. LSU fans hung out the open door shouting "Go Tigers" and chanting "LSU, LSU ..."

The Mississippi State fans responded by rattling their cowbells with the same amount of enthusiasm. The Bulldogs fans that I saw were more amused than they were perturbed. Behind me was a group of ladies laughing about the whole scene. Their cheerful perspective was fully represented in the name of their tailgate: "Malfunction Junction Tailgate Group." I took a picture beside the CBS bus (with all of the teams logos in view), and I made my way up the hill toward the Bost Extension Building. This is where I found a great group of guys with the best name of a tailgate.

They were known as the "Hailgaters," and their tagline was "Bulldawgs, Brews, Bells, & BBQ." The sign featured a bulldog head in the middle with crossed bones behind it. They even had drink holders with their unique logo on them. They were all family men whose kids were having a great time. They had a lot of good food already prepared and another batch in process. It even had some Cajun flavor amongst it all.

It was entertaining talking with the guys about their history of coming to Bulldogs games and their tailgating experiences. They informed me that it was a good crowd today, but there have been times when it was much larger. I was having a good time, but I had to go meet up with my new pal Brad. I said goodbye to the Hailgaters and slipped through the opening between Bost and the Cullis Wade Depot.

I passed by the CBS trucks and was happy to see that my truck hadn't been disturbed. I found Brad and his tailgate crew on the grass next to the stadium. The event was in full swing. Brad introduced me to some of his friends. They had a nice set up full of meal and beverage choices. There was even a dessert table, which included a large bowl with an assortment of Moon Pies. We went over to talk with his wife, Mary, and he introduced me to their respectful and humble grandson. He is a proficient golfer. I tried to get some tips, but he didn't feel qualified, saying "I just get up there and hit the ball." Little does he know that's about all I do too!

Brad asked if I had a ticket, which I confirmed that I did. As I continued a pleasant conversation with Mary, he went to talk to some of the other guests. When he returned, he handed me a laminated pass to the State Level Loge. He told me that it was an extra that wasn't going to be used. He mentioned that there might be some people that would sit with me. I was very appreciative and had no problem sharing the space. Not long after, we all decided that it was about time to enter the stadium. I had one more thing that I needed to do before going inside.

I hustled down to the southwest corner of Davis Wade Stadium. Earlier, I had seen a lot of people bargaining for tickets in that area. I sat back and watched the trade activity. I saw a young couple looking for tickets. They had just failed to negotiate a deal. I approached them and inquired if they needed a ticket. They were actually newlyweds and needed two tickets. I asked if it would be helpful for me to give them one and then they find a second one. They were open to that scenario, so I handed them my printed ticket.

They were thrilled with the opportunity to get a free ticket. I assured them that it was legitimate and explained that I'd bought it from the university. They kept thanking me, and I refused to take any money. I left them with "Enjoy the game. This is a wedding gift from Brad." Then I rushed back to the other end of the stadium and got in line to go through the metal detectors. If that couple is reading this, then you now know why I did that. I hope that you found another ticket and enjoyed the game. Be kind to each other the way Brad and his family were to me.

I cleared the gate, found the elevators, and rode to the State Level. It is a wonderful addition to the north end of the stadium that was completed in time for the 2014 season. I popped out of the hallway into a large linear room with floor to ceiling windows exposing the field. There were food and dessert tables flanked by drink stations. Suites wrapping around the sides of the north end zone continued down both sides. I went straight ahead through the glass door, down a few steps, and two loges over to the left. It was a private outdoor box like one you might find at the horse races. There were four rolling chairs and a small flat panel television. On the counter sat a tri-fold with game day information and a guide to every televised game in the country.

I was getting my bearings when Brad came over to check on me. He and his family were sitting a few loges down over my right shoulder. I was doing fantastic and told Brad that I would take any seat when the other people came. The look on his face gave me the impression that I might not share the box that day (in fact, I had it to myself because the others were invited to a suite). On the south end zone video board, they played the "More Cowbell" skit from *Saturday Night Live*. When Christopher Walken says "I got a fever ... and the only prescription is more cowbell," the place went bananas. The crowd hollered its approval, and the cowbells squealed to honored Walken's request.

The band played the national anthem, and the cowbells joined in at its completion. The costumed Bully rode a golf cart, which was decorated as a mobile doghouse, through a tunnel of cheerleaders and band members. Bully jumped off the cart just shy of mid-field and worked the crowd into a frenzy. The LSU team then left its locker room, which paused the celebration. Then, the cheerleaders flags started waving as the State players bunched up in the northwest corner with the cowbells rocking. The smoke from the fire extinguishers started to billow, flames shot up from two temporary towers and the team exploded onto the field behind a bunting of Mississippi State flags. The cowbells were ringing very loud and proud. The place was amped.

Mississippi State received the ball first. The Bulldogs attained a quick first down, but then faced a fourth-and-one at their own 45-yard line. MSU decided to go for it, and the fans appreciated the aggressiveness. That is, until the Bulldogs were stopped for no gain. LSU used the good field position and drove down to the 3-yard line. The MSU defense walled up, and the Tigers settled for a field goal.

That scenario basically repeated itself during the next possession for each team. The Bulldogs put together a few plays, but a penalty left them with a longer distance to reach on this fourth down. They decided to punt. The Tigers went on a long drive that exhausted the first quarter clock. The drive stalled at the 5-yard line, and LSU kicked a second field goal for a 6-0 lead.

The cowbells are remarkable. People ring them with a passion and fervor that is not often seen. It sounds like you are in a hyperbaric chamber surrounded by train whistles. From where I was sitting (above the student section), I couldn't hear much from the PA announcer the whole game. I did hear him after some first downs say "First Down Bulldogs..." to which the crowd responded "Hail State!" When the crowd responds, the fans also ring their cowbells in unison. It's actually pretty cool because it sounds like the cowbells are vocalizing the words.

The other neat thing about the cowbells is the control they show during the game. They ring loudly throughout the game, but as soon as the teams line up over the ball - bam! It stops. Of course, that's the rule that they have to follow, but it is remarkable how disciplined they are about it. The clanging returns as soon as the ball is snapped.

The cowbells weren't ringing after State's second play of the next series. It was a fumble that LSU recovered. LSU drove to the 7-yard line this time before kicking yet another short field goal. Bulldogs linebacker Errol Thompson made some tremendous plays to keep Mississippi State's defense competitive. Not all of them resulted in a statistic, but he was a force in the first half. Louisiana native, C.J. Morgan also made some big plays in the secondary for the Bulldogs. The State offense chipped in during the next series. They were finally able to string positive plays together. A 12-yard touchdown run from quarterback Garrett Shrader cut the LSU lead to 9-7.

When the Tigers' offense went back onto the field, they didn't mess around with trying to drive for a score. Joe Burrow threw a strike to wide receiver Racey McMath for a 60-yard touchdown on the first play. But after the extra point was no good, MSU still felt good about their chances only down 15-7. The team's confidence started to build when Shrader hit receiver Stephen Guidry for a first down at the 44. It all came to a halt when LSU safety Jacoby Stevens took back possession with an interception. The LSU offense didn't waste time and scored a touchdown in about a minute. After the LSU touchdown, there was little time left in the second quarter and the half ended with the Bulldogs down 22-7.

The third quarter started slow for both offenses. They traded punts before LSU replicated a quick touchdown drive from the first half. After another MSU punt, the Tigers finally converted an extended drive. Burrow patiently sat behind the offensive line and analyzed the defensive scheme. When the ball was snapped, and the cowbells rang out, the quarterback sent a decisive rocket into receiver Justin Jefferson's hands for a touchdown and a 36-7 advantage.

Another turnover kept the Bulldogs at bay through the rest of the third quarter. With the Bulldogs in possession of the ball, the State fans soaked in one of their newest traditions. Journey's "Don't Stop Believin'" was played before the fourth quarter starts. The crowd cheered and sang along as the cowbells rendered a similar tune. The fourth quarter began new hope as MSU drove the ball inside of LSU's 25-yard line. Trailing by multiple scores, State went for it on fourth down, and the Tigers defense thwarted the attempt.

From that point, the punters started getting more playing time. Mississippi State never quit. They put together an impressive 90-yard drive that resulted in a Shrader to Guidry touchdown pass, but the two-point conversion failed, and LSU ran out the last minute on the clock. The final score was LSU 36, Mississippi State 13.

At the completion of the game, I talked with Brad and his family. I was quizzed about my impression of the game and the atmosphere. My thoughts kept going back to one thing - the best moment that I had seen for the entirety of my journey.

It was Mississippi State University's Salute to Service that day, and Sergeant Matt Zajac was the day's honoree. He honored us all with his presence that day. Everyone there was proud to be Americans and proud to have Zajac home after representing us overseas.

During a television timeout, Mississippi State rolled out a red carpet for Sgt. Matt Zajac to enter the field area. As he came out onto the field in his wheelchair, the PA announcer introduced us to the Veteran. Zajac looked humbled with his head slumped as "God Bless the USA" triumphantly played over the loud speakers. The cowbells reached a rare decibel level. Zajac clapped his appreciation for their recognition. My line of sight began to get blurry when he raised his arms to the sky. It was as if he opened up his chest to receive the adulation into his heart. I didn't know what it was, but you could tell that it meant something more to him. Everyone was standing and cheering. Most of us had tears in our eyes.

As the commercial clock dipped under 20 seconds, someone walked behind Zajac's chair and cued him with a slight nudge. That's when he gently put his hands on the wheels to stop the momentum. Sergeant Zajac positioned his prosthetic legs to the side, shoved himself up out of the wheelchair and walked off the field. The cheers somehow got louder. A powerful USA chant started right in front of him. My hands were throbbing and my tears were flowing, but I didn't care. This was a special moment. The game had resumed, but some Mississippi State players didn't care either. They came down the sideline to show their respect to the soldier.

After doing some research, I learned more about the man who inspired us all that day. He was injured in Baghdad in 2007 while serving during Operation Iraqi Freedom. When he returned home, he faced a tough road to repair his body and mind. When he stabilized physically, he began to pursue a degree in engineering. That was cut short when his father, who raised him, fell ill and passed away. His father was the caretaker for his grandmother. Zajac assumed that role until she also passed. He had lost his only family and was dealing with a divorce. Zajac was trying to figure out how to live life again. After some coaxing, Sgt. Zajac packed up and moved from Arizona to

Arkansas. He had never been to the state of Mississippi before his visit that weekend.

There are videos on the Internet that show him talking about his journey. That day, I felt that it meant more to him than just adulation. His story explained the sense of meaning that circled him in that moment. The video ends with him talking about making the choice to walk off rather than "shuffle off" in his chair. He continued with words that can help us complete every challenge. He stated "We all go through some hard times, but you can't let it beat you ... Just don't let it win, that's all!"

Matt Zajac proved his indomitable American spirit that day. He made us all stronger individuals by helping us realize our capabilities. Thank you for your service and sacrifice Sergeant Matt Zajac! Thank you, Matt, for being you and teaching us what is possible with perseverance. You continue to be a light of inspiration for many of us that were in attendance that day.

I couldn't stop thinking about that moment. Brad's family was about to leave, so we took a few photos before they went on their way. I stayed in the spot and watch (on the TV monitor) Kentucky play in a downpour at Georgia. Well, the rest of the first half anyway. The stadium was empty except for the few people cleaning. The large video board at the other end of the stadium played the press conference that was happening underneath the stands. I watched the UGA-UK game in an empty stadium. It was kind of a wild experience. Finally, it was time for the crew to shut down my area, so I had to find somewhere else to find out who swam to the top in Athens.

When I left the stadium, I decided to go back over to where the Hailgaters were set up. They had packed up and took their families home already. Many others had done the same, but there were still plenty of parties still underway. It wasn't hard to find people tuned in to the other SEC games. I bounced around during commercials to see the most action that I could. Suddenly, I heard a minor commotion. It was the LSU equipment truck lumbering down Stone Blvd. As the LSU staff bid farewell to Stark Vegas,

MSU fans wished them well in no uncertain terms. The State faithful were happy to have them gone so they could go back to watching the games.

When Georgia completed the victory over Kentucky, I went back out exploring the rest of campus. I realized that about two-thirds of the people had departed, but that still left a considerable amount of people making the most of their day at MSU. It was like a big campground without people telling ghost stories (although there were some roasting marshmallows). I set a path toward my truck while still scouting the festivities.

When I reached the parking lot, it had almost returned to the empty state that I found it in the early morning. The big Mississippi State logo on the stadium was now aglow. I got in my truck, took a deep breath, and started toward the campus' exit. I wasn't serenaded like the LSU equipment truck, but there was a faint sound echoing in my ears. It was cowbells ringing in unison with the battle cry, Hail State!

Mississippi State Bulldogs

Defensive Backs

Jonathan Abram (2017-18)

Ashley Cooper (1998-99)

Ken Phares (1970-72)

Jonathan Banks (2009-12)

Frank Dowsing (1970-72)

Pig Prather (1998-2001)

Fred Smoot (1999-2000)

Stan Black (1973-76)

Walt Harris (1992-95)

Darius Slay (2011-12)

My favorite players to watch at other defensive positions:

DL - Greg Favors (1994-97)   LB - Erroll Thompson (2017-20)

DL - Fletcher Cox (2009-11)   LB - Mario Haggan (1999-2002)

Offensive Linemen

Eric Allen (1995-98)

Gabe Jackson (2010-13)

Derek Sherrod (2007-10)

Ben Beckwith (2011-14)

Jesse James (1991-94)

Brent Smith (1993-96)

Pork Chop Womack (1997-2000)

Wayne Harris (1979-82)

John James (1989-92)

Randy Thomas (1997-98)

My favorite players to watch at other offensive positions:

WR - Eric Moulds (1993-95)   QB - Dak Prescott (2012-15)

WR - Kevin Prentiss (1997-98)   RB - Anthony Dixon (2006-09)

*Fan Favorites: QB - Dak Prescott, LB - Johnie Cooks, DL - Fletcher Cox

10

HOLD THAT TIGER

Week of October 26, 2019 game against Auburn

My trip to Baton Rouge began with the truest definition of a homecoming. I was welcomed to Baton Rouge that evening with a family gathering. The family, of my friend David Day, came together to share some wine and homemade gumbo. It was a special way to begin my Louisiana quest. The gathering was at the home of Susan and Don, who would be my gracious hosts for the week. It was apparent early on that this gathering was going to be more of a benefit to me than just the wonderful company and scrumptious medley of flavors that we enjoyed that night. At the dinner table, the family accepted assignments that would help me become fully immersed into the cultures of Baton Rouge and Louisiana State University.

The family has a long history in South Louisiana. David's grandparents both served as sheriff of East Baton Rouge Parish. Robert Day was a two-term sheriff who had already received the Democratic Party's nomination for the 1924 election. Sheriff Day was tragically shot and killed, only weeks before the vote, as he attempted to break up a gambling operation. Governor John M. Parker appointed Robert's wife (Eudora Slaughter Day) as sheriff the next day. As the election neared, without an endorsement from the Democratic Party, E.S. Day campaigned for the post. With the help of newly righted female voters, Day won the election and served the next four years as the state's first elected female sheriff. Even to this day, Eudora Slaughter Day is the only female in history to serve as sheriff of East Baton Rouge Parish.

The Day family also has a long lineage of LSU graduates. It all began with John Wilton Day Sr., who was the son of Robert and Eudora. He attended on a track scholarship and attained his engineering degree from LSU in 1929. Mr. Day was part of the first class to complete its studies at LSU's current campus in Baton Rouge. His wife, Kitty Lanius Day, completed her studies in 1940, and their children would earn another 12 degrees from LSU. The Day family's academic achievements include bachelor's, master's, and doctorate degrees. LSU has conferred 26 degrees to three generations of the Day family.

LSU was established in 1860 in Pineville, Louisiana as the Louisiana State Seminary for Learning and Military Academy. Its first superintendent was none other than Colonel William Tecumseh Sherman. Sherman subsequently resigned from his duties to enlist in the U.S. Army when Louisiana seceded from the Union in 1861. The school closed when many of the students and faculty left to fight for the Confederacy during the Civil War. The school building largely survived the destruction of the war and reopened in 1865. It remained in Pineville until October 1869, when a fire destroyed the seminary building.

After the fire, the school relocated to Baton Rouge. The move was meant to be temporary, but support to rebuild in Pineville never materialized. In 1886, LSU occupied the former military post in Baton Rouge, which was referred to as the "pentagon barracks." The "Old War Skule" continued to grow and needed more room for expansion as early as 1915. Land from plantations in south Baton Rouge was purchased in 1918. After extensive construction, LSU began classes at the contemporary campus in 1925 and dedicated it in April of 1926. Currently, the LSU campus is larger than 2,000 acres and is home to more than 31,000 students.

Louisiana State University has substantial research initiatives. LSU is included on an elite list of national universities that serve as land grant, sea grant and space grant institutions. According to the school's web site, this is the 11th straight year that LSU has been ranked in the top tier for "Best National Universities." The National College Learning Center Association has recognized the Center for Academic Success as one of only two Learning Centers of Excellence in the country.

DesignIntelligence magazine rated the LSU Landscape Architecture undergraduate program No. 1 and the graduate program No. 5 in the country. *The National Jurist* magazine ranks the LSU Law Center as the No. 8 best value law school in the nation.

Kiplinger recognizes LSU as one of the Top 100 public colleges in the country. All of these achievements have been accomplished with LSU maintaining that two in every three students graduate with zero debt. As for the school colors, gold is a reminder to strive for greatness while purple embodies the passionate, spirited Louisiana culture.

I was able to experience some of that Louisiana culture with William Day. He

Louisiana State, LSU

School Colors:

Purple & Gold

Traditions:

Walk Down Victory Hill

First, Second, & Third Down Cheers

"Saturday Night in Death Valley"

Jersey No. 18

H-Style Goalposts

The Golden Band From Tigerland

Fight Song - Fight For LSU

Hey Fighting Tigers

Touchdown For LSU

Favorite Battle Cries:

Geaux Tigers

Tiger Bait

had some time in the morning, so we toured downtown Baton Rouge. William took me to the Louisiana State Capital, which still is the tallest capital in the U.S. The building was the brainchild of Louisiana's infamous Governor Huey Long. It was built in a relatively short amount of time (14 months) and it was completed in 1932. "The Kingfish" was very proud of the building. Ironically, it was also where he was assassinated in a marbled hallway in 1935. The recent patches to the bullet holes still show witness to the attack. Long is buried on the grounds and a statue of him faces the capital building.

We took two elevator rides up to the observation deck on the 27th floor. Standing 350 feet above the ground, the observation deck shows a great view of Baton Rouge in all directions. The capital is still a beautiful working building that is symbolic of the entire state. Just a few steps away, Veteran's Memorial Park is a gorgeous green space dedicated to the throngs of Louisianans who have served in the United States Military. The Baton Rouge Gold Star Families Memorial Monument is a powerful tribute to the veterans and their families who paid the ultimate price.

William and I walked down to the USS Kidd, which is anchored on the banks of the Mississippi River. We walked out on an elevated pier that allowed us different views of the destroyer, the casino boats and the towering Horace Wilkinson Bridge. We were right across the street from the Raising Cane's River Center Arena. On our way back, we saw the Louisiana Old State Capital which resembles a medieval castle. It is a fabulous historic building that now serves as the Museum of Political History. It was designated as a National Historic Landmark in 1974.

We continued on toward the Pentagon Barracks. This is where the LSU campus was located from 1886-1925. The buildings now house offices and private apartments for government officials. They have a terrific view of the Louisiana State Capital Building.

William then had a special treat for me. We drove past where his father worked as an engineer for almost 50 years and went to Southern University. He showed me Scott's Bluffs, which had stunning views of the Mississippi River. I also saw the "Red Stick Sculpture." Legend has it that French explorers saw a tall post with red markings (thought to be animal blood) that delineated the boundary of hunting grounds for local tribes. This is thought to be the genesis of how the town came to be called Baton Rouge (French for red stick).

I made it to the edge of campus in time for a late lunch. The Chimes Restaurant & Tap Room on Highland Drive couldn't have been a better place to get indoctrinated to the LSU culture. This Baton Rouge tradition sits just outside of the northern gates of the university. Afterward, I walked down Highland to the welcome center. Across the street from the welcome center is the delightful parade ground outlined by ancestral oaks. At the midpoint of the parade ground, one can look across Highland Road to the stately Paul M. Hebert Law Center. Staying on the west side, a brick-lined path leads to the LSU War Memorial in the center of the parade ground.

The LSU War Memorial honors those who lost their lives in military conflict. Starting with WWII, those names are carved into the circular memorial. In the center is a tall flag-pole waving a yellow LSU flag. A larger blue state of Louisiana flag and a grand flag of the United States of America fly above it. The backdrop is the majestic 175-foot tall Memorial Tower. The stirring clock tower was built in memory of the 1,447 Louisiana soldiers who died during WWI. The chimes above the clock face sing every 15 minutes and play the *Alma Mater* each day at noon.

The stunning student union resides on the southern edge of the parade ground. The student union offers an array of amenities and services to the LSU students. There are many dining options, an art gallery, the Union Theater, offices for student government and much more. There is constant activity in and around the student union. Just outside its doors is a more docile and reflective place. The Memorial Oak Grove houses thirty live oaks that were dedicated to a fallen soldier. One of the remarkable trees is dedicated to "The Unknown," which represents those missing in action.

I ambled between many of the engineering buildings. Eventually, I wound up standing next to the T-33 aircraft on the corner of South Stadium Drive and Field House Drive. It is right across the street from the Military Sciences and Aerospace Studies complex.

The plane hasn't always been at this location. From December 1966 when it was loaned to the university until November 2016, the plane was located closer to Tiger Stadium. The expansion of the stadium caused the "T-Bird" to relocate to its new spot.

As I traversed under the shadow of the stadium's southeastern corner, it looked much different since I had last visited fewer than ten years prior. It was no longer the view of the back of the scoreboard (displaying the national championship years) that I remembered being perched on top of five steel columns. The view has become a mass of suites and club level seating that connects the east and west stands. I entered through the unlocked doors and took an elevator to the suite level. At the top, I could see across Baton Rouge to the State Capital. I wasn't as high up, but from that distance it seemed as if I was looking at it from its Southern counterpoint.

My trek took me down the east side of the stadium past the journalism building and the Hill Memorial Library. I arrived at the LSU Campus Mounds and saw that they were fenced off, which is normal during a home football week. The mounds are estimated to be thousands of years old. In an effort to preserve them, tailgating is no longer permitted in the area. Further Northeast is the amazing Greek Theatre. It is a gem of an assembly point surrounded by artistic landscaping and trees full of Spanish moss. I joined a few students who also found the spot to be a perfect retreat from the constant activity on campus.

My expedition around campus resumed the next morning. I parked outside of the southwest corner of Tiger Stadium. I had a meeting in the athletic administration building and then explored North Stadium Drive. The mostly shaded road runs right between Tiger Stadium and the Pete Maravich Assembly Center (PMAC). On that end of the stadium, there are plaques dedicated to the LSU football players that have won national awards. The entrance to the football locker room and a weight room for many LSU athletes is also located there.

I went across the street and up the ramps to enter the PMAC. It was built in 1971, but it is still in great condition. The lights highlighted the phenomenal looking basketball court. I walked around the concourse and witnessed many acknowledgements of prominent LSU athletes. There were mentions of players like Joe Dean, Seimone Augustus, Sylvia Fowles, and fellow Louisville (KY) native Rudy Macklin. Also on North Stadium Drive is Mike the Tiger's Habitat. The current live tiger mascot is Mike VII. He has been at LSU since 2017. Mike's magnificent home encompasses over 15,000 square feet and includes many amenities for him to enjoy. On the outside, there is a tiger statue, multiple large bay windows for viewing, and many educational displays. After my introduction to Mike VII, I had another meeting before a lunch appointment at one of Baton Rouge's favorite restaurants.

Not only is Mike Anderson's Seafood Restaurant a town treasure, but Mike Anderson himself is literally an LSU legend. He was honored as LSU's SEC Legend in 2002. Anderson was a standout linebacker for the Tigers from 1968-1970. He earned consensus All-American honors in 1970. He opened Mike Anderson's College Town Seafood and Oyster Bar in November of 1975, and he has enjoyed immense success ever since. I had the pleasure to have a great conversation with Mike as I ate lunch in the restaurant's bar area. He was happy to talk about Baton Rouge and the LSU Tigers as he drank a glass of iced tea.

Anderson discussed how he went to Lee High School just down the road from where we sat. He recalled, "This area was all woods. We used to come here and play when I was a boy." He is Baton Rouge through and through. When it came time to pick a college, there was only one option. "This is my home. I never considered playing anywhere else," Anderson told me. Playing at LSU also meant being in the SEC, something Mike made sure that he emphasized.

"The SEC was the premier football conference and I wanted to be a part of it." He feels fortunate to have had the opportunity to play at LSU, in the SEC and to start a successful business all right here in his hometown.

There are odes to LSU and his playing days throughout the bar area. Team pictures and photographs of his best tackles, his old helmet (adorned with "45" on the side) and even framed photos of every modern-day LSU head football coach are on display. His favorite is the large frame holding a black and white print with an overhead view of an empty Tiger Stadium. Written in black marker on the picture, are the words "Death Valley," the date (Dec. 5, 1970) and final score of LSU 61 Ole Miss 17. Beating Ole Miss with Archie Manning was special because, as Anderson explains it, "Archie had beaten us single-handedly the two years before."

Mike Anderson is a hometown success story in Baton Rouge.

Later that afternoon, I experienced another delight. I met up with local attorney Joe Simmons at the new Alex Box Stadium to watch the LSU baseball team compete in an intrasquad scrimmage. Simmons has been a long-time attendee of LSU games in Tiger Stadium and Alex Box Stadium. He also travels to Omaha when the LSU baseball team qualifies for the College World Series. It was odd for me to watch baseball in the middle of football season, but it was a fantastic experience. In the late innings, we explored the entire stadium. We made it to the press box, locker room, coaches' offices, meeting room (filled with postseason trophies) and the LSU Baseball Hall of Fame. As we exited the stadium, we were able to observe the Championship Plaza and the Legacy Plaza (with the new Skip Bertman statue).

Joe's enthusiasm was even more refreshing than the infusion of a different sport. We eventually left campus and went to meet with his wife, Patricia Day. They took me to an old haunt that they visited as kids and still enjoy today. Fleur de Lis Pizza has been around since 1946. The inside had a pinball machine and a true jukebox. The pizza was fantastic, and the restaurant reminded me of a scene from *Happy Days*. We talked about their families and

Tiger Stadium

AKA – "Death Valley"

Surface: Grass

Built in 1924

Capacity: 102,321

Record Attendance: 102,321 - Multiple Times

Nickname: Tigers

Mascot:

Costumed: Mike the Tiger

Live: Mike VII

*Fans' Favorite Home Games:

Won 28-21 over Florida in 1997

Won 7-6 over Auburn in 1988

tailgating experiences. I even learned about the gas-powered blender that they used for a while. It was a nice and relaxing evening with two great Baton Rouge natives.

I left for Lafayette early the next morning to pick up my nephew at the bus station. Josiah has been a loyal LSU Tiger fan for many years. He had been texting me every week asking when I was going to LSU. Susan and Don were very generous in offering to let Josiah stay at their home. The 19-year old used his own money to pay for the 12-hour bus ride. When I picked him up, he didn't want to eat or sleep. He just wanted to get to Baton Rouge. Josiah's excitement rejuvenated me, and we were off to indulge in the campus at LSU.

I paced the discoveries, as I knew we had a long three days ahead of us. As I drove through campus, Josiah marveled at the sights. We parked at Tiger Stadium and saw CBS was already in town preparing to televise the game. I led him around the west side of the stadium viewing all of the team and player plaques along with the tiger and Billy Cannon statues. I was trying to save the north side to surprise him later. Fortunately, his adrenaline leveled out and his teenage hunger kicked in.

We went to eat at the original Walk-On's Sports Bistreaux. The atmosphere and the plate left Josiah's eyes wide open. I was pleased to see the helmets from every SEC team hanging from the ceiling. After satisfying his hunger, Josiah was ready to join me on a personalized tour of campus.

We met John W. Day Jr. outside of the Energy, Coast, and Environment Building, where he has earned the title Distinguished Professor. Dr. Day has taught at LSU since he returned in 1971 with his Ph. D. in Marine Sciences and Environmental Sciences. He has conducted research in many areas of the country and around the world. Dr. Day has received numerous awards including the Lipsey Professional Educator Award (2000) and the William A. Niering Outstanding Educator Award (2003).

I am hardly qualified to explain Dr. Day's expertise, but it was obvious that he has a great grasp on the history of LSU. We toured much of the Historic District of campus including the quad. Dr. Day provided a wealth of information about the use of Northern Italian Renaissance style of architecture and how the azaleas and crepe myrtles have been blended with the oaks and magnolias on the quad. He recalled when Middleton Library was added, and he walked us through the fresco murals of Allen Hall.

When we were finished, I requested directions to the Lod Cook Alumni Center. I was made aware that the patriarch of the Day Family (John Sr.) had purchased bricks for his children who had earned degrees from LSU. Instead of giving us directions, Dr. Day drove us there. We were able to quickly find the bricks for his parents, siblings, and even his own, which he hadn't seen before. We thanked him for his hospitality, and he was off to a previously scheduled engagement.

On our walk back toward the stadium, Josiah and I stopped by the unbelievable University Recreation Center. Neither one of us had seen anything quite like it. It has been recently updated with additions that include an indoor jogging trail one-third of a mile long, a large climbing wall, turf training area and a leisure river in the shape of the LSU logo. Across the street is a phenomenal challenge course. As we continued the march back through campus, I was able to point out things that I had seen earlier in the week. When we neared the stadium, I prepared to unveil the attractions north of the stadium to my awestruck nephew.

We checked out the weight room before Josiah perused the plaques on the stadium wall. I pointed out the number of awards Glenn Dorsey had won in 2007, alluding to how dominant he was that year. Josiah was itching to visit the PMAC, but I veered him left toward Mike's Habitat. I think that he was glad that I did. Mike VII is still fairly young and is a showman. The 400-pound cat's playful antics, like bobbing his head back and forth and seemingly posing for pictures, were entertaining to witness.

As we observed Mike VII, there was man who sat on a bench and monitored the area like an incognito secret service agent. Not long after, that man went through the outer gate on the side and interacted with Mike VII through the inner fencing. The man was Dr. David Baker, Mike VII's personal veterinarian. It was incredible to view the connection between the two of them. We were privy to an impromptu Q&A session that Dr. Baker had with some visitors. It was interesting and informative. One lady had tears in her eyes as she confessed to Dr. Baker, "Mike represents the spirit of LSU for all of us!"

When we finally left, I took Josiah up through the PMAC. He had as much fun as I did seeing the tributes to the past players and teams. We then walked behind Mike's Habitat, past the Bernie Moore Track Stadium and to the entrance of the basketball practice facility. At that point, Josiah was able to see the statues of Naismith Hall of Fame players Bob Pettit and Shaquille O'Neal. The statues were as impressive as each of the players' careers. The statues sit on an individual stone base that has a plaque on all four sides. The plaques have pictures, stats, and small bios of each player.

Josiah eagerly consumed every facility that we encountered. The athletic facilities were his favorites. I took him over to the Football Operations Center across Nicholson Drive. There is an impressive entrance for the players. A replica of the famed white H-style goalpost frames the opening of the hallway leading to the inner workings of the facility. The hallway is lined with trophy displays lit in a vibrant yellow. At the end of the hallway are the National Championship trophies melded with two yellow LSU helmets against a purple backdrop. We walked around the facility, saw the practice fields, and traversed to Alex Box Stadium. The baseball Tigers were having another scrimmage that I knew Josiah would enjoy.

The gray skies constantly released raindrops and made Friday wet and soggy. Josiah and I began by visiting the John M. Parker Agricultural Coliseum. I explained the fact that the "Cow Palace" was where "Pistol" Pete Maravich played his games while attending LSU. Josiah appreciated that, but as a horseman, he liked the current arrangement, which included a dirt floor set up for rodeos and horse shows. The concourse looked like a gym from the movie Hoosiers and has large display windows (like trophy cases) that show off old 4-H projects. When we left, I informed Josiah of a surprise that I had planned for us.

We joined Grant, a graduate-assistant with communications, for a tour of Tiger Stadium. It started out in the locker room area where there were tributes to NFL draft picks, current players in the NFL and a list of the biggest wins in Tiger Stadium history. The tour continued through the locker room and out to the doors that led to the field. The doors were painted with the "Tiger Eye" and sat just underneath "The Win Bar." We made sure to touch the piece of the goalpost painted with a purple and gold "WIN!" as we exited toward the field. Above the exterior of the doors was a sign displaying SEC championships covered by a white awning listing the years of national championships.

Standing behind the north end zone, we were able to take in the cavernous stadium. It was eerily similar to the last time I visited, yet it was also much larger. The expansion has increased the size, but the stadium maintains the feel and mystique that it has always presented. We followed Grant up to the press box and were able to consume the beauty of the entire stadium. The field looked pristine with its traditional numerical markings every five yards and SEC logos on each 25-yard line. We had a great conversation with Grant, and he bid us adieu outside the north end of the stadium.

We moved across Nicholson Drive to the set of *SEC Nation*. Josiah was able to get a picture with Tim Tebow. We talked with Laura Rutledge on her return after becoming a new mother. She is always so cordial and talked with many of the fans. Marcus Spears was thrilled to be home. We were separated by a barrier and about five feet of space as we talked with Spears. Despite the rain pouring down, he left the cover of the tent and came over to speak with us more personably. The SEC personalities gave Josiah another example of greatness in the conference.

That evening was spent in the company of our wonderful hosts Susan and Don. They had prepared a meal for us, and it was nice to spend some personal time with them. As Tropical Storm Olga intensified over Baton Rouge, we remained in the comforts of a dry home and good company. Our night ended fairly early as we prepared for a 6:00 am departure the next morning.

An autumn Saturday in Baton Rouge is special no matter what the weather conditions happen to be. I had an idea of what to expect, and I wondered what Josiah's thoughts were heading to campus. This pre-dawn morning was fairly silent except for the constant drip of water from every overhead perch. We parked in a lot next to the Charles McClendon Practice Facility and gravitated to the warm glow of golden lights declaring "Tiger Stadium." We made our way to one of the larger RV lots off the Nicholson Drive Extension. Josiah was astounded by the number and extravagance of the RV's. He kept looking up their value on his phone.

It wasn't much longer before a group invited us into their circle. The group of friends had gotten together to cook for a co-worker's tailgate party. The chef had prepared some deer sausage to hold the crowd over until the fried chicken and ribs were ready. We had some good conversation and laughs. Before we left, the guys made us promise to return for the chicken. We continued touring the RV lot meeting people setting up for the day's events. As the dawn gave way to an overcast sky, we had already racked up more than a handful of tailgate invites.

I took Josiah back over to the set of *SEC Nation* so he could experience the atmosphere of the live show. We indulged in the festival of sponsors by accumulating give-away t-shirts for his siblings. We met some LSU cheerleaders who gladly recorded a video wishing Joey (Josiah's brother) good luck at his play-off game. We dropped by a few other tailgates where people welcomed us and apologized for the rain. The weather had limited the crowd, but it was still in excess of the 100,000 plus ticket-holders.

As we headed back to the acres of RV's, we saw people dressed in purple and gold diamond patterned suits and LSU visors with silver-plated hair extending from the top. One guy was dressed as a Mardi Gras version of Gene Simmons. The parties were now in full force. People warmed themselves with beverages of all sorts, and we were propositioned with a plethora of Cajun flavors. When we arrived to revisit our first friends of the day, we indulged in the fried chicken. It was the best fried chicken that either of us had ever sampled. We shared some more laughs and pulled ourselves away to fulfill our promise of returning to other tailgates.

The WTF (We're Tiger Fans) tailgate had us feeling gluttonous all over again. The jambalaya was extraordinary. Gene Plauche was the host of the marvelous tailgate scene, and he gave us a tour of the inside of the RV. The outside was wrapped with historic scenes of LSU football, Mike the Tiger and a list of every LSU athletics conference and national championship. By the way, the jambalaya was delectable. There were purple and gold tents designating places to eat and drink. The music had people using the parking lot as a dance floor. Did I mention that the jambalaya was tasty?

We made a few more stops on our way to North Stadium Drive, getting there in time for the Tiger Walk. It was an epic college football scene. People were ten rows deep on each side of the road and the ramps to the PMAC were also packed. Motorcycled troopers rode through with their sirens alerting people that the team was coming. Friends and acquaintances led the way before Coach Orgeron came through delivering hooks and uppercuts to the air. He was pumped and so was the crowd. An "LSU" chant endured as the team made its way to the locker room. There was another younger uncle and nephew pairing that stood in front of us against the barrier. The uncle made sure that we didn't leave before the band came through.

"The Golden Band from Tigerland" started at the Greek Theatre and marched down between Tiger Stadium and the PMAC. The "Golden Girls" and majorettes led the band down Victory Hill. They stopped right in front of us. The drummers began to tap a different beat and then BUM ... BUM BUM ... BUM, the "The Pregame Salute!" It welled emotion inside of me that I didn't know I had for LSU. The crowd exploded as the beat was repeated toward all four sides. The entire band then continued with "Touchdown for LSU" as they energetically danced toward the stadium as the crowd passionately chanted "LSU, LSU, LSU..."

It electrified Josiah and I. We did make appearances at a few more tailgates on the west side, but we were soon ready to get into the stadium. We stood in line for several minutes before we gained admittance and immediately started the climb to our seats. Josiah had a puzzled look when LSU PA announcer Dan Borne' said over the loud speaker "...chance of rain" and the crowd hollered "Never!" It has become lore in Baton Rouge that "it never rains in Tiger Stadium" and as an LSU fan, Josiah readily accepted it.

Even if it did rain, we wouldn't get wet because we were seemingly sitting above the clouds. In fact, after Borne' announced "It's Saturday afternoon in

Death Valley," some of the fireworks (shot from the field during the team's entrance) actually exploded below us. It was time for a showdown with No. 9 Auburn.

The kickoff went to the Auburn Tigers. Their first play went for 11 yards and a first down. The LSU defense allowed them three more plays before forcing them to punt. LSU's offense could only manage three plays of its own before punting.

A penalty on the punt gave Auburn the ball at its own 46-yard line. Auburn took advantage of the field position and drove deep into LSU territory. The 14-play (42 yards) drive ended with a field goal from kicker Anders Carlson that gave Auburn an early 3-0 advantage. LSU essentially reciprocated Auburn's previous drive, going 41 yards on 11 plays. A negative play on a first down and a penalty on third down undermined the drive and forced LSU to punt. LSU's defense held Auburn in check and gave the band another opportunity to play "Tiger Bandits." The song is played when the defense forces the opponent to give the ball back to LSU. The fans raise their arms overhead and repeat a bowing motion.

LSU's next drive started out poorly as Auburn's defensive tackle Derrick Brown sacked Joe Burrow. After a short completion, the first quarter ended with LSU facing a third-and-twelve at their own 9-yard line. The second quarter began with Burrow using his legs to convert the long third-down attempt. He used his arm the rest of the way and the LSU Tigers found themselves in the end zone after a 10-play 89-yard drive. LSU forced Auburn to punt again, and the Bayou Bengals looked to add to its 7-3 lead.

They moved 43 yards down to Auburn's 29-yard line, where they faced a second-and-one. It turned into a third-and-one and then a fourth-and-one. LSU tried for a third time but still couldn't gain a yard. Auburn's defense had stepped up in a big way. Auburn's offense couldn't follow suit and punted again. The punt sailed 44 yards before LSU fumbled on the return. The Auburn coverage unit pounced on the ball and gave the offense a reprieve. It took Auburn seven plays to navigate the 22 yards, but quarterback Bo Nix finally converted on fourth down from the 1-yard line. Auburn led 10-7 with three minutes left in the half.

LSU used 2:22 of that time to go 73 yards down to Auburn's 2. Facing a fourth-and-one, Orgeron decided not to pass up points. LSU kicker Cade York made the short field goal and the game was tied 10-10.

But Auburn had no intention of letting the game stay tied. Running back D.J. Williams busted a 41-yard run into LSU's territory with 13 seconds remaining before half. Two plays later, LSU corner Derek Stingley Jr. came up with an interception at the 2-yard line, and the score remained LSU 10, Auburn 10 at the half.

During halftime, Josiah and I moved to the other side of the stadium to watch the second half from a different angle and a lower level. LSU started the second half with a quick first down but then had to punt. On Auburn's first play, Williams gashed the defense again. He broke through the line, angled left and rumbled toward the end zone. It looked like he was close to scoring, but the replay proved that he stepped out of bounds at LSU's 9-yard line after a 70-yard gain. The offense couldn't progress much further, so Auburn settled for a field goal and a 13-10 lead.

LSU would once again have a drive (74 yards) that resembled the previous Auburn possession's output (73 yards). The Auburn defense would also mirror something it did in the first half, stopping LSU on downs. This time it happened at the 1-yard line. Afterward, Auburn's offense was backed up and not able to break out. The next possession was similar, and Auburn punted again.

The Auburn offense became impotent against the LSU defense, while running back Clyde Edwards-Helaire gave LSU a kick start. Four straight carries from the scrappy back produced 45 yards and a touchdown. After the PAT was missed, LSU was on top, 16-13.

When LSU got the ball back, Burrow kept the momentum going. He ran for a big third-down conversion that started the drive. A few Edwards-Helaire runs sandwiched a completion to wide receiver Justin Jefferson, and LSU was at Auburn's 27 as the third quarter ended. During the break, Garth Brooks' "Callin' Baton Rouge" came over the loud speaker. The majority of the stadium clapped and sang along with the beloved tune. The energy stayed elevated as the fourth quarter began.

LSU continued clicking off positive gains. They eventually faced a third-and-2 at Auburn's 7-yard line. This was a crucial play for both teams. LSU came out in an empty set that left Burrow as the only LSU player in the backfield. Players for both teams were strewn across the width of the field. The ball was snapped, players ran to the edges of the field, and Burrow jaunted up the middle for a 7-yard touchdown. The band played the "Hold That Tiger" portion of "Tiger Rag," and the fans chanted "T..I..G..E..R..S, Tigers!" LSU's lead was now 23-13.

From there, both offenses were stagnant. LSU's band continued practicing "Tiger Bandits" as Auburn punted three more times. After LSU's third consecutive punt, Auburn took over at the LSU 49-yard line with 3:19 left to play. A few completions (and a pass interference call against LSU) put Auburn at LSU's 5-yard line. Bo Nix paid it off with a touchdown pass to wide receiver Seth Williams. The lead was down to three, and people started feeling a little anxious. LSU covered the onside kick and proceeded to run out the clock. The final score was LSU 23, Auburn 20.

LSU had 508 yards compared to Auburn's 287, and they had 30 first downs against 16 for Auburn. Two turnovers and failures on two fourth-downs made LSU fans sweat it out. Ultimately, the LSU Tigers obtained a tough conference victory over a ranked team and sat at 8-0 on the season. The fans cherished the victory and took it as a good reason to recommence the celebrations. Josiah and I soaked up more time in "Death Valley" and then re-joined the festivities.

We made a few stops at familiar tailgates, and then were invited to join a new set of friends. The people were wonderful and so was the boudin they served us.

One of the most iconic plays in Tiger Stadium history is the Billy Cannon punt return touchdown on Halloween in 1959. It gave No. 1 LSU a 7-3 lead late in the fourth quarter against No. 3 Ole Miss. Many people claim to have been there, but I believe that I finally met someone who saw the famed run! Well, sort of. He was nine years old at the time. He saw Cannon catch the ball and make his first cut. He saw nothing after that. Everyone stood up in front of him, and he could only hear the crowd roar. What he did see was Ole Miss drive down to the 5-yard line with a precious few seconds left in the game. He remembers a huge hole opening for the Ole Miss runner. About that time, Billy Cannon and a teammate stepped in and collided with the ball carrier. Ole Miss was thwarted and LSU held on for the 7-3 victory.

We said our goodbyes and fulfilled our desire to take another loop around the stadium, PMAC and Mike's Habitat. Then we reluctantly retreated to my truck. We leaned on the tailgate and gazed over at the illuminated battlefield. Together, we understood each other's unspoken desire to stick around just a little longer. It was about relishing the time spent together at a college football game. Recognizing everything that this game meant for the seasons of both teams. Appreciating the hospitality of LSU and the people of Louisiana. Experiencing a fall Saturday with family in the SEC. A perfect Louisiana Saturday night! Geaux Tigers!

LSU Tigers

Defensive Backs

Tommy Casanova
(1969-71)
LaRon Landry
(2003-06)
Eric Reid
(2010-12)

Morris Claiborne
(2009-11)
Tyrann Mathieu
(2010-11)
Corey Webster
(2001-04)
Greedy Williams
(2017-18)

Greg Jackson
(1985-88)
Patrick Peterson
(2008-10)
Tre'Davious White
(2013-16)

My favorite players to watch at other defensive positions:

LB - Bradie James (1999-2002)   LB - Ron Sancho (1985-88)
DL - Glenn Dorsey (2004-07)   DL - Marcus Spears (2001-04)

Running Backs

Joseph Addai
(2002-05)
Kevin Faulk
(1995-98)
Derrius Guice
(2015-17)

Charles Alexander
(1975-78)
Leonard Fournette
(2014-16)
Dalton Hilliard
(1982-85)
Harvey Williams
(1986-90)

Billy Cannon
(1957-59)
Eddie Fuller
(1986-89)
Jim Taylor
(1956-57)

My favorite players to watch at other offensive positions:

WR - Wendell Davis (1984-87)   OL - Nacho Albergamo (1984-87)
WR - Eddie Kennison (1993-95)   QB - Joe Burrow (2018-19)

Fan Favorites: QB - Joe Burrow, DB - Tyrann Mathieu, RB - Jacob Hester

11

ON THE HILL

Week of the November 2, 2019 game against Mississippi State

The drive through Fort Smith was peaceful and aesthetically pleasing. It was an early iridescent morning with the sun peaking through an autumn color wheel of trees. There wasn't much traffic besides the occasional truck or school bus passing by in the opposite direction. I was headed to Fayetteville, and it wouldn't be much further now. There's never been a very easy way to get to Fayetteville, but a newer addition to I-49 sure does help. Forty-five minutes later, the drive was winding through mountains and I knew that I was close. Entering Northwest Arkansas, I could sense that it was a different type of place. It was different than I had imagined, and it had a distinct feel.

It didn't take very long for me to figure out that Northwest Arkansas is a hidden gem. There has been continued growth in industry, infrastructure and amenities in the area. There's diversity in its people and its economy. There is an endless variety of dining, entertainment, and shopping. Northwest Arkansas is booming, yet it maintains a small-town feel, as every town in that part of the state seemingly has its own town square. The towns mesh together, but they continue to preserve their autonomy.

The region is home to an array of outdoor activities. There are literally hundreds of miles of trails for hiking or mountain-biking and it also offers many choices of destinations for fishing, camping or rock climbing. It is a progressive and beautiful area.

Bentonville is recognized as the retail capital of the world. Of course, it is also the home of Wal-Mart, the world's largest company. There are hubs of major businesses all around Northwest Arkansas. Lowell houses the headquarters for trucking giant J.B. Hunt and a massive Fed Ex facility. Tyson Foods has its home base in Springdale. Those are just the companies on the Fortune 500 list. Many other well-known companies have operation centers scattered throughout the area. The increase in businesses is accompanied by an inflow of jobs, higher wages and transplants. The southern gateway to Northwest Arkansas (NWA) is Fayetteville.

Fayetteville is experiencing its own growth spurt. The town square features historic buildings combined with newer structures. While there, visitors can see a waterfall, do business at the old bank and get some good eats at Cheers at the OPO (old post office) or Hugo's. Dickson Street, which runs directly into campus, is a convergence of shops and restaurants and is the epicenter of entertainment in Fayetteville. Also located on Dickson is the Walton Arts Center. The Walton Arts Center hosts numerous events including musicals, recitals, concerts and weddings. A block down from there, I saw an old train that was converted into a bank. It was pretty neat. A couple of weeks before I arrived, Fayetteville hosted the annual Bikes Blues and BBQ motorcycle rally, which is one of the biggest in the nation.

Fayetteville's crown jewel is the University of Arkansas. It is the flagship university in the state of Arkansas. The school was founded in 1871 and has an enrollment exceeding 27,000 students. It is referred to as "The Hill" because it was created on the land of a farm that sat on a hilltop with terrific views of the Ozark Mountains. The Hill offers more degree programs than any other school in the state. The University of Arkansas is ranked 15th in the nation for the number of NSF (National Science Foundation) CAREER Awards for research. It is also the 15th fastest growing university in the country.

Driving onto campus, the first building I saw was Baum-Walker Stadium, on the south end. The stadium is where the baseball team plays and it is a grand stage. I was able to get a good view of the facilities from the right-field corner. Outside of left field is an inviting picnic area nicknamed the "Hog Pen." Right next door to the stadium is the indoor facility that serves both the baseball and indoor track teams. It is a huge modern facility. This place gives both squads a great advantage with preparation. There is no wonder why Arkansas fields successful baseball and indoor track squads on a consistent basis.

Arkansas athletics, in total, has a long history of success. Even before joining the SEC, Arkansas had produced many notable victories and national championships. Since joining the conference, the totals have only increased. In fact, the University of Arkansas has won more team national championships, across all sports, than any other school in the SEC, and has the sixth most in the country.

Indoor and outdoor track, coupled with the cross-country teams, have led the way. The men's cross-country team was a dynasty between 1984-2000, winning 11 national championships. That's hard to beat. Unless, of course, it's the men's indoor track and field team at Arkansas. They won 16 national titles in that same span. They won another three over the

Arkansas, UA

School Colors:

Cardinal & White

Traditions:

Calling The Hogs

Running Through The "A"

"Go Hogs!" Spellout

"Wild Band of Razorbacks"

Home Games at War Memorial Stadium

Best in Sight and Sound

Fight Song - Arkansas Fight

Swing March

Cowbell Cheer

Favorite Battle Cries:

Woo, Pig, Sooie

Go Hogs

following six years. That's 19 national championships in 23 years! I'd say that is the epitome of a dynasty.

The Hogs added another title to the SEC's ledger when Nolan Richardson's basketball team cut the nets down in 1994. The legendary cagers only lost three games all season (one was by two points and another by one). The women's running program has produced notoriety as well. Their cross-country team and indoor and outdoor track and field teams have combined to win five national championships in the last five years. The Hogs brought a storied athletic history to the SEC, and they have continued to add to it as a valued member of the conference.

The campus on the hill has its own storied history. It all starts with "Old Main." Old Main is the oldest building on campus. It is a gorgeous red brick structure with limestone inset around the windows. It has both a clock tower and a bell tower. The towers were actually built on opposite sides from what the original plans prescribed. The shorter clock tower rests on the south end while the slightly taller bell tower occupies the north end. A few popular theories, why the switch occurred, have been passed down and debated ever since. One of those tales states that the foreman had too much to drink and read the plans upside down. Either way, it has turned out to be a majestic symbol of higher education in the state of Arkansas.

The bell tower chimes ring at the top of the hour throughout each day. At 5:00 pm every day, the Arkansas *Alma Mater* can be heard playing from the tower. The clock tower did not have a functioning clock for well over a hundred years. That ended in 2005, when a clock was installed on the south tower. The building, and the area around it, is a directional beacon for people on campus. People routinely start their explanations based on the direction from or proximity to Old Main. There is an arboretum in the front lawn that is occupied only by trees native to Arkansas. The area around Old Main is home to numerous landmarks that are popular destinations for students and visitors alike.

The Spoofer's Stone is one such case that has a history as long as Old Main itself. It is a block of limestone that is thought to have been left behind after the construction of Old Main. The large stone hasn't been moved since then. At the start, the University of Arkansas was an all-male school. When women were allowed to attend, the fraternization between male and female students was prohibited. The stone became a popular spot for the students to exchange correspondence. That secret activity helped maintain a healthy morale and many relationships. There is a plaque, from students in the early 1930's, signifying its importance. The lore has continued through the years, and the Spoofer's Stone has become a very popular place for marriage proposals.

On the opposite side of Old Main stands the J. William Fulbright statue. Fulbright was a prominent U.S. Senator and alum of the University of Arkansas. He is also the namesake of the Fulbright Program. The program is one of the more well-known cultural exchange programs in the world. There have been countless students, professors, researchers, and others than have earned grants to do research and study around the world. Fulbright also had a reputation for opposing military conflicts. Across from his statue, at the University of Arkansas, sits the Fulbright Peace Fountain. It represents Fulbright's opinions of peaceful resolution and his belief in the benefits of studying abroad.

Old Main is also the origin of a very unique tradition at Arkansas. The senior walk is where names of graduates from the school are stamped in the sidewalk according to class year. The tradition was started by the Class of 1905. It incorporates every class of graduates all the way back to the first graduates in the late 1800s. The earliest graduates' names start just out from the front steps at Old Main. The Senior Walk covers over five miles of walkway and consists of more than 200,000 names. The names used to be etched in the concrete by hand, but now there is a machine that does it more efficiently. The school's Physical Plant Department developed a machine called the "Senior Sand Hog," and it sandblasts the names after the poured pavement has cured.

The University of Arkansas has a splendid campus. There is a great combination of historic beauty and elegant modern construction. Razorback Road and Stadium Drive run north and south with the majority of the athletic buildings splitting them down the middle. Every so often there is a street from east to west that connects them like railroad ties. That area really sits a lot lower than the rest of campus. Travelling east from the athletic facilities, people have to navigate various levels of inclines to reach the main academic part of campus. The inclines appear to be steeper and longer the farther south on Stadium Drive. Once at the crest, the inclines aren't nearly as severe through the rest of campus. For instance, the area around Old Main is comparably flat.

I was on campus for a variety of weather. The mornings were all chilly or downright cold. Most of the mornings I had to clear frost or ice off my windshield. As the days wore on, it usually unveiled a paradise of conditions. Sunrays floated around the campus like a golden fog. The breeze gently blew vibrant leaves across the walking paths. People considerately made their way through campus for meetings and classes. Even with large groups touring the campus, it never felt crowded. On the days that it rained even the showers were convenient. It never poured on me like it had at other places. It was an overall nice experience that the UA students get to experience each day. I noticed that the students were a cheerful bunch - never really rambunctious, but smiling and energetic.

On one of the radiant afternoons, I stumbled into the Chi Omega Greek Theatre. It was an unexpected but majestic scene. Students sat around its bowl talking and studying. The sky was clear, allowing the sun to warm the students on the stone bleachers. I walked up to the stage and examined the columns lining the back edge. I didn't venture out to the front of the stage because I felt like the current audience might demand a scene from *Macbeth*. The venue is a replica of the Theatre of Dionysus (Greece), and it was donated to the University of Arkansas by the Chi Omega sisters. It was their way of saying thank you to the university for sponsoring their foundation chapter. The project was completed in 1930 and has been a favorite spot since then. The area hosts concerts, movies, plays and at one point it was where the commencements took place.

The Greek life is a huge aspect of the college experience at Arkansas. I went by a bunch of frat houses on Arkansas Avenue going toward Dickson Street. Across Dickson, there is another frat nestled in between a bank and the Nanoscience Building. It is thought to be the nicest one on campus. I went inside the Kappa Sigma Fraternity as the freshmen were setting up for the approaching Homecoming events. One group of freshmen (many of them were legacies) was excited about having their families come for a visit. There are also fraternities sitting atop the hill on the western side of Stadium Drive. These frat houses had great access and a terrific view of Razorback Stadium, Barnhill Arena, the Bev Lewis Center and the campus rec center. The same type of scenes played out for them as they readied for Homecoming.

On a day when the wet drizzle hung around all morning, I was going to have the fortune of being indoors. I met with Randy Ross, the director of football operations at Arkansas. Coach Ross has been working in college football since 1987. He has been employed by a member of the SEC for 22 of those years. We sat in the dry office and talked about the season, coaching, recruiting, and the SEC through the years. We discussed players and coaches with which we shared connections. I also learned a little about Coach Gene Stallings, who Coach Ross had worked with at Alabama. It was fun to spend some time with him. Randy Ross is very affable person, and there is no wonder why he has spent so much time in the SEC.

Coach Ross arranged for me to tour the facilities. I was able to see the unique weight room setup, the indoor facility (which they would use that day), meeting rooms and the outdoor fields. I had already seen the outdoor practice fields from a distance. Walking out to them was a different story. It wasn't that they were any better than any other practice field that I have been on. It was because they are on top of a parking garage. It was the exact parking garage that I had parked in, so I knew what lay underneath it. The fields were durable, cushioned and functional, and I was impressed.

I have to be getting old when something like that impresses me. I saw something else there that I thought was pretty cool. It was recognition of the rest of the Southeastern Conference. It had a big SEC logo with the teams from the west on the left side and the eastern teams on the right. It had their name and logo at the top with a picture of when the Razorbacks played them underneath. For the Arkansas picture, they had a picture of the team huddled around each other.

After leaving there, we went over to Razorback Stadium. I was able to see the locker room and go out onto the field. I was really impressed with the loge seats that wrapped around behind the north end zone. The innermost loges were next to the gate where the players enter the field. The gate was metal and had "Razorbacks" written across the top in black with a Razorback logo underneath. It looked like a chute at a rodeo although it opened from the middle. I saw the SEC Club and the 1964 Grantland Rice Championship trophy outside the 64 Club. Those two areas were particularly fun for me.

The following day, it was supposed to be raining again, so I planned my schedule away from the campus. I went to Bentonville to visit the Wal-Mart museum. It is on the square in Bentonville in the spot where Walton's 5-10 (Sam Walton's first store) was located. The museum was very interesting. There was Sam's Rules for Building a Business, a Flying with Sam exhibit and one of his old trucks all on display. Visitors can also see Sam Walton's office enclosed behind Plexiglas. It is really amazing that the biggest company in the world originated from this tiny town square. It's also amazing that the town and its square have maintained it roots through all of it. It is a true testament to the American Spirit.

While in Bentonville, I also went to the Crystal Bridges Museum of American Art. The museum was founded by Alice Walton (Sam's daughter). Crystal Bridges was dripping with interesting and unique architecture. It started before even entering. There was a 30-foot tall silver tree greeting people at the entrance. The museum contained numerous pieces of art that reflect diversity, culture, and history. There are options to visit the Bachman-Wilson House, have lunch at "Eleven" (the name of the restaurant) overlooking the water or shop for souvenirs in the gift shop. There are temporary exhibits throughout the year. The exhibit that I liked the best is actually a permanent one. It was the

Donald W. Reynolds Razorback Stadium

Frank Broyles Field

Surface: Grass

Built in 1938

Capacity: 76,212

Record Attendance: 76,808 - 9/25/10 vs Alabama

Nickname: Razorbacks

Costumed - Big Red

Live - Tusk V

*Fans' Favorite Home Games:

Won 31-14 over Tennessee in 2006

Won 38-14 over Auburn in 2011

popular Yayoi Kusama - Infinity Mirrored Room. Visitors had to schedule a time and have a ticket, but it was certainly worth seeing in person. There were so many things to take in that I could have spent a whole day there.

Friday was a glorious day. No rain, plenty of sun, and the temperature was climbing faster than it had all week. I started off the day talking with the Mississippi State equipment truck driver who was waiting on the equipment staff to show up. He was a nice man, and we discussed different routes to take through SEC country. I decided to walk around the stadium so that I could see it as the fans do. Red seatbacks were scattered around the bleachers. The field had been fully painted and roped off. I saw championship teams and moments memorialized on concrete bases. There were Razorback greats like Felix Jones, Dan Hampton, Ken Hamlin and Leotis Harris honored around the concourse. One corner had a bust of Donald W. Reynolds, who the stadium is named after.

I inspected the second level loge seats, the Razorback Room and the Touchdown Club. The Touchdown Club looked like a fun place. It was near the locker room doors and there were a lot of places to sit and socialize. There were images of Arkansas players like Darren McFadden embossed on the wall. Large displays detailed famous Arkansas plays like "Double Post Redemption" against Tennessee in 1999. There was plenty to see. It looked like there was plenty for Hogs fans to do during the time before and after the game. From there, I walked out of the north end of the stadium to see two specific statues.

The first was the Frank Broyles statue. Coach Broyles was a very influential person for Arkansas and college football. I remember watching Broyles call some of the biggest college football games on television with his distinct southern voice describing formations and strategies. It was truly entertaining for a young boy that knew he was going to be a coach. His name has been pinned to the award (the Broyles Award) honoring the best assistant coaches in college football. That speaks to the success that he had as a leader. Many of the coaches under his tutelage went on to successful coaching careers of their own. Johnny Majors, Doug Dickey and Hootie Ingram (Alabama AD) were his former assistants who made an impact in the SEC. Jimmy Johnson, Joe Gibbs and Barry Switzer are Super Bowl champion coaches that also coached under Broyles.

In 19 seasons as head coach at Arkansas, Coach Broyles had a record of 144-58-5 (.708) with ten bowl appearances and the 1964 national championship. Those 144 wins is the most in school history, and it's 69 more wins than Houston Nutt (who has the second most in school history - 75 wins). Broyles also served for 33 years as the men's athletic director. The University of Arkansas left the Southwest Conference and moved to the SEC under his leadership. Frank Broyles was no stranger to the league. As a quarterback for Georgia Tech (when they were part of the SEC), he won the 1944 Southeastern Conference Player of the Year Award. Coach Broyles was inducted into the College Football Hall of Fame in 1983.

The other statue that I wanted to view was the "Wild Band of Razorbacks" outside of the northeast corner of Razorback Stadium. It is a massive structure that reaches to 25 feet in height and 50 feet wide. The monument was dedicated to the memory of the 1964 national championship team. Its title comes from a speech in 1909 that led to Arkansas becoming the Razorbacks. At the train station after a victory over LSU (16-0) in Memphis, Coach Hugo Bezdek told the crowd that "The team played like a wild band of razorback hogs." That led to the students of the university voting to change the mascot from the Cardinals to the Razorbacks. The monument is impressive, especially in that location where the inside of the stadium is visible as the backdrop.

I walked around other parts of the campus until I found myself at Bud Walton Arena. It is a fantastic place for basketball. The outside even states that it is the "Basketball Palace Of Mid-America." There was a Hall of Champions Museum in Bud Walton Arena that brought back a lot of memories of past Razorback teams. I walked around and saw some of the dressing rooms, including the work they were doing to upgrade the main locker room. After leaving, I went over to the basketball practice facility. I was invited to watch practice, so I did for a little while. They had a great observation deck with comfortable theater seating.

Just past Bud Walton Arena was the Jerry and Gene Jones Family Student-Athlete Success Center. It is one of the newest buildings on campus, and it was phenomenal. It had anything that a student-athlete should need to be successful in the classroom and many resources that will help them as athletes as well. The Bogle Academic Center is now located there. It had three computer labs, a math lab, a writing lab, a language lab, multiple tutor rooms and an auditorium. There are areas designated for wellness, educational enrichment and student-athlete development. There was also a large dining hall. There were sports nutritionists and sports psychologists available too. The Jones family helped create a facility that will have a lasting impact on every student-athlete that utilizes it.

As the sun began to fade on Friday afternoon, I was walking beside the stadium on Razorback Road. I was on my phone and heard what sounded like a car with its music turned up loud. The noise became louder and louder. As I reached the parking lot, the sound was intense. I looked over my left shoulder to see a tow truck (fully painted with Razorback colors and logos) pulling a trailer containing Tusk, who is the official live mascot of the University of Arkansas. The music was blaring the Arkansas fight song from speakers atop the truck and trailer. The cheerleaders were perched on a platform on top of the trailer. The truck stopped in front of the entrance to the stadium next to the Broyles statue. They too were preparing for the parade and subsequent pep rally. The cheerleaders climbed down from the top, and they (like me) were excited for the chance to observe Tusk in person.

It is *A Season of Homecomings*, as you already know, so it was bound to be Homecoming week for my visit. Homecoming kicked off with Chancellor's Ball, which was a concert where the Homecoming court is announced. It featured a student band (Right field) and was free for the Arkansas students. That happened the week before I arrived. This year's theme was "Etched in Stone," which is an ode to Senior Walk. Glimpses of the Greek Life lawn decorations could be seen sporadically all week, but they were out in full force throughout the day on Friday, which was also the day of the parade. The Homecoming parade has been occurring at Arkansas since 1922.

The parade started at 6:00 pm. It was a big event for the Greek organizations on campus, especially those housed down by Dickson Street. There were a lot of people down there for the parade. It seemed like many of the students had family who had come in for the event. Unfortunately, I didn't see any of the freshmen that I had met earlier in the week. The celebration continued all the way to the Chi Omega Greek Theatre where it concluded with a pep rally that started at 7:30 pm.

But, this was no ordinary pep rally. The Greek Theatre was full, and it was spirited. The excitement stems from what was about to take place. At the end of the pep rally after the parade, they announced the Homecoming King and Queen. That's new to me. I haven't heard of another school announcing the king and queen the night before a game. I think that it's pretty neat that Arkansas has a different tradition than others.

The game was scheduled to start at 3:00 pm CT, and I was there way too early as usual. I parked at 7:30 am and saw some tailgaters before I even got out of my truck. I figured that it was going to be a good day if people were already out in this weather. With it being just after dawn, the light was still dim in the gray sky. The people all were wearing jackets and gloves. They seemed half asleep, but hey, they were there. I went exploring down Razorback Road. I walked toward the baseball stadium to see how much activity was happening there. The walk kept me warm, but it uncovered a similar morning malaise. I noticed more activity as I made my way back up Stadium Drive.

Saturday was another brisk morning, but it mimicked Friday's quick rush to being comfortable. More people arrived and began to set up as mid-morning approached. I made my way over to the Alumni Center. There was certainly going to be a lot of activity there, but just not at the moment, as they were still setting up. The only thing happening at the time was former Razorback D.J. Williams recording some television spots for a local station.

I walked over to "Hog Town" and found that a party had started. Hog Town is north of the stadium on Maple Street. The street is closed and there are a number of family-friendly activities for fans. The music was loud and people were starting to populate the area. Tusk was even making an appearance for the fans. I made it through to the east end of the party to watch a little bit of *SEC Nation* on a huge screen set up for fans. They were analyzing the "World's Largest Cocktail Party," which was going to be played around the same time as the game here at Donald W. Reynolds Razorback Stadium.

I continued east and visited some areas on campus, and then I circled back north of Hog Town. I found a tailgate that had one of my favorite titles of the whole season. It was the "Hog Trough." The title probably isn't as eye-popping as you expected. I just liked it because it reminded me of when I was an offensive line coach. I regularly named our practice area the "Hog Trough," so I was intrigued. I had to stop and introduce myself. The man in charge of the tailgate was a great guy and a fantastic host. There was good food, happy people and kids running around having a blast. The Hog Walk went right past his tent too. As the team came through, we were standing and talking right next to the walkway. The kids all rushed over from their make-shift football games to greet the players. I saw Coach Ross, wished him luck and watched the fans' giddiness as the players strutted through the crowd. When it was over, I thanked my host, took a picture of us with the Hog Trough sign and I kept moving.

As I made my way down the same hill as the team, I ran into the "Tusk to Tail" tailgate. It had a good layout with a couple of large tents with food on one end and televisions on the other. There was plenty of seating all around and a frequented bar in the middle. The guys were very nice and personable people. This tailgate party wasn't one that you could just walk through and say hello. These guys were like when you visit your grandma and she makes you eat something. They made sure that I had something to eat. It was also highly suggested that I try the "John Daly" (the drink of the day), complete with my own "Tusk to Tail" cup. The party provided me with something else that I didn't have yet - a ticket. A quick ten dollars, and I had admission into the game. It wasn't a bad seat either.

I made it to a few more stops before I finally saw another SEC flag. I went by to show my appreciation. It was a group of friends and family with a great disposition. They had a great setup. A tent with a side wall that had a banner that read "Eat, Drink, and Watch Football." It also had a few Yeti coolers, a couple of more ice chests, a cart with supplies and a fryer. Next to the tents sat an ambulance that anchored two flag poles. One had an American flag flying above the Arkansas state flag. The other had a Razorback flag flying over the SEC flag.

It was obvious that this was no ordinary ambulance. I received a tour of the ambulance and found that it was a mobile tailgate unit. It was decorated inside with Hog regalia and was stocked with supplies for particular emergencies. The crew was on call if anyone needed fluids. There was an IV bag with brown fluid hanging in the interior. The exterior cargo bin contained a microwave and a small refrigerator. The refrigerator held collection tubes of another brown liquid and syringe barrels filled with jello shots. If anyone needed assistance, then they were on call.

I entered the stadium at Gate 1 in the southwest corner. While walking in, I passed the Donald W. Reynolds monument. It didn't take me long to find my seat because it was in the lower level of that same corner. Before long, the guy who I bought the ticket from and his friend showed up. The pre-game program performed by the band was crisp. They were very good snapping off every part of the routine. The crowd participated in an obligatory manner. The national anthem was nice as the crowd sang along in a soft and reverent unified voice.

Then, everyone did the cheer spelling out "H--O--G--S, H-O-G-S.." and finished it with "Arkansas Razorbacks GO!" Periodically, it would be time to "Call the Hogs," and the crowd would oblige.

Calling the Hogs is probably the most famous tradition at Arkansas. The words "Wooo Pig Sooie" is well-known, but the procedure is often misrepresented. It starts by raising your straight arms from your side into the air, saying "Woooooo..." the whole time. At the top, continue the "Woo"

and start wiggling your fingers. After several seconds, drive your elbows down with clenched fists and yell "Pig." Immediately following that, punch through the air with the right fist and yell "Sooie." This is repeated and after the third time, you finish it by yelling "Razorbacks."

This happens all throughout the pre-game rituals. What surprised me was how deliberate it is. It isn't three quick "Whooo, Pig Sooies." It's slow and methodical, and Hogs fans cherish it.

When all of it was completed, it was time for the team to run through the "A." The band forms the Arkansas "A" for the team to enter the playing surface. This has become a treasured scene over the years. It is a special tradition that the players embrace every home game.

After Mississippi State received the opening kickoff, the Bulldogs came out running the ball. They scored on the opening drive to take a 7-0 lead. Arkansas looked to answer when running back Rakeem Boyd ran for 22 on the first play. The offense then went stagnant and had to punt. The Bulldogs had another 80-plus-yard drive and scored through the air this time. Arkansas had a quick possession that didn't yield much. MSU began marching again when the first quarter ended with the Bulldogs holding a 14-0 advantage.

The Arkansas defense stiffened when the second quarter started. With Mississippi State already inside the 20, the Hogs held them to a field goal. The Razorbacks defense later forced a punt. It gave Boyd the opportunity to race 52 yards for a touchdown, to make the score Mississippi State 17, Arkansas 7.

MSU continued to have long touchdown drives (75 and 84 yards). Sandwiched between them was a fumble on a punt return that Arkansas recovered. The Razorbacks managed a field goal from it. Then, it was Mississippi State's defense that scored on a pick-six. That drove the fans crazy. They were incensed, and venom was spewing. The eventual halftime score was 38-10 with the Hogs trailing.

Halftime was a little different because it was Homecoming. They presented (the announcement was made Friday night) the king and queen to applause. The band did its routine concluding with its formation spelling "Go Hogs" as the finale. The guys that I was sitting with left the seats to go join their wives in another section. I decided to walk around and experience other sections as well, since there were now plenty of seats available.

John Stephen Jones started the second half at quarterback for Arkansas. The remaining Hogs fans were happy to see it. The first drive ended in a punt, and the Bulldogs had another lengthy scoring drive. The next Arkansas possession showed promise as Jones capped it with a touchdown pass to wide receiver Mike Woods. Mississippi State expired the third quarter and used over three minutes of the fourth quarter to add a field goal.

Then, the fans in attendance went wild when K.J. Jefferson entered as quarterback for Arkansas. People had wanted this for a while. The energy in the building ramped up when the Razorback offense zipped down the field for a touchdown. People were buzzing about the Hogs' potential with Jefferson. I think most of them missed State's next score that took only three plays to reach the end zone after running for another 75 yards. Jefferson did indeed come back in at quarterback. The Razorbacks were trying to move the ball, but they fumbled at the end of a run that would have given them a first down. MSU ran out the last eight minutes of the game to win 54-24.

I didn't pay close attention to that last drive. I was actually about to go back to my section when I met a huge Arkansas fan. His name was Mac Reeves, and he is a perfect example of the type of person in which I wrote this book. Reeves is a young veteran from Southern Arkansas. He and his parents have been big fans of the Razorbacks for as long as they can remember. It was Reeves' first time in Razorback Stadium to watch his Hogs play. He was thrilled to be there no matter the score. Reeves told me about the field being grass for the first time in a while and the end zones being painted red for the first time that he has ever known. He was like the way "Rudy" was for Notre Dame. His father sat quietly next to him. Reeves told me that his father had tears in his eyes as he came up the ramp and saw the inside of the stadium.

Like I said, they are all fanatics about University of Arkansas sports, particularly football. Reeves told me that his mother was the biggest fan of them all. She was not there because she had passed away almost two years ago to the day. His father was just cleared medically for the trip the previous day, and they drove up early that morning. Reeves was going to do whatever he had to do to share this moment with his dad, and they surely weren't going to leave early. I told him how much I admired him for what he had done for his father, and I stated that people like him all over the south are what makes the SEC so great. I thanked him for his service and for being a good son to his father. We hugged and I departed. As I looked back from the bottom of the stairs, Reeves and his father sat side-by-side reflecting on the day as they gazed out onto the field. Here is to you, Reeves family! Go Hogs!

Arkansas Razorbacks

Defensive Linemen

Dick Bumpas
(1968-70)

Tony Cherico
(1984-87)

Ron Faurot
(1980-83)

Henry Ford
(1990-93)

Dan Hampton
(1975-78)

Wayne Martin
(1985-88)

Loyd Phillips
(1964-66)

Billy Ray Smith Sr.
(1954, 1956)

Billy Ray Smith Jr.
(1979-82)

Jimmy Walker
(1975-78)

My favorite players to watch at other defensive positions:

DB - Steve Atwater (1985-88)   DB - Ken Hamlin (2000-02)

LB - Jermaine Petty (1999-2001)   DB - Kenoy Kennedy (1996-99)

Offensive Linemen

Shawn Andrews
(2001-03)

Brandon Burlsworth
(1995-98)

Freddie Childress
(1985-88)

Leotis Harris
(1974-77)

Glen Ray Hines
(1963-65)

Greg Kolenda
(1976-79)

Steve Korte
(1981-82)

Jonathan Luigs
(2005-08)

Jim Mabry
(1986-89)

Tony Ugoh
(2003-06)

My favorite players to watch at other offensive positions:

RB - Darren McFadden (2005-07)   QB - Quinn Grovey (1987-90)

RB - Madre Hill (1994-95, 1998)   WR - Anthony Lucas (1995, 1997-99)

*Fan Favorites: RB - Darren McFadden, OL - Brandon Burlsworth, RB - Felix Jones

12

Roll Tide Roll

Week of November 9, 2019 game against LSU

The University of Alabama was founded in 1831, and it's the oldest and largest university in the state of Alabama. It is a sea grant and space grant institution that is known to alumni and friends as "The Capstone." The nickname, meaning the top stone or high point, originated from a George H. Denny speech in 1913. As the president of the university and a staunch advocate for education, Denny set out to advance public education in Alabama. During the noted speech, Denny made reference to the University of Alabama as "the capstone of the public school system of the state." His actions as the school's president backed up those ideals, and the university has followed through on them ever since.

There was tremendous growth at the University of Alabama during President Denny's tenure, as the number of students and facilities increased dramatically. In similar fashion, the past 15-plus years has been a period of great expansion for UA. The enrollment has nearly doubled since the early 2000s. As of 2019, the number of students is more than 38,000, which is the third consecutive year the university has exceeded that milestone. The campus continues to expand to accommodate the growth in student population. With the purchase of the Bryce Hospital property, the campus now encompasses over 1,200 acres.

UA is one of the fastest growing flagships in the country, but the goal is not to just simply grow. The University of Alabama is continuously working to maintain its legacy as the place "Where Legends Are Made," as they are actively recruiting quality students.

According to UA's web-site, the university had 256 National Merit Scholars entering in 2019. The new enrollees also include three Goldwater Scholars and two Boren Scholars. The University of Alabama also boasts 12 graduates that won Fulbright awards for 2019-20. *U.S. News and World Report* ranks Alabama Law in the top 25, and the Manderson Online Business Master's programs 10th in the country. The University of Alabama is also listed as one of the top doctoral research universities in the nation.

The university has grown at such a high rate partly because of the ability to recruit an influx of out-of-state students with vast abilities. Recently, the number of high caliber in-state students has increased as well. The combination has led to a wonderfully diverse and capable student body. It is understandable why students would choose to attend the University of Alabama. The campus is a great college setting with beautiful buildings and scenery. In addition, the town of Tuscaloosa has been voted as one of the 30 best college towns in America according to *USA Today*.

Many UA graduates have decided to make the region home. Their contributions to local industries have led the area to prosper economically. The area surrounding Tuscaloosa is home to multiple major manufacturers like Michelin/BF Goodrich, Phifer, Mercedes-Benz, Peco Foods and Nucor Steel. Tuscaloosa is also full of culture. Places like the Bama Theater and Tuscaloosa Amphitheater provide citizens opportunities to divulge into the arts. Exploring natural wonders is always a viable option at the University of Alabama Arboretum and Moundville Archaeological Park too. It is no wonder why Tuscaloosa also ranks as one of the most livable cities in America.

Before I made it to Tuscaloosa, I had to stop and visit "The Old Gray Lady" - Legion Field in Birmingham. Legion Field has a long and storied history with college football, particularly with the Southeastern Conference.

The first two SEC Championship football games (1992 & 1993) were played in the stadium, and the Iron Bowl was played at Legion Field 47 times. In fact, Auburn and Alabama used to play a lot of their home games at the venue. Auburn started phasing out its home games at Legion Field in the late 1970s. Alabama played at least three home games a year at Legion Field up until the late 1990s. As Bryant-Denny Stadium expanded, and Legion Field grew more outdated, Alabama began to move more of its home contests to campus.

The history of Alabama football has many of its roots buried in Birmingham. Most of the bigger home games were contested right there in Legion Field. One major example is "The Third Saturday in October" game against Tennessee. For many years, when Alabama was the host school, it was held in Birmingham. The tradition of Alabama home games at Legion Field runs so deep that there is a monument of coach Paul "Bear" Bryant that still stands outside of the stadium. Legion Field's legacy also includes the Magic City Classic, Steel City Classic, the SWAC Championship and a variety of bowl games. Legion Field has earned its title as "The Football Capital of the South."

Alabama, Bama, UA

School Colors:

Crimson & White

Traditions:

Houndstooth

The Walk of Champions

"Sweet Home Alabama"

The Elephant Stomp

"Dixieland Delight"

Million Dollar Band

Fight Song - Yea Alabama

Roll Tide, Roll

Are You From Dixie

Favorite Battle Cries:

Roll Tide

Rammer Jammer

Birmingham is also the home of the Alabama Sports Hall of Fame. There is an appropriate monument outside of the museum that features both coach Paul "Bear" Bryant and legendary Auburn coach Ralph "Shug" Jordan. The museum honors coaches like Bobby Bowden, Danny Ford and Erk Russell along with great athletes such as Hank Aaron, Jesse Owens, Willie Mays, Evander Holyfield, Mia Hamm, Willie McCovey, Carl Lewis, Billy Williams, Joe Louis and Ozzie Smith. I also went across the intersection to visit the Southeastern Conference offices. All of the SEC's official business is handled in this location. The lobby is unmistakably SEC. There is a banner for every school hanging from the ceiling, and there are marble posts recognizing the reigning champion of every team sport that the conference sponsors.

When I arrived in Tuscaloosa, the beauty of the University of Alabama campus immediately struck me. It is straight out of central casting for an idyllic college campus. Distinguished monuments and magnificent houses of learning populated the gorgeous tree-lined walkways. Stately fraternity and sorority houses present jaw-dropping architecture that only the other Greek houses' magnificence can rival. On top of that, there's a majestic centralized tower that serves as a beacon to all pedestrians and an opulent president's mansion that seems to have been plucked right from the state capital - tucked into just the right spot to keep an eye on things. The campus is filled with a casual flow of focused students and renowned professors.

And, of course, this all resides in the shadow of the massive iconic football stadium.

I started my expedition going up Bryant Drive past the alluring Alumni Hall. I turned onto Second Avenue and made my way up to University Boulevard. I went west and passed the Frank Moody Music Building on my left and fraternity houses on my right. Getting deeper into campus, I came upon Farrah Hall. It is a red brick building with lots of windows. The dramatic corner entrance faces the southeast corner of the quad. The building behind Farrah Hall is the Foster Auditorium where commencements, concerts and athletic events have been held. Currently, the Foster Auditorium hosts the women's basketball and volleyball teams.

In front of Foster Auditorium is the meticulously manicured Malone-Hood Plaza, which includes the evocative Autherine Lucy Clock Tower. The landmarks were named in honor of the first three Black students to register at the University of Alabama. Autherine Lucy Foster, Vivian Malone Jones, and James Hood were trailblazers in the effort to desegregate higher education in the state of Alabama. Their efforts and resolve through the years have inspired many. The appropriate space outside of Foster Auditorium will serve to inspire more generations to come.

Across Sixth Avenue sits A. B. Moore Hall where Coach Bryant's office was during his first few years as head coach. It connects to Little Hall, which used to be the athletic dorm, via a classic portico. Porticos are a popular feature in the architecture at the University of Alabama. It is a major reason why the campus has such a classic stately look and feel. Another feature that Moore Hall and Little Hall share with the rest of the campus is the pristine landscaping. All of the flowers and hedges combine with mature oaks, magnolias, and crape myrtles to form an aesthetic utopia.

One look down University Boulevard provides a view to the symmetric rows of glorious oaks rising above the activity below. Many of the oaks were planted nearly one hundred years ago in honor of the Tuscaloosa County natives who were killed in World War I. The Memorial Oaks frame out a section of University Boulevard where the president's mansion and the quad sit across from each other. It is a glorious location that makes one want to sit on a swing and enjoy the day with some sweet tea.

The focal point of the quad is Denny Chimes. The iconic edifice was made from red brick and Alabama limestone. It was made for and named after George H. Denny who served as president of the university for over twenty-five years. Surrounding the base of Denny Chimes is the Walk of Fame, which is a collection of cement slabs that preserve the handprint and footprint of every captain of the football team since 1948. It's one of the most unique and revered traditions at the University of Alabama.

A straight shot north of Denny Chimes is the Amelia Gayle Gorgas Library. The building's portico serves as the backdrop for a newer (but still cherished) tradition on campus. The Elephant Stomp is the premier pregame pep rally. The cheerleaders perform while the "Million Dollar Band" plays its opening numbers on the voluminous staircase. Then they move west and form at Colonial Drive to lead a march to Bryant-Denny Stadium.

On this afternoon, students have commandeered the platforms and stairs of Gorgas. They use that area of the quad as a base to socialize and study. A treasure called the Little Round House sits on the northwest side of the library and is one of the few structures that survived the destruction from the Civil War in 1865. It gives the visual impression of the highest portion of a castle turret. The small white building was the headquarters for the Jasons, a men's honors society. In 1990, the Little Round House became a memorial for all of UA' honor societies.

The next day, I visited the Walk of Champions and Bryant-Denny Stadium. From the various expansions to the numerous upgrades, the stadium has changed so much over the years. It is now a massive modern cathedral for football in Tuscaloosa. With the suites and upper levels, the big screens in all four corners, and the brick post and wrought iron railing that divides the stands from the field, it's the perfect football venue for the school who owns the most bowl appearances and victories in the country.

The outside of the stadium memorializes Alabama's 17 national championships, which is the most in college football, and the 27 SEC championships, which is the most in the conference. The Walk Of Champions commemorates each team that has won a conference or national championships with plaques situated in the brick paver layout. All five head coaches who have led the Crimson Tide to a national championship have a statue erected to the west of the walkway. It is an incredible area filled with history and excellence.

Across the street from the southwest corner of the stadium was Rama Jama's. It's a uniquely oriented place that was covered with Crimson Tide spirit from the outside in. It was a fun diner type restaurant that will have one staring at the wealth of memorabilia while waiting for your delicious hamburger. There is always a party on game days, but during the week was a lot of fun too. Evan and Sam were always around to answer questions and talk Alabama football. I wish every lunch could be filled with good food and SEC football like it was at Rama Jama's.

Thursday morning offered me the opportunity to meet with Ken Gaddy, the director of the Paul W. Bryant Museum. He was gracious with his time as we walked through the museum. We talked about the history of the museum and Alabama football. He shared with me that Coach Bryant had a real desire to have all of his players, coaches and teams represented. Hence, the Paul W. Bryant Wall of Honor that had touch screens with a Rolodex of the players, coaches and all of the teams that he coached. They have done a wonderful job of gathering data, but Gaddy admitted that it's still not complete. The museum always welcomes new information about any of those individuals regardless of the school where they played for Coach Bryant.

The museum was really about the history of Alabama football. Of course there is a lot about Coach Bryant, but that's because Coach Bryant was such a big part of Alabama football. There is a replica of Coach Bryant's office for visitors to observe. There were also trophies from the past and present and game balls from Coach Bryant's record setting victories. The display of the six national championship rings that Coach Bryant won was massively impressive. There was one of the houndstooth hats that he wore and the megaphone that he used at practice. To cap it all off, there was even a Waterford crystal replica of his houndstooth hat.

An iconic photograph of Coach Bryant leaning against the goalpost is stamped with one of his great quotes. It reads:

"I'd like for people to remember me as a winner,
because I ain't never been nothin' but a winner."

Coach Paul W. Bryant

Gaddy pointed out a few relics that sometimes go unnoticed and then some pictures and exhibits of people that I know. The whole museum was captivating. From the "Thin Red Line" to the jersey Tua Tagovailoa wore during the victory in the Orange Bowl over Oklahoma and Kyler Murray - it's all chronicled here. My favorite thing was the digital displays of programs and tickets. Every head coach since Bryant has an exhibit about their era. In each space, there were two digital displays. One showed a highlight reel of plays during those times. The other cycled through pictures of tickets and program-covers from every game that person coached at Alabama. I can confirm the accuracy because I had some of those same tickets and programs.

I couldn't help but spend the rest of the morning in the Paul W. Bryant Museum, but I eventually pulled myself away. I walked through Hotel Capstone, which sits next door. This is where the Crimson Tide team stays on Friday nights before home games. Inside the hotel is the Legends Bistro, which features houndstooth upholstered chairs at its entrance. Then I went north to and across University Boulevard. I passed some fraternity houses, Bryant Hall and some more fraternity houses. From my experience, I think that there might possibly have been more fraternity and sorority houses on Alabama's campus than any school in the country. They were virtually everywhere around UA's campus.

Bryant-Denny Stadium

Surface: Grass

Built in 1929

Capacity: 101,821

Record Attendance: 101,821 - Multiple Times

Nickname: Crimson Tide

Mascot: Costumed - Big Al (Elephant)

*Fans' Favorite Home Games:

Won 55-44 over Auburn in 2014

Won 24-15 over LSU in 2009

I eventually emerged at the Science and Engineering Quad. It is an excellent area containing buildings with marvelous architecture. Stone columns are a popular theme and none are more striking than the entrance to Shelby Hall. It is a gorgeous building that was named after U.S. Senator and Tuscaloosa native Richard Shelby. At 33 years of service, and counting, Shelby is the longest serving U.S. Senator from the state of Alabama. The impressive building is the epicenter of much of the research done at the university. As I approached Shelby Hall, the skies opened and sheets of water fell down upon me. Many students joined me in seeking shelter in the large portico. Some of them waited it out while I went inside to inspect the pentagon-shaped structure. Shelby Hall was a modern facility with large lecture halls, research labs and plenty of office space.

As I made it around Shelby Hall, the view of the courtyard informed me that the rain had stopped, so I resumed my outdoor exploration. As soon as I put some distance between myself and Shelby Hall, the rain came again. I sought shelter in the closest buildings, but I had little luck. It seemed that every door that I tried was locked. I tried desperately to keep my notes and map dry. The rain came the hardest as I trudged toward a bus shelter in the lakeside area. I had bad timing because the rain dissipated as soon as I reached the covering. As I waited for the bus, I laid everything out to dry.

The bus came and carried me to the transportation hub. I connected with another bus that would take me around to the athletics facilities. We stopped at several notable places along the way. There was Carmichael Hall, Reese Phifer Hall, Tutwiler Hall and finally the Mal Moore Athletic Facility. I sloshed my way to my truck as the betraying winds knocked raindrops off of the trees and onto my wet shoulders. While changing into dry socks and shoes, I decided to take a different approach. It was 4:30 pm and I figured that it was time to partake in a different Alabama tradition.

There is no shortage of great barbeque restaurants in the area around Tuscaloosa. There's Full Moon Bar-B-Que, Jim 'N Nick's Bar-B-Q and, of course, Dreamland BBQ. On a recommendation, I searched out the original

Archibald's Bar-B-Q in nearby Northport. The unassuming cinderblock building sat right smack dab in the middle of a neighborhood across the river from Tuscaloosa. The family-run business has been in continuous operation since 1962.

Archibald's was one of the inaugural inductees into the Alabama Barbeque Hall of Fame, and there is no wonder why. They have been featured in magazines and other media publications for years. Their accolades came honestly. The hickory-smoked fare was phenomenal. Ribs have never been my favorite choice, but Archibald's made them hard to dismiss. I felt like I was consuming the best kept secret in the food world. The only thing better than the meal was the people. It felt like I was having a meal with long lost family. I wanted to give them all a hug before I left. I'm not even from the area, but I was proud of them for what they built from this location.

Friday morning continued to be cool and rainy. I found a spot in the parking lot of Hotel Capstone. The lot was nearly full because many people showed up to hear Rece Davis deliver an address for the Alabama basketball tipoff event. I sat in my truck and listened to raindrops and acorns slap the roof while I worked on my schedule for the day. As the weather subsided, I proceeded over to Marr's Spring. This water supply was a major reason that the University of Alabama was founded on this plot of land. It is now a peaceful retreat for students and visitors alike.

I then hiked back over to Coleman Coliseum. I perused the area uncovering homage to Crimson Tide greats like Robert Horry, C.M. Newton, Antonio McDyess and Wimp Sanderson. The place was more active than I expected. Many people were there to pick up their reserved tickets for the football game. There was also preparation underway for the Nick at Noon luncheon. On the Friday's before home games, UA has a luncheon featuring coach Nick Saban. I had different lunch plans, so I soon exited and went over in front of the Mal Moore facility.

I was there to meet with Tommy Ford, a recent retiree from the athletics department. He had worked for UA for over 37 years. We ate at the Levee Bar & Grill next door to Dreamland in Northport. It turns out that he helped start the Tide Pride program with people that I've come to know through the years. He has authored or co-authored 11 books related to UA Athletics, and he has proven to be a wealth of knowledge about the University of Alabama. It was an enjoyable afternoon reliving poignant moments in Crimson Tide history. After several stories, we headed back to campus.

The rain clouds relented and the sun made brief appearances through an overcast sky. The crispness of the afternoon air confirmed the season. I popped in at the *SEC Nation* set to see my buddy, Darion. I found out that he was looking for a ticket just like I was. This wasn't going to be an easy ticket to find. The teams were ranked No. 1 and No. 2 in the polls while the CFP (College Football Playoff) rankings had them at No. 2 and No. 3 respectively. They were calling it "The Game of the Century II." Media outlets from around the country were in town to cover the game. There were even reports that the President of the United States would be in attendance. All of it coupled with the fact that it was a traditional rivalry game was going to make it difficult to gain access to the event.

To accentuate the point, all I had to do was cross the street to be transported from the *SEC Nation* set to the location of ESPN's *College GameDay*. There were tailgate tents blanketing the east side of the quad while the loud speakers from *College GameDay* played "Sweet Home Alabama." Students and fans paced all around as they waited for production to start. I walked over to Denny Chimes and heard its sweet song at the top of the hour. Groups took pictures in front of the 115-feet tall bell tower. Other guests moseyed about inspecting the cement slabs of the Walk of Fame. A throng of tailgate tents began covering the west side of the quad as well.

As the afternoon faded into darkness, I traveled down to The Strip just off the western edge of campus. The Strip is an area of University Boulevard that contains an abundance of restaurants, storefronts and bars. There were patrons all over The Strip on this early Friday evening. I was informed that the crowd would only get bigger, and it would go well into the night.

The Strip on Friday nights before game days has been compared to Bourbon Street. At Gallettes (Campus Party Store), Tide fans started the game weekend with a Yellow Hammer. Down a little further, The Houndstooth was serving people all throughout its inside and outdoor seating areas. Fans of all ages could be found down on The Strip, and the regular announcement of "Roll Tide" left little doubt who they supported.

Saturday was a brisk clear morning. I parked downtown where I finally secured a ticket, and then I walked to campus. On my way down Paul W Bryant Drive, there was frost on windshields and clouds of breath pumping out of joggers. At one house, only small patches of the crystallized blades of grass were visible. The rest was covered with aluminum cans from the night before. I walked between Bryant-Denny Stadium and Evergreen Cemetery and found groups of fans walking north. They were headed to the vicinity where *College GameDay* and *SEC Nation* would broadcast their live shows.

I weaved my way through unbelievable sorority houses and academic buildings. The uniformed beauty of each structure made them hard to distinguish without reading the signs out front. The occasional cheering of the crowd reverberated through the campus. People were migrating to the area from all directions. A roar exploded from the masses when alumnus Rece Davis addressed the audience. I arrived to find an energy that promised to immortalize the day's game.

It wasn't even 8:00 am yet, and I had already seen a full days worth of entertaining fans. There was a couple that stumbled to the scene with beverages and a blanket to lay on the wet grass. One guy had a stick adorned with two rolls of toilet paper sandwiching an empty box of Tide laundry detergent (Roll-Tide-Roll). Many Tigers fans wore purple and gold beads. One stylish LSU backer was wearing a purple suit with gold tiger stripes. I saw Bama fans wearing Joe Namath jerseys, cowboy hats with script A's on them and a houndstooth patterned sports coat. I thought, "this might turn into the Tailgate of the Century."

I covered the short distance across the street to where *Marty & McGee* were concluding its preamble to *SEC Nation*. The enthusiasm of loyal fans had everyone excited for the matchup. Sponsors' exhibits peppered the landscape, and they had a variety of offerings for the public. A few lots to the west of that location, I witnessed a memorable elephant topiary in front of the Rose Administration Building. I continued down University past Reese Phifer Hall and beyond the Walk of Champions.

On the lawn northwest of the stadium, a completely separate group of exhibits appeared. The Nissan Heisman House was present, as was the AFCA Coaches' Trophy presented by Amway. Regions Bank had a huge green tent, and Tailgate Nation had a nice area set up. On my way down Wallace Wade Avenue, I spotted Secret Service agents outside of the stadium. I guess that the president was going to show up after all. As I continued toward Rama Jama's, Eli Gold (the voice of the Crimson Tide) was making his way into the stadium. He cordially stopped every few feet to take a picture or sign an autograph.

Eventually, I made it back over to the quad. Family gatherings, fan fiestas and corporate soirees were underway all around the famed field. Fathers threw footballs to their sons and mothers shared recipes with their friends. It was a community park hosting reunions from a broad spectrum of its citizens. The people were friendly and cordial with each other. The decorations ranged from as simple as a company flag or as complex as a mixture of red, white, and houndstooth regalia lining the outer edges of tents. At "Crawford's Corner," the whole set up was entertaining. On this day, it included a makeshift "Cajun Graveyard," complete with gravestones that recounted past scores of Alabama victories against LSU.

As it approached noon, I had to get over to the Walk of Champions to observe the moment the team arrived. There was already a mob of people bunched up against the barricades. I was surprised to see so many LSU and Alabama fans paired up. There was some fun-loving banter with each other, but everyone seemed to get along very well. That was good because we were all packed together. The team finally came, and they approached the stadium to AC/DC's "Thunderstruck." The music was loud, but the cheers of the crowd mostly drowned it out. A nice young lady used my phone to video the event from her boyfriend's shoulders.

After the players went through, the quagmire of people began to break up. Just before we were about to be freed, "Sweet Home Alabama" bellowed from the speakers. The Alabama supporters had a whole new exhilaration. Our migratory progress was stopped as people danced, sang and showed reverence. After every "Sweet Home Alabama" refrain, the assemblage responded with the obligatory "Roll Tide Roll."

I spent some time engaging the tailgates around the stadium. I pondered whether to go across the street to the frat houses or over to Gorgas Library for Elephant Stomp. There were mentions all week about the president attending and advisements to enter the stadium early because of extra security. After witnessing Secret Service earlier, I decided to heed that advice. I got in line and had a good conversation with a father and son from Tennessee. We passed through the special metal detectors and were in the stadium with plenty of time before the game.

I circled my way to the heavens via the ramp on the northeast corner of the stadium. I say it that way because it never seemed to end. I kept going higher and higher as I passed entrances to subsequent levels. When I finally reached the top, I was able to watch some of the other games on screens around the Bear's Den, a concessions area above the north end zone that features a gigantic replica of Coach Bryant's houndstooth hat. I then went out on the perch to watch the "Million Dollar Band" perform its pregame routine far below.

The stadium was filling up fast, and the energy was palpable. A parachute team from Army Special Forces dropped into the delirious stadium. The three soldiers individually delivered the game ball, an Alabama flag and a POW flag. The fans went ballistic with their appreciation for the veterans. Then the stadium joined together to sing a heartfelt version of "God Bless America." "Thunderstruck" came on again as the Crimson Tide players assembled in the north end zone. A sea of crimson and white shakers pumped back and forth to the rock tune. The teams entered to different reactions from the crowd, and it was on!

The biggest college game of the year - Game of the Century II.

Alabama would receive the ball, and the Bryant-Denny faithful only got louder with the first few plays. Alabama wide receiver Henry Ruggs III started it off with an effective kickoff return, and then he complimented it with a nice reception on the first play. Running back Najee Harris followed with a long run, and Alabama was already in the red zone. The Crimson Tide moved the ball inside the 10 before they called a timeout facing third down. During the timeout, the President of the United States was introduced to a standing ovation that endured the entire timeout. The ribbon boards displayed American flags, and some sections chanted, "USA, USA."

Alabama was looking to score on third-and-goal. Quarterback Tua Tagovailoa took the snap, looked downfield and quickly felt pressure. He stepped up and to his right. He began to run up field and as he attempted to tuck the ball into his side, it popped out behind him. LSU linebacker Ray Thornton was able to get to it before anyone else.

The raucous crowd went into a surprised silence.

Starting at its own 8-yard line, LSU had three successful run plays that preceded three consecutive completions. The finale was a 33-yard touchdown reception by receiver Ja'Marr Chase. LSU led 7-0.

The Alabama offense started the second drive much like the first. A 15-yard strike to receiver Jerry Jeudy was supplemented with a 15-yard penalty by LSU. The Crimson Tide was past midfield again. However, a couple of incomplete pass attempts forced a punt. The long snap was mishandled and LSU made a stop on fourth down to give its offense a short field.

LSU's offense didn't do a lot with it on its second possession. In fact, Alabama intercepted quarterback Joe Burrow, but it did not stand because of a penalty. Burrow did complete a pass that made a field-goal attempt manageable. The kick was good, and LSU now led 10-0.

On the next series, the Alabama possession didn't start as promising, and the Crimson Tide was forced to punt after three plays. In similar fashion, the Tigers' offense was forced off of the field after three plays. As the LSU cover man took a high aim at him, Alabama's Jaylen Waddle received the punt. The collision with the gunner spun Waddle backwards, but did not bring him down. The Crimson Tide's ace returner jetted across the field and down the sideline for a 77-yard touchdown return. That quickly revised the score to 10-7. LSU started the next march by barely converting a third-and-one before the first quarter ended.

After the teams switched ends, LSU began to rip off chunks of yards that ended in the end zone. Alabama blocked the extra point to keep the deficit at nine points. The Tide was in danger of giving the ball right back before

Tagovailoa ripped a 20-yarder to Jeudy. A subsequent penalty left Alabama behind the chains. The Tide fought back to fourth-and-one right around midfield. Coach Nick Saban was confident in his defense and decided to let the offense try to convert. They did not, and LSU took back the possession. Coach Saban's defense rewarded his confidence, though, and forced the Tigers to punt.

The punt left the ball at the 10-yard line, but a false start truthfully forced the Crimson Tide to start at its own 5. Jeudy came up big on third down again. His 26-yard catch gave Alabama a first down and some relief from their own end zone. The next play saw Alabama receiver Devonta Smith advance the ball into LSU's end zone. The extra point attempt was no good, but the 90-yard drive made the score 16-13 with around seven minutes left in the half. The crowd had settled in the way the teams seemed to have done. This was already becoming a great SEC battle.

LSU responded with a drive into the red zone. A sack on third down eliminated any hope for a touchdown. The Tigers would have to be content with adding three points to the lead. That was until a few minutes later when they quickly forced Alabama to punt the ball back to them. With just over two minutes remaining, the Tigers were on a mission. They wanted a touchdown. Effectively, they moved the ball down the field, and running back Clyde Edwards-Helaire finished it with a one-yard plunge. The score was 26-13 with only 26 seconds left in the half.

The next two plays were huge in the outcome of the game. The first was a Patrick Queen interception of Tagovailoa. It gave LSU the ball back, and a penalty by Alabama put the spot at the 13. It took only one play for Joe Burrow to make the Tide pay. A touchdown pass put LSU ahead 33-13 at halftime. The first half had the Bama fans absolutely stunned. They made so many mistakes and then gave up 14 quick points right before the half. Plus, LSU would receive the ball to start the third quarter. The Tide faithful weren't in despair, but they were concerned.

The Bayou Bengals took the ball and methodically moved inside of the Crimson Tide's 40 to begin the second half. Then, Alabama surprised LSU with a blitz. Xavier McKinney sacked Burrow and forced a fumble. Alabama avoided giving up any more points, even though its offense didn't do anything with the extra possession. The Bama defense stepped up again to force an LSU punt. This time the Alabama offense had their best drive of the game. In total, it went for 95 yards (and seven points). LSU punted again, and the Crimson Tide was certainly rolling. Bama moved the ball to LSU's 14 as the third quarter came to an end.

The crowd had come alive. Their team was back into the game, but they also knew what was coming. It started out with "We Will Rock You" and a show from the recently installed LED lighting system. There were lots of shakers being whipped about in the crowd. Fans waited and wondered if it was going to happen - and it did. Yes, they did play "Dixieland Delight." The place went wild. Every shaker in the building was in rhythm like a beater tapping a kick drum. It was as if one was trapped under a massive red and white amoeba of shakers. The additional lyrics were sung more loudly by Bama fans than the originals of the song. It was a party in Bryant-Denny Stadium.

As the game continued, Alabama had to convert a crucial fourth-and-one. Najee Harris delivered a powerful run that converted the first down and put the Tide at the 1-yard line. He then punched it across the goal line and brought his team to within 33-27. LSU responded on its next possession. Burrow converted three huge third downs on the 75-yard drive. The conversion was unsuccessful leaving the lead at 12 points. Tagovailoa and the Tide reciprocated the 75-yard drive, converting two third downs and two fourth downs to keep UA in the game. The score now rested at 39-34.

With 5:32 remaining in regulation, LSU set out to direct another 75-yard drive. Fifty yards later, the Tigers faced a consequential third-and-two with 2:21 left. Burrow took the snap, held it out for the running back, and then pulled the ball back to his body as he ran around the left side. He made a few guys miss and was finally brought down after gaining 18 critical yards. Edwards-Helaire completed the mission on the next play. Alabama was now down 46-34 with 1:37 on the clock.

It only took ten seconds and one play for Alabama to stay within striking distance. Devonta Smith caught Tua's offering and raced to the end zone for an 85-yard score on the first play. Tide fans believed this could be one of those rare comeback wins that would be remembered forever. It all depended on the onside kick. The kick didn't produce any drama, though, as LSU recovered. The Tigers gained a first down and ran out the remaining time. The game finished with a final score of LSU 46, Alabama 41.

Despite the result, there was still positive energy outside the stadium. Even with the close loss, Alabama was still in contention for the College Football Playoff. "Roll Tide" was a commonly heard phrase as I walked by the cars stuck in traffic. I walked by the house with all of the cans in the yard. It looked more orderly, but maybe that was because the yard was now completely covered. There were two girls walking toward me. When they saw the LSU fan in front of me, they said, "Geaux Tigers" and "Good game." They gave him a high-five and said, "We hope you guys win it all, but we still love our boys. Roll Tide!" As I got closer to my truck, a car passed playing "Yea Alabama!" People from each side of the street hollered "Roll Tide Roll!"

Alabama Crimson Tide

Linebackers

Cornelius Bennett (1983-86)	Dont'a Hightower (2008-11)	Lee Roy Jordan (1960-62)
Barry Krauss (1976-78)	Woodrow Lowe (1972-75)	Keith McCants (1988-89)
C.J. Mosley (2010-13)	Dwayne Rudd (1994-96)	DeMeco Ryans (2002-05)
	Derrick Thomas (1985-88)	

My favorite players to watch at other defensive positions:

DB - George Teague (1989-92)   DB - John Mangum (1986-89)

DL - Jonathan Allen (2013-16)   DB - Landon Collins (2012-14)

Running backs

Shaun Alexander (1996-99)	Derrick Henry (2013-15)	Bobby Humphrey (1985-88)
Mark Ingram (2008-10)	Derrick Lassic (1989-92)	Bobby Marlow (1950-52)
Johnny Musso (1969-71)	Trent Richardson (2009-11)	Siran Stacy (1989-91)
	Sherman Williams (1991-94)	

My favorite players to watch at other offensive positions:

WR - David Palmer (1991-93)   OL - Chris Samuels (1996-99)

WR - Tyrone Prothro (2003-07)   QB - Tua Tagovailoa (2017-19)

*Fan Favorites: LB - Derrick Thomas, QB - Tua Tagovailoa, RB - Mark Ingram

13

THERE'S A SPIRIT CAN NE'ER BE TOLD

Week of the November 16, 2019 game against South Carolina

As the popular saying goes, "Everything is bigger in Texas!" Texas A&M University is no exception. Not even close. The College Station campus boasts one of the highest enrollments in the nation. The 2019 figure stood at more than 64,000 students. The Corps of Cadets is the largest uniformed student body outside of the U.S. military academies. A huge band of former students can be found throughout Texas, around the country and across the world. Visitors will be greeted with a hearty smile and a gregarious "Howdy." While there, it isn't difficult to discover massive statues, huge monuments and, of course, a gigantic football stadium. The list of traditions is as long as a lottery winner's Christmas list. All of the traditions have a meaning as deep and wide as the state itself. The only thing bigger and more meaningful than the traditions is the "Spirit of Aggieland."

"The Spirit of Aggieland" is more than the *Alma Mater*. It is something uncovered in every current and former student - a way of giving, a way of improving and a way of living. It has been molded from the six core values and the culture at Texas A&M. It was manifested from the hard work, sacrifices and accomplishments of those who came before. It is developed through every Aggie's own personality and their personal experiences. The Aggie Spirit has been explained as "to stand ready to help one another and be loyal to one another." I believe that is true, but I also believe that it's not something that you can fully encapsulate with words. Being an Aggie has a unique significance for each, and the spirit lives in all of them. The Aggie Spirit corrals all of that gumption and wisdom and points it toward improving the world.

Although it is fairly new to the Southeastern Conference, Texas A&M University has a long and illustrious history. The school was opened in 1876. The town of College Station received its name because of the demand for the railroads to stop to service the multitude of students. For a long time, the school was restricted to males, and they were all required to join the Corps of Cadets. During both World Wars, Texas A&M was an integral supply chain of servicemen and commissioned officers. Since 1965, joining the Corps was no longer mandatory, although Texas A&M remains one of only six Senior Military Colleges. It is one of only 17 land, sea and space grant universities in the country, and the only one in Texas. It is consistently ranked one of the best values in higher education, and the campus also contains the Presidential Library of George H. W. Bush.

Texas A&M University is widely known as "The Home Of The 12th Man." That started in 1922 with a student named E. King Gill. The Aggies were playing the Dixie Classic versus No. 1 ranked Centre College in Dallas. The injuries were mounting, and the roster of available players was dwindling. In fact, they were down to only the 11 players that were on the field. Coach D.X. Bible needed options. He spotted Gill in the stands and asked him to suit up. Gill had previously played football and was currently an Aggie basketball player. He answered the call for the A&M football team and readied to help if needed. The Aggies eventually took advantage of Centre's turnovers and won 22-14. They never had to use Gill, but his eagerness to help the team became legendary, thus, beginning the 12th Man tradition.

The 12th Man designation is attributed to the student body whose support is monumental for the Aggies. The current students stand throughout home games in an effort to assist their Aggie teams to victory. Coach Jackie Sherrill utilized the students' fervor when he developed the

"12th Man Kick-Off Team" in the 1980s. It was a unit consisting of non-scholarship players, and their passion and drive made them one of the best cover units in the nation.

After Sherrill, the idea was revised to use one walk-on (who wore No. 12) on the kick-off coverage unit. The strategy of fielding a kick-off team totally with walk-ons was later brought back and used sparingly for a while. For several years now, the No. 12 has been awarded to the player who exhibits hard work and determination. Donning the No. 12 jersey for Texas A&M is one of the highest honors at the university. Throughout the year, and especially on game days, you see the No. 12 jersey worn by fans young and old. It represents the 12th Man, and it is a great symbol of Texas A&M University.

The 12th Man is just the beginning of the traditions at Texas A&M. There is the Corps of Cadets, the Yell Leaders, Reveille, Bonfire, the Aggie War Hymn, Silver Taps, the MSC, Pennies on Sully, the Century Tree, Muster, Elephant Walk, the Flag Room, Replant, the Aggie Ring, Midnight Yell, Gig 'Em, Big Event, "Whoop" and the "Fightin' Texas Aggie Band." They each have their own subset of traditional procedures, and all of them bear a significant meaning to being an Aggie. Every tradition individually helps bond the Aggie Family in its own unique way. Together, they are the heartbeat of the Spirit of Aggieland.

The Texas A&M campus is a sprawling 5,500 acres that represents the great state of Texas in a myriad of ways. From the majestic Albritton Bell Tower to the historic Williams Administration Building to the giant Aggie Ring statue or the "Welcome To Aggieland" water tower, it is undeniably Texan. A jaunt through campus will almost certainly expose one to mesquites and live oaks, people wearing cowboy boots, military references and appreciation and many things marked with a Texas Lone Star emblem. Something that is harder to see, but not difficult to feel, is the Texas hospitality. There is always someone willing to point visitors in the right direction or lend a hand to someone in need. Many visiting fans know that if it's game day, then there is always plenty of Aggies willing to offer an invitation to their tailgate.

My week in College Station also allowed me to experience the ever-changing fall weather in Texas. The week started off gray and cold. The temperature even dipped down into the 20s at night. There was rain during the middle of the week before it was predicted to turn nice for the weekend. The lack of rest and erratic weather was enough for a cold to set in on me. But it was game week in the SEC and there was plenty of work left to do. I had to keep pushing forward because there wasn't time for me to be sick. I carried more water with me, and I was a little more deliberate with my schedule. It was a great benefit that I was always close to somewhere to warm up with some fantastic Texas cooking.

The Dixie Chicken (the Chicken as it's known locally) is a long-time favorite of Aggies everywhere. This place is legendary, and it's Texas A&M through and through. It's not hard to get some tasty grub and have a little fun there. You can prop your boots up, carve the SEC logo on a table or throw a bottle cap down the alley. Just a pooch punt from there, I found BBQ 13-0. Its name comes from the score, from a legendary Aggie victory over Texas, that was branded on Texas's longhorn mascot. The place was littered with all things Texas Aggies. If someone is looking to talk Texas A&M and get some great Texas BBQ, then Juan is always ready to serve it up. Speaking of good Texas eats, Good Bull BBQ borders the other side of campus. They are proud to be Aggie owned and operated, and it shows in the decor. They also must be proud of their BBQ because it was really good. Throughout the week, those places provided nourishment and helped re-energize my excitement about Texas A&M.

When one says "good bull," it's speaking Aggie vernacular. Good bull is a way to designate approval of something worthwhile or something that upholds the Aggie traditions. There is a whole supplementary language in Aggieland. Did you notice that I haven't used the term ex-student? That's because at Texas A&M, an enrollee of the school is always an Aggie. If someone is no longer enrolled, then they become a former student. Here are other examples of Aggie lingo:

> The official greeting at Texas A&M is "Howdy." While that may not be an odd word, it certainly gets the attention of visitors when everyone walking by says "Howdy!"
> The Aggies don't have cheers, they have "yells" and "yell leaders." The yell leaders lead the student body in yells designated to support their team.
> "Whoop" is a word that you don't normally hear being used unless it's after an A&M yell. Whoop is used like a climactic affirmation.
> "Miss Rev" refers to Texas A&M's mascot. She is a purebred American collie named Reveille. Reveille is the highest-ranking member of the Corps of Cadets, and the students address her as "Miss Rev."

There is also muster, pass back, boot line, hullabaloo, humping it, wildcat, other education, fish, red ass, pull out, non-regs, pots, load, stack and many more. They each have a meaning that all former students and currently-enrolled Aggies completely understand.

The Aggie Family has a fraternal feel to it. There is a bond never to be broken. As the *Alma Mater* says, "... there's a spirit can ne'er be told ..." It is formed from the entirety of the A&M experience, but it originates from two very distinct sources - the Code of Honor and the six core values at Texas A&M University. The Code of Honor declares, "Aggies do not lie, cheat, or steal, nor do they tolerate those who do." It is an oath that I witnessed in action. A student forgot to zip up her backpack, and some cash was blown from it as she was walking on campus. A male student saw it, retrieved it and chased her down to return it. It was a moment that strengthened my faith in the good of people.

That same rainy day, I found myself outside of the Alumni Center, where the Association of Former Students is housed. It is easily recognizable because it's the building with the big Aggie Ring statue in front of its entrance. On both sides of the entrance are three horizontal monoliths. On the end of each block (six in total), one of the core values is etched into the stone. Down the length of each monolith is a quote from a former student about what that specific core value means to them. The Texas A&M University core values are Respect, Leadership, Integrity, Loyalty, Excellence, and Selfless Service.

I stayed in the same vicinity and spent some time on the outside of Kyle Field. There is a lot to observe and learn around the stadium. There are monuments for the "Fightin' Texas Aggie Band" and the Texas A&M University Corps of Cadets. The band is comprised of members of the Corps, and they are deemed "The Pulse of The Spirit of Aggieland." The Corps, in its entirety, is considered "The Keepers of the Spirit." A little further down the road is the War Hymn Monument. It is an impressive monument of 12 students locked arm-in-arm and swaying to the chorus of the Aggie War Hymn. Just past that is a monument to honor the yell leaders, who are considered the "Ambassadors of the Aggie Spirit." Once at the corner, the statue to honor E. King Gill (the original 12th Man) stands tall.

Continuing around, there is the Texas A&M Lettermen's Association and some ticket windows. A short distance further is the Reveille Memorial. This is where past Reveille's have been laid to rest. Directly in front of it is a small scoreboard that will operate during the games so the former "Miss Revs" will know how her beloved Aggies are faring. Behind the Reveille Memorial is a plaza with four stone pillars. Each pillar has four sides that are each designated to recount the accolades of the football program. There are national championship teams, All-American players, College Hall of Famers and national award winners displayed. Just down from there is the John David Crow statue honoring Texas A&M's first Heisman Trophy winner.

Moving to the west side of the stadium, in front of the Hall of Champions, one will be able to observe the 24-feet tall Core Values monument. It has a limestone base and proudly lists the six core values. The football facilities are around the next corner, outside of the south end zone. In the lobby, the national awards won by Aggie players are proudly on display. The locker rooms, indoor facility, weight room and practice fields are also in the area. The walk around the stadium is certainly a lot to absorb, but every bit of it is significant. It is just as significant as all of their contributions to the Aggie Spirit.

The Texas sun returned to greet me on Thursday morning. The sunshine increased the temperature and made the campus even more spectacular. I stepped down Military Walk retracing the steps that the Corps of Cadets would take to Sbisa dining hall. I saw the "fish pond" (a fountain outside of Sbisa) and doubled back to make my way to the Academic Plaza. The area is bustling with students, but it is an appealing and harmonious setting. This area alone is filled with history and tradition. There are markers for Silver Taps and Muster, the Sul Ross statue and the Century Tree.

The Century Tree is a majestic live oak, and is one of the first trees to be planted on the campus. It is a very popular destination for photo shoots. There have been numerous proposals and wedding ceremonies under the tree. The story goes that couples who walk under the tree together will eventually get married, and if the proposal happens there, then the marriage will last forever. I didn't witness any proposals that day, nor could I find anyone who had witnessed one. I also didn't find anyone who would dispel it as myth. I just know that the couples I saw liked taking pictures, but weren't quite ready to take the walk underneath it.

Students weren't quite as apprehensive about the tradition associated with the statue of Lawrence Sullivan Ross. During his life, "Sully," as he was known, served as both president of the school and governor of Texas. The legend has it that while Sully served as president, he would regularly help students with their homework. When they asked how they could repay him, his reply would be "A penny for your thoughts." Now, students "put a penny on Sully" for luck with tests, projects and even in their personal life. I didn't actually ask anyone what luck they were searching for (for fear of jinxing it), but it was obvious that they believed. There were mounds of pennies and a few bills piled on the base of the statue. It is my understanding that the money is picked up regularly and donated to a local charity each semester.

My trek took me past the academic building, through the Evans Library and the Pavilion and down to the quad. Not far from there is the Sam Houston Sanders Corps of Cadets Center. Inside, I found a museum that has a countless array of pictures, relics and archives. It was a very interesting place with plenty of military and Aggie history. After an hour of exploring, it was finally time to visit the MSC (Memorial Student Center). The MSC is a wonderful combination of a reverential memorial and modern resources. Because it is a memorial, it is requested to refrain from walking on the grass outside and uncover (take off your hat) when entering. Inside, there's the bookstore and then the Flag Room across the hall. The Flag Room is like a big elegant living room, and it's a special place for Aggie students. While I was there, a student came in and started playing the piano. I had no idea what he was playing, but it was a beautiful melody that was calming to the soul.

I knew from the start that Friday was going to be a challenge. It began with an interview at 7:30 am, and it wasn't going to end until "Midnight Yell" was completed. The good news was that most of it was going to be fun, and I had another clear day to do it. What I realized that day was that Texas A&M really appreciates and embraces being a member of the Southeastern Conference. I saw a multitude of signs, banners and murals that stated, "This is SEC Country!" Fans and

Texas A&M, A&M, TAMU

School Colors:

Maroon & White

Traditions:

Midnight Yell

12th Man

Yell Leaders

Corps of Cadets March-In

"Wrecking Crew"

Fightin' Texas Aggie Band

Fight Song - Aggie War Hymn

The Spirit of Aggieland

Noble Men of Kyle

Favorite Battle Cries:

Gig 'em or Gig 'em Aggies

Farmers Fight

administrators alike are proud to be playing against such good competition. They are thrilled to be in a conference that is so similar to them and appreciates them for who they are.

Who are they? A respected member of the SEC Family!

It was a big weekend for Texas A&M athletics. In the afternoon, the women's soccer team was hosting an NCAA tournament matchup against the University of Texas (or t.u. as Aggies call them). The men's basketball team was hosting Gonzaga later that evening. Then, it all culminated the next night with the football game against South Carolina. I was able to catch some of the soccer match before I headed to my next destination. The Aggies seemed to be in control when I left. That proved to be true as they vanquished their rival and advanced to the next round.

Unfortunately, the same couldn't be said for the men's basketball team. My plan was to make it back for the second half of that game, but when I heard the halftime score, I knew my time would be better served staying right where I was.

My location that night was the site of the Student Bonfire, which is the continuance of Bonfire, but away from the campus at Texas A&M. "Bonfire is the undying flame of love that every loyal Aggie carries in their heart for the school." Bonfire was a long-standing tradition at A&M until the stack collapsed in 1999. The center pole buckled and sent the stacked logs crumbling to the ground. The accident took the lives of 12 people and injured another 27. Student Bonfire renewed the tradition in 2003 as a way to honor those lost and to guarantee what they helped build will continue on. The Student Bonfire is held off-campus because it is independent of the school and not sanctioned by Texas A&M University in any manner. Student Bonfire maintains many of the traditional procedures of Bonfire although it has been active in implementing advanced techniques and safety precautions. It is built strictly by students, and all need to have a "cut card" and must always be wearing their steel-toed boots and the respective pot during the procedures.

The pot refers to the helmet that everyone must wear at the site. The color of the pot designates one's position on the crew, and many times it determines whether someone is a freshman, sophomore or upperclassman. For instance, Red Pots are seniors that lead Student Bonfire. There are brown, yellow, green, blue, orange and others - all have specific ranks and responsibilities (a huge shout out to all of the existing Gray Pots). The logs are cut (with an axe), "shouldered" (thrown on the shoulders of a group and carried to the destination) and "slammed" by using human power and determination. Slamming the logs is when they stand it upright into the stack. Trucks are used to transport the logs from the load site to the stack site, and chainsaws are used to "butt" (to trim and cut to the prescribed length) the logs. Everything else is done by hand.

I spent most of the evening learning from Dion McInnis and Ashton Vara. McInnis was Head Stack in 2003, and I would wager that his knowledge of Bonfire exceeds anyone else's. Vara was Head Stack for 2019, and he is an impressive young man. He exudes Texas A&M's core values, and his leadership was the beacon for building such an impressive stack in 2019. They explained how Student Bonfire is a 12-month process and is made possible by the generous support of so many in the community. I discovered more traditions, unearthed famed stories and learned important procedures. I observed the dedication, loyalty and selfless service that the students display throughout the build. It was very interesting and entertaining. Because I learned the procedures, I was lucky to have the opportunity to help shoulder a log up to the stack. It was something that I did not expect, but I was proud to be a very small part of the build. The crews continued to work, but it was time for me to hit the road so that I could make it back to College Station for Midnight Yell.

There are yell practices held at different times throughout the year. They even schedule the event on the road for away football games. Midnight Yell practice in Kyle Field at midnight on Fridays before home football games is one of the most popular traditions in Aggieland. The gates at Kyle Field are opened about 45 minutes before Midnight Yell begins. The stadium is illuminated and the big screens proudly display a Midnight Yell graphic. I saw the special logo at midfield fully painted for the first time (earlier in the week, it was just an outline). It was a Texas A&M logo with a maroon ribbon wrapped around the stem of the "T." Painted under the "A" was 1999 and 2019 was painted under the "M." This special logo was being used for the 20-year remembrance of the Bonfire falling in 1999.

There were probably only a few hundred people there when I first arrived. I was hoping to spot my friend's son, Cole. He is a freshman in the Corps at A&M, and I assumed that he would be at yell practice. At around 11:50 pm, there was a mad rush of people that lasted until well after yell practice began. The lower level on the visitor side was eventually filled and began to wrap around the end zones. With another 500 or so on the sidelines, I estimate that there was easily 15,000 people in attendance. There was no way that I was going to find Cole now. I positioned myself on the rail in the concourse to get a good view of the scene and for an easy exit when it was over.

The yell leaders run the show. There are five of them in total. There are three seniors and two juniors, and all five of them have been elected into the position. It was the seniors' last yell practice, so they each got a chance to address the crowd individually. They spoke about what the experience has meant to them, what Bible verse is on their towel, and the legacy they've hoped to leave.

One of the seniors had a special request for everyone in the stands. He explained how the South Carolina fans show respect to the Hilinski family. Ryan Hilinski is South Carolina's quarterback who lost his brother (Tyler) after a battle with mental illness. Tyler wore the No. 3 at Washington State, and Ryan does the same at South Carolina. The South Carolina fans hold up three fingers and are silent for the first play of the third quarter. The senior yell leader asked that we all do the same to show support and welcome the Hilinski family. I was impressed by it, and South Carolina fans were appreciative of the gesture.

As the yells and chants began, I was totally lost. I had never experienced anything like that, and it was surreal. The vast majority of the fans (mostly students) were having a great time and followed along quite nicely. I was starting to understand some of it, and then BANG! A huge cannon blast came from the opposite corner of the end zone. It elicited a roar of approval from most, but my section contained many who were caught off guard. There were more cannon blasts periodically, but none as stirring as that first one. The yell leaders continued to guide everyone through the specific yells and songs just as they were to be performed during the game. The mass of people uniformly locked arms and swayed right on cue with the playing of the Aggie War Hymn. A few more yells were performed, a final cannon blast went off and the rehearsal was complete. I was on my way to get some rest with the satisfaction of participating in two of A&M's most cherished traditions and the anticipation of a terrific game day experience in Aggieland.

Kyle Field

AKA – "Home of the 12th Man"

Surface: Grass

Built in 1927

Capacity: 102,733

Record Attendance: 110,633 - 10/11/14 vs Ole Miss

Nickname: Aggies

Mascot:

Costumed - Ol' Sarge

Live - Reveille IX

*Fans' Favorite Home Games:

Won 20-16 over Texas in 1999

Won 74-72 over LSU in 2018

I arrived on campus eight hours before kickoff. By that time, a plethora of activity had commenced all over the grounds. My designated area to park was largely at capacity already. I walked down the long row of cars and emerged next to a sizeable group of people having a sit-down meal on picnic tables under staked-down tents. There were kids tossing a football around while the men were next to the pits throwing down cans of their favorite Texas brews. The enticing smell of smoked brisket filled the breezy air. As I walked on by, I had a feeling that I might regret not seeking a sample. Not to worry. Within minutes, my senses were again bombarded with the inviting aroma of Texas cooking. The landscape was dotted with camps set up for Aggie fiestas. Many of the spots had signs displaying the name of the tailgate with the names of the hosts (complete with the class year of every Aggie). While those spots enjoyed the festivities, other groups were working diligently to get their own parties started. I witnessed the Cavalry arrive, and then I went exploring other parts of the campus.

On the other side of the tracks (railroad tracks split the campus), I saw something that intrigued me. It was a group of flags that included one for all of the members of the Southeastern Conference. At first, I thought that it might be a corporate sponsor set up to promote their affiliation with the SEC. I wasn't sure, but I knew that I wanted to go there.

On a corner spot near a walkway jutting from Reed Arena, I found a tailgate spot called "The Aggie Embassy." Eight flagpoles distinctly marked its outer perimeter. Austin, who runs the tailgate, explained the setup. The first pole flies the SEC flag. Each pole after that holds two flags representing that week's conference match-ups, with his preference on top. The teams without conference games are grouped together in order of Austin's favorites. There was a large inflatable A&M helmet, and the door to the trailer revealed unique signs from each conference road trip. I was offered food and drink just like anyone who stops by. At The Aggie Embassy, everyone is welcome. You would be safe to say that it was my kind of place.

It wasn't difficult to see an SEC flag flying over a tailgate or to find a tailgate sign that displayed the SEC logo. There was one large tent that had pennants for every SEC school hanging from its ceiling. I even saw a maroon and gray tent with SEC markings all over it. The only Aggie mention was a Texas A&M banner zip-tied to one of its sides.

The Texas A&M folks are truly excited and appreciative to be in the Southeastern Conference. One tailgate host even told me, "I'd rather go 7-5 in the SEC than win ten games in another conference." He has experienced it for a few years now. He knows that there are great traditions and difficult competition, but that's what makes it so fun. His trailer is painted with an SEC logo and the phrase "This is SEC Country." He boastfully reports to me that he has "hauled that thing all over Texas."

The tailgate scene at Texas A&M is massive. On every side of the stadium, and throughout most of the campus, there are large garrisons of Texas A&M supporters. Each outpost has Aggies of old and new. They are enthusiastic and loyal. They are also very hospitable. Visiting fans are always welcome and are usually treated as a guest of honor. At Aggie tailgates, traditions are exalted and the stories of Aggie games and legends are spoken with reverence. A former student recounted how they used to camp out so they could watch the games from the track that previously surrounded the turf. All one had to do was mention a name and the stories started flowing. The Wrecking Crew, Ja'Mar Toombs, Sam Adams, Dat Nguyen, Jeff Fuller,

The Hit, Richmond Webb, Aaron Glenn, Ray Childress, Jack Pardee, Kevin Smith, Greg Hill or any of the others. There were stories for all of them.

I met up with my wife (who drove in for the game), and we progressed over toward the 12th Man statue. We watched the "Fightin' Texas Aggie Band" perform on their way down Houston St. They were advancing to where they enter the stadium, and we agreed that we should do the same. After gaining entrance, we walked past the visitor's locker room and watched the Corps of Cadets march in at that gate. I tried unsuccessfully to spot Cole, but we did get a great view of Reveille as she walked past. It took a good while for every company in the Corps to parade past us down the tunnel, out onto the field and back up the tunnel on the opposite corner of that end zone.

We watched the teams warm up and talked about the changes since the last time we were on the sidelines (a few years back we took a recruiting visit with one of the kids I coached). After the warm ups were complete, the security personnel started clearing the sidelines. We were about to decide where we were going to go sit, when some people challenged security to stay on the field. The lead security guy pointed to the passes around our necks and said, "That's what you have to have to stay down here." After it thinned out, my wife and I decided that the sideline was as good a place as any to watch the game. A few moments later, the "Fightin' Texas Aggie Band" snapped off a meticulous pre-game performance that readied the crowd for the ensuing battle.

This permanent crossover game, between South Carolina and Texas A&M, is actually a trophy game. The winner of the game receives the Bonham Trophy. It is named after James Bonham, who is a native of South Carolina and died fighting at the Alamo. The trophy idea was developed when Texas A&M joined the SEC and was annually pitted against South Carolina. Then-governors Nikki Haley (South Carolina) and Rick Perry (Texas) had the trophy constructed and agreed to house it in the winning governor's office. Texas A&M has never lost to South Carolina, so the trophy has stayed in Texas. With Rick Perry no longer in office, the Bonham Trophy is now kept at the Alamo. It's odd, but it is hard to get information about the trophy. Not many people (from South Carolina or Texas A&M) know much about it, and even fewer have actually seen it.

Early on, the game was played pretty tightly. There were some interesting strategies that kept the score close. My wife was more interested in the crowd. The chants and yells, coupled with the towel waving and swaying, really fascinated her. We discussed the symbolism of it all, and I tipped her off to the plan to honor the Hilinski family. It was a loud and spirited home crowd. The game remained close until A&M's running game began to be more effective. Texas A&M scored twice in the second quarter to take a 13-3 lead at halftime. Before the half ended, the Corps started filing out of the stands to prepare for their halftime duties. With my wife's help, I was finally able to spot Cole. We briefly caught up and took a picture before he rejoined his unit.

As the third quarter began, we were primed to witness the Texas A&M tribute to the Hilinski's. At first, the only real sound was the South Carolina band. Then, all I really heard were the whistles at the end of the play. It was remarkable how quiet 100,000 fans were able to be, especially considering how loud they had been. The third quarter was all about the defenses from both teams. There were a lot of punts and not much offense. Between the third and fourth quarters, the place came alive. Hearing the Aggie War Hymn and seeing the stadium swaying must have fired up the Texas A&M players. They came out on fire to start the fourth quarter. The running game wore down the South Carolina front, and the Aggies scored two touchdowns. Texas A&M had over 300 rushing yards and won the game 30-6.

The reason that I chose this week to visit Texas A&M was because it was the 20-year remembrance of the collapse of Bonfire. I wanted to attend and pay my respects at the events held to honor those who had fallen. I postponed my departure a full day so that I could attend the Bonfire Remembrance Ceremony at 2:42 am on Monday, November 18th. The ceremony happens at that exact time every year because it was the date and time that the tragedy occurred. The ceremony takes place at the Bonfire Memorial and is attended by thousands of students and citizens.

The Bonfire Memorial is a powerful and poignant spot to gather and remember those that were lost and injured. It consists of three main elements; Traditions Plaza, History Walk, and Spirit Ring. The Bonfire Memorial is filled with thoughtful and meaningful aspects. The Spirit Ring is comprised of 27 blocks of granite (for the 27 injured) that connect 12 portals (for the 12 that perished). The ring symbolized the perimeter fence around Bonfire, and there is a black granite marker in the center at the exact spot of the last center pole. The portals each have a bronze inlay where a portrait and information about the fallen person is engraved. The portals look to be placed randomly, but they are not. The portals are individually situated around the Spirit Ring so that it faces in the direction of the lost Aggie's hometown.

As we approached the Spirit Ring (where the remembrance took place), there was a somberness that I have never felt before. It was a feeling of loneliness but also of support, a feeling of sadness but also pride and a sense of loss but perseverance. I stood on the ridge, which shields the memorial from the outside world, and watched people silently walk in from every direction.

The Remembrance Ceremony is directed by the yell leaders. Prayers, tributes and traditions make up the program. Two particular traditions hit me the hardest.

The singing of "The Spirit of Aggieland" was something to behold. The words, movements and meaning were the same as they had been on Saturday night when there was a party at Kyle Field. This version, unprompted and in unison, was sang in a whisper. And the off-script parts, that are normally sung louder, were quieter than a whisper. I don't have the words to describe the emotion on that cold and damp morning. The other tradition was "Roll Call for the Absent." The yell leaders called the names and class years of the fallen Aggies. Those in attendance replied "Here" in unison for each one individually. That was followed by singing the first verse of "Amazing Grace."

The yell leader softly spoke a few words that ended with "...May your experience here this morning burn in your heart forever, and may you never forget what it means to be a Fightin' Texas Aggie." With that, the assembly was dismissed until 2:42 am on November 18, 2020. The Remembrance Ceremony was traditional, heartfelt and appropriate, just like the Bonfire Memorial itself. It was driven by the Aggie Spirit.

It was pure Texas A&M through and through. Just as it is carved into the stone at the entrance of Tradition Plaza, "There's a spirit can ne'er be told ..."

Texas A&M Aggies

Linebackers

Antonio Armstrong
(1991-94)

Marcus Buckley
(1990-92)

Quentin Coryatt
(1990-91)

Bill Hobbs
(1966-68)

Johnny Holland
(1983-86)

Robert Jackson
(1975-76)

Von Miller
(2007-10)

Dat Nguyen
(1995-98)

John Roper
(1985-88)

Ed Simonini
(1972-75)

My favorite players to watch at other defensive positions:

DB - Aaron Glenn (1992-93)

DB - Kevin Smith (1988-91)

DL - Ty Warren (1999-2002)

DL - Sam Adams (1991-93)

Running Backs

John David Crow
(1955-57)

Cyrus Gray
(2008-11)

Greg Hill
(1991-93)

John Kimbrough
(1938-40)

Darren Lewis
(1987-90)

Leeland McElroy
(1993-95)

Rodney Thomas
(1991-94)

Ja'Mar Toombs
(1998-2000)

Trayveon Williams
(2016-18)

George Woodard
(1975-79)

My favorite players to watch at other offensive positions:

OL - Richmond Webb (1986-89)

OL - Jake Matthews (2010-13)

WR - Jeff Fuller (2008-11)

QB - Bucky Richardson
(1987-88, 1990-91)

*Fan Favorites: QB - Johnny Manziel, LB - Von Miller, LB - Dat Nguyen

14

GLORY, GLORY

Week of the November 23, 2019 game against Texas A&M

The University of Georgia has a football program with a long and storied history. It is a history chocked full of championships, All-Americans and traditions. The university as a whole has a strong history of excelling in education as well. The alumni are proud that the University of Georgia always has been and always will be the flagship university in the state. It is a top notch research school and has produced a plethora of talented people who have made contributions in the fields of medicine, law, banking, music, media, athletics and many more industries. The scenic southern campus resides in Athens, which is known as the "Classic City." It's much more than just a pretty campus in a neat college town. The University of Georgia is a leader in higher education.

One of the school's earliest claims to fame is that it's the "Birthplace of Public Higher Education in America." It began when the state chartered the school back in 1785. It was the first institution of higher learning to be state run rather than by a religious organization. The university hasn't rested on that distinction, as it has set out to set itself apart. It starts with a commitment to excellence. It is an idea that is constantly repeated within its mission statement. Those efforts have produced results nationally and around the world. The University of Georgia is consistently ranked as one of the top colleges and best values for education in the U.S. It has produced 24 Rhodes Scholars, 143 Fulbright Scholars, 21 Truman Scholars, 60 Goldwater

Scholars and many more achievements. The Honors Program has been recognized as one of the top 10 honors programs in the country.

The academic success of the university has been a constant for a long time. It used to be that most of the engineering students attended a school in Atlanta, and everyone else went to Georgia. It seemed as if the majority of doctors, economists, teachers, bankers, lawyers and all the rest enrolled at the University of Georgia. There are always some exceptions, but that was the stereotype for a long time.

But recent history has shown UGA has even been attracting more quality engineering students to its improved program. The quality of education is certainly a factor in choosing Georgia, but there are so many other things that attract students to Athens. It's a comprehensive experience that helps students thrive in any career they choose.

The Georgia campus runs north and south along the Oconee River. The river runs along the east side while the north end of campus butts up against downtown Athens. The north campus is considered the "old campus" because of its many historic sites. One of my favorites places is Herty Field. The field is the site of the first intercollegiate football game ever contested in the state of Georgia. It's name comes from Dr. Charles Herty. He was a chemistry professor who is credited with being the first football coach at Georgia. The small field is a peaceful setting for students and teachers to escape the rigors of the day. A small walking path that runs by a lovely fountain encircles the field. The opposite end from the fountain is marked with a historic plaque explaining the spot's significance.

Dr. Herty introduced the game of football to the students at the University of Georgia. He was exposed to the sport while earning his doctorate of chemistry at Johns Hopkins University. He was a good friend of George Petrie, another student who received his doctoral degree (history) from Johns Hopkins the same year (1890). They both enjoyed the game and implemented it on their respective campuses. Dr. Petrie is recognized as his school's (Auburn University) first football coach too. When the teams began competition, the friends scheduled a game against each other. The contest took place at Atlanta's Piedmont Park in 1892, and it was the first installment of what we now know as "The Deep South's Oldest Rivalry" (Georgia versus Auburn).

Just a stone's throw away from Herty Field is the Chapel Bell. The bell used to sit in a tower above the old chapel. It is now located in the rear of the building atop its own tower. The current tower resembles an oil derrick. The wooden tower is painted white and is topped with a metal roof to protect the bell from the elements. The Chapel Bell is regularly clanged all night long after the Bulldogs attain a victory on the gridiron. Traditionally, the freshmen were tasked with keeping it ringing throughout the night, but now everyone wants to get in on the act. The ringing of the Chapel Bell tradition is so loved that it has been adopted for many other purposes. People ring the bell when they graduate, get engaged or just plain feel happy. Students, alumni and fans all find good reasons to tug on the rope, so they can hear its song echo through the buildings of north campus.

When walking around to the front of the Chapel, it's easy to realize how beautiful of a place it is. The Chapel's six white columns provide for a terrific backdrop. As I walked past, a student was in a cap and gown for a photo shoot. While those pictures were being taken, another student, with photographer in tow, was waiting for her turn. To the right, there was a family having pictures taken as they walked side-by-side up the walkway. They were southbound so the Arch would be in the background. People really have an affinity for the area, and it's not difficult to see why, as the whole area bursts with southern charm. It is a place where someone could sit on the grass, have a glass of sweet tea and not have a worry in the world.

After the family took the shot they wanted, I walked past to go see the Arch. Of course, there was another future graduate having her photo taken in front of the Arch. I suspect that professional photographers in Athens don't have to worry about too much with their jobs. They were performing sessions the whole week that I was there, and there is never a shortage of places with iconic backdrops. The Arch is the most iconic of them all.

The Arch serves as the northern gate to the campus. The polished and painted cast iron forms an arch that has three pillars reaching to the ground below. The three pillars represent wisdom, justice and moderation. The Arch, as a whole, symbolizes the past and future of the university. Even the official logo of the University of Georgia predominantly displays a representation of the Arch. Many people have framed prints of the Arch hanging on the wall in their office. Whether it was covered in snow or surrounded by a crowd of people, the Arch stood tall with a beauty and strength in every picture. It is said that if a freshman walks under the Arch, then that person will never graduate. I'm not sure about the validity of the tale, but I would advise the freshmen not to test it and stay in the library.

The next morning, I parked at the Tate Center Deck, which is close to the stadium and a fairly centralized location. I started south down Lumpkin Street toward the athletic complex. I should say "up" Lumpkin Street because it is a pretty decent incline in that direction. In reality, it's an incline in every direction from the Tate Center Deck. The students were on the move and so were the squirrels. There were squirrels in trees and bushes, running across fence posts and maneuvering their way through the pedestrians. I think that

I even saw one waiting for an Uber. Seriously, there were a lot of squirrels, and it made perfect sense. The campus is a beautiful sanctuary. It's like a college and a nature preserve combined to form an oasis in the middle of Athens.

Something else that I noticed was the amount of buses. Other campuses had buses, but they also had many more students riding scooters, bikes and skateboards. At Georgia, the students who wanted to ride were going to ride on the buses. However, I had no problem walking. It is an exquisite campus with many alluring buildings. The walk through campus revealed the varying stages of the autumn transformation for the numerous trees on campus. There were dry crackling leaves strewn across the ground, but many of them still grasped to the perch from which they were sprouted. At the bend in Lumpkin, I veered left down Carlton Street toward Stegeman Coliseum.

This building was the site of a basketball game that increased my passion for SEC sports. It was the 1981 contest between the Georgia Bulldogs and Kentucky Wildcats. I listened to the game with my grandpa, and I was enthralled. Kentucky's legendary radio man, Cawood Ledford, was enamored with the talents of

Georgia, UGA

School Colors:
Red & Black

Traditions:
Between The Hedges
Silver Britches
Running Through The "G" Banner
Ringing The Chapel Bell
Light Up Sanford

Redcoat Marching Band
Fight Song - Hail to Georgia
Glory
Battle Hymn of the Bulldog Nation

Favorite Battle Cries:
Go Dawgs
How 'bout Them Dawgs

Georgia's Dominique Wilkins. Ledford's descriptions of Wilkins made me envision a basketball superman that could only be conquered by a true team effort. Ledford voiced "Wilkins glides in and scores with a finger roll ... over to Wilkins, lays it up and in ... Wilkins will fire; Got it!"

Wilkins ended with 32 points, but Sam Bowie and Kentucky eventually won the instant classic in double overtime. On top of that, the Georgia coach, Hugh Durham was a Louisville native (he and my mom were actually cousins). With that game, I discovered the conference that I already supported was good at basketball too! It cemented my admiration for the SEC and opened my rooting interest to sports other than football.

Sitting outside of Stegeman, there is the UGA Olympians Memorial Plaza. Stegeman Coliseum is the site where the rhythmic gymnastics and volleyball competitions were held during the 1996 Olympics. The facility has recently undergone major renovations, and it looks brand new. It's a great venue that hosts various UGA sporting events and concerts. Stegeman is actually two different structures - the roof and the building. The inside is really nice with displays of athletes that have excelled at Georgia. Yes, I was able to find multiple places where "the human highlight film" (Dominique Wilkins) was honored.

Leaving Stegeman, I walked down the backside of the football facility toward Foley Field. I explored the Bulldogs' baseball stadium and the Dan Magill Tennis Complex. The tennis facility is a little ways past the centerfield wall. Hiking up the other side of Foley Field, I came to Pinecrest Drive. I was able to take it past the front of the baseball stadium and up to Butts-Mehre Heritage Hall. The Butts-Mehre building has a public area that includes a sports museum with trophies, pictures and history of University of Georgia sports. The complex also houses the athletic administration and football facilities, including the indoor practice field. Walking past the Butts-Mehre Heritage Hall complex, a real gem awaits.

That gem is the Vince Dooley Sculpture Garden. It is on the corner at Lumpkin, and it serves as an introductory foyer to the Vince Dooley Athletic Complex. It has a plaza featuring, "The Character of a Champion" (the statue of Dooley on his players' shoulders). Numerous black marble plaques encircle the sculpture. The plaques detail his performance, accomplishments and service as head football coach and athletic director. The plaques also list the achievements of the athletes and teams during his reign. The area is surrounded by beautiful gardens, which is something that I am sure Coach Dooley appreciates since he has a well-known fondness for gardening. The area is a fantastic tribute to a man who did so much for Georgia Athletics and the Athens community.

Coach Vince Dooley was raised in Mobile, Alabama and he played football at Auburn. After graduation, he was an assistant coach at his alma mater before he became the head coach at Georgia in 1964. Coach Dooley won a national title in 1980, coached Heisman winner Hershel Walker and retired from coaching in 1988 with the second most (at the time) victories in SEC history. Dooley also served as Georgia's Athletic Director from 1979-2004, overseeing 23 national championship teams. When I asked Coach Dooley what the SEC meant to him, he explained "I was born in 1932. The conference started in 1933. I went to Auburn and then came here to Georgia. I've been here since, so you can kind of say that it's been a part of me since the beginning."

I can't argue with that, but I would say that Coach Dooley has meant just as much to the SEC as it has to him. The Southeastern Conference and UGA seem to agree because Dooley has been named the University of Georgia's SEC Legend for 2019. Congratulations! It was a well-deserved honor.

My journey took me to the Richard B. Russell Special Collections Library. The place is a treasure trove of interesting and significant artifacts. It is named after Senator Richard Russell to honor his 50 years of public service. Mr. Russell was born in Georgia, graduated from UGA Law and served as governor of Georgia before being elected to the U.S. Senate. He served in the Senate from 1933 until his death in 1971. The Russell Senate Office Building (in Washington D.C.) is also named in his honor, and it's the oldest of the U.S. Senate office buildings. The Special Collections Library, at the University of Georgia, contains the Hargrett Rare Book and Manuscript Library, the Richard B. Russell Library for Political Research and Studies and the Walter J. Brown Media Archives and Peabody Awards Collection. Each one is filled with its own historic relics.

Outside of the Special Collections Library is where *SEC Nation* was setting up to air. I stopped by to visit with my friend Darion as they were constructing the set. We enjoyed the sunshine and a few stories. As I was headed to my next meeting, I had to stop and make a quick phone call. I called Augusta National Golf Club to inquire about setting up a visit after I completed my duties in Athens. I just wanted to drive over and see the home of the Masters Tournament. I was told that it was a private club and the only way for access was as a guest of a member. Since I don't know any members personally, my hope to see the famed place was thwarted. It was actually the nicest rejection that I had ever experienced, and at least I didn't waste time driving over there. See, in the South people are congenial even when you aren't welcome. That probably wouldn't have been as true if I had just shown up unannounced.

You can find traditions just about everywhere around the University of Georgia. Traditions play a big part in the affinity that people have for their schools. Some things are more traditional landmarks than actual traditions, and some landmarks get embellished and become lore.

Take Tanyard Creek for example. For years, I've heard stories that Sanford Stadium had a river buried underneath it. Supposedly, that's why the field drained so well when it rained. The reality is that there is a creek that runs under the Georgia sideline. In fact, it runs under a lot of the campus. There are certain spots where it is visible around campus, and one of those spots is outside the southwest corner of Sanford Stadium. There is no access point into the stadium, so any stories of people sneaking in that way is more urban legend than tradition.

Every group of fans has their own personal traditions whether it's tailgate procedures or stadium rituals that make Saturday game days special. Sometimes those traditions are noticed and embraced by the masses. That's what happened to Mike Woods.

Woods, known as "Big Dawg," would paint the top of his head with a classic Georgia Dawgs logo. Actually, it was his loving wife that did the painting most of the time. It was common to see a representation of the opponent's mascot clutched in Uga's jaws in the artwork. Mike Woods was a natural for an activity like this, as he was a successful salesman with a big personality and a huge heart. He entertained and brought smiles to the faces of many fans (of UGA and other teams). Woods loved it, and so did flocks of Georgia fans. They always wanted to take pictures with him showing off his painted dome. The "Big Dawg" tradition was well-known in UGA circles, but it really took off with the popularity of social media.

The tradition actually began with Big Mike's father Lonnie, who started painting his head during the magical 1980 season. Lonnie Woods was friends with Erk Russell, the famed defensive coordinator for Georgia. Russell was a fiery coach who would regularly clash heads with his players (they had on helmets and he did not). Often times when he did this, Russell's head would start to bleed and blood trickled down his forehead. Lonnie Woods teased his friend by telling him that he should do something with the blood, like form a bulldog with it. Russell was coaching and didn't have time for that. So, Lonnie did it with paint on his own bald head.

The first time Lonnie did it as a way to razz Russell more than anything. When Lonnie did it in New Orleans for the Sugar Bowl, the fans embraced it, and it grew from there. After Lonnie passed away, Mike eventually decided to carry on the tradition.

Mike's sudden passing a few years ago changed everything for his family, particularly for his youngest son. Trent Woods was always the planned replacement as "Big Dawg." When he was younger, Trent accompanied his father to games and regularly served as the unofficial photographer. Trent wasn't sure that he was ready, yet duty called - a duty that has become a tribute to his father and the Georgia Bulldog fans.

It can be overwhelming at times. It might take him two hours to get from his tailgate into the game. It can also be therapeutic. I watched people in Knoxville (Tennessee fans) flock to Trent to show their appreciation and tell stories about times they spent with his father. "It's amazing how many lives Daddy touched," said a proud son. Trent echoed his father's words when he told me "I do it in honor of my Daddy. It's my way of continuing what he did." Sometimes a tradition grows into something more meaningful. Now, it has been solidified as a family tradition, and all of us in the SEC can appreciate that.

"Calling the Dawgs" is always a welcome tradition at Georgia. Traditionally, it is done during kickoffs. The crowd says "Goooooo," until the ball is kicked, and then they finish with "Dawgs. Sic 'em. Woof. Woof. Woof." It's even popular before the game at tailgate events. Many times it is interactive. Someone will say "Go Dawgs" and the response will be "Sic 'em," which usually elicits barking sounds. If it's a more refined setting or it's not game day, then the reply is typically a reciprocal "Go Dawgs."

The English bulldog mascot is named Uga, and he is one of the most beloved mascots in the entire country.

Uga is owned and cared for by the Seiler family out of Savannah. Every Uga has been a descendant of the original Uga, "Hood's Ole Dan" from 1956-1966.

Since 2015, "Que" has served as Uga X. He is more than just a mascot, as he is part of the team. Uga travels to games with the team and gets a special jersey made just for him. The previous Uga mascots are all buried in a mausoleum in the southwest corner of Sanford Stadium. Each has a plaque with an epitaph and a summary of its reign as Uga. When Georgia plays a home game, there are many people who stop to pay their respects. Some even bring flowers. The current Uga always has a great seat for the game. The viewpoint is from a custom doghouse on the east sideline, complete with air-conditioning.

The Georgia fans and the city of Athens love their bulldogs. There are more than three-dozen bulldog statues around campus and the city. Local artists uniquely designed each "dawg" as part of a project initiated by the city. The statues stand guard at local businesses, buildings on campus and around other Athens destinations. I wish that I had known about their existence earlier in the week. As it was, I only discovered 11 of the 38 pieces of art. Still, my favorite probably wouldn't have changed if I did see them all. It was titled "Dawg Walker," and it sat in the front yard of the Wray-Nicholson House (Alumni Association). The design was a tribute to Hershel Walker. It was red, black, and silver with his number and pictures of his biggest moments painted around it.

Another amenity in Athens is called Bulldog Park, and it's a luxury RV facility. It was developed by Phil Nichols, a long time supporter of the

University of Georgia and one of five investors for the project. The park is a gated community that can house over 280 RV's, complete with restroom and shower facilities. There are private structures built on some of the lots, and they all have fun and unique names. They range from being garages for golf carts to full-blown party decks. It is a great place for fans to park their RV's for sporting events and to enjoy the company of other faithful Dawg fans. I made it out there on Friday night when people were starting their tailgate parties early enough to avoid the impending rain.

Saturday morning fulfilled the promise of wet conditions. Thankfully, the rain was intermittent. At 7:00 am, the campus was already alive for the 3:30 pm start. Smokers, manned by their covered operators, were billowing with the aromas of the day's menu. Tents emblazoned with huge "G's" shielded guests from the raindrops and leaves that were falling out of trees. Red and black flags whipped in the gusts of crisp air. There were "Go Dawgs" calls and "UGA" chants. Joggers worked their way through it all as if they were completing the last mile of a marathon. This was the last home game, and the Bulldog faithful were going to make full use of the opportunity despite the conditions.

I made a visit to the *SEC Nation* set and saw both "Que" and Trent "Big Dawg" Woods. The students were ready to cheer, and they brought plenty of signs. My favorite said "Get Well Soon, Tua" with Georgia's famed "G" starting the first word. In an effort to support our Veterans, I helped Oscar La Madrid throw red shirts into the crowd. The shirts help assist Angels Alive Inc. in giving Veterans a better quality of life. The chest of the shirt said R E D, with Remember Everyone Deployed written underneath the large white letters. The rain didn't hamper the attendance, as everyone was excited for a good late-season test against Texas A&M.

The tailgate scene was vast. There was a sea of tents set up in every direction from the stadium. There was no way that I could get to every area. It looked like one big party, and in a way, it was. From one tent to the next, it seemed like everyone was connected. They shared music, drinks, food and a love for Georgia football. They even shared acquaintances. Every setup that I visited had someone that knew someone from the neighboring tents. It was a cordial atmosphere, like a big family reunion. It was a nation indivisible. A Bulldog Nation! I shouldn't have expected anything less. The Georgia fans had shown up in full force at the two UGA road games that I attended (Vanderbilt & Tennessee). A home game, rain or not, wasn't going to be any different.

The Dawg Walk was predictably full of people. That is where the team walks to the stadium from Lumpkin Street. I had an overhead view from Sanford Drive (directly above Tanyard Creek). There were people on top of the parking deck, standing on outdoor staircases and at least ten people deep on Sanford Drive (where I was). "The Redcoat Band" was spirited as they chanted and serenaded the players and coaches walking into the stadium. Fans reached over the ropes to touch hands with the players passing by. Red appeared to be the color of the day, but it was broken up with the clashing hues of yellow, blue, orange and green ponchos. Nonetheless, the fans were enjoying the event, and they were prepared to support their Dawgs.

I changed into some dry clothes and made it into the stadium right before the

Sanford Stadium

Dooley Field

AKA – "Between the Hedges"

Surface: Grass

Built in 1929

Capacity: 92,746

Record Attendance: 93,246 - 9/21/19 vs Notre Dame

Nickname: Bulldogs

Mascot:

Costumed - UGA

Live - UGA X (Que)

*Fans' Favorite Home Games:

Won 23-17 over Notre Dame in 2019

Won 18-13 over Tennessee in 2002

skies opened again. The rain appeared to energize the crowd and the players during warm-ups. I hoped that the rain would subside as the game neared. It eventually lightened, but not for the senior introductions. Being the last home game, the football seniors and their families were recognized for their contributions to Georgia football. As they continued through the introductions, the rain intensified. By the time they reached the end of the list, the skies and the crowd gushed. The crowd did so in appreciation for the last honoree, Rodrigo Blankenship. "Hot Rod", as the fans affectionately refer to him, is a favorite for many reasons, but mainly because he excelled as the team's kicker.

The pre-game festivities continued to build into a crescendo. "The Redcoat Band" scurried onto the field in their clear ponchos after hearing "Hey, what's that coming down the track? It's the heart of the Bulldog spirit." It continued, "A huge machine in red and black ... Ain't nothing finer in the land than the 115th edition of the University of Georgia Redcoat Band!"

The band's performance was very interactive with the fans. "The Redcoat Band" morphed in to the shape of the Arch as they played "Glory, Glory" and then the *Alma Mater*. As if that wasn't enough, the audience sang along with the national anthem. Then followed the "spell Georgia" cheer and the "Georgia Bulldogs Cheer" coupled with the "Calling of the Dawgs." After that, the band played "Hail to Georgia," the University of Georgia fight song. Finally, the performance hit the high note with the "Lone Trumpeter."

The Lone Trumpeter tradition is fairly new by tradition standards, but it is awesome. A note is begun and held while people point to the section marked "South." Behind the word is a single trumpet player who slowly exhales the first few notes of the "Battle Hymn of the Bulldog Nation." The video board plays a riveting montage featuring Larry Munson as narrator while the rest of the band lightly continues the song. It ends with everyone saying "Go Dawgs" in unison. It was one of those moments that I didn't expect. Thirty seconds ago, I was getting ready to watch Georgia play Texas A&M for the first time since 1980. Now, I'm standing hear with tears in my eyes and my heart pounding out of my chest. It was stirring, and I loved it! I guess readers could say that I have too much SEC in me!

I don't know if much could top that, but it's always fun to watch the teams enter the field. The band formed a tunnel for the team and played "Krypton." I have always liked the tradition of the Georgia players running through the "G" banner, and I was ready.

Or so I thought. I planned to record it, but instead I took two pictures - one of the banner and one after the fact. Maybe I wasn't ready after all. Well, let's just say that my phone wasn't ready. I did get to witness the whole scene (complete with the boos as Texas A&M ran on the field). It was a sight to behold with the Bulldogs jogging out and the gigantic Georgia flags flying. It was a very cool moment.

The day continued to be promising when I heard Brook Whitmire (the PA announcer) convey, "Welcome back between the hedges" over the PA system. The crowd was excited and only became more raucous when the rain fell harder.

Georgia has two of the most renowned traditions in the SEC.

At home, the Bulldogs play "between the hedges," which refers to the Chinese privet hedges that surround the field. They have been around since 1929. The hedges have been removed only twice. Once for 2017 expansion and once for the soccer medal round games of the 1996 Olympics. It isn't the only stadium in the country (or the SEC) with hedges, but it is the only stadium where the game is played "between the hedges."

Also, Georgia wears "silver britches." They have been a staple in the Georgia uniform for many years. It started when new coach Wally Butts introduced them in 1939. There was a time when Coach Dooley went with white pants, but he reverted back to the "silver britches" in 1980 - just in time for the Dawgs to wear them through the entire national championship season.

Larry Munson was Georgia's radio play-by-play man for more than 40 years. He had a unique and recognizable voice that immediately told listeners Georgia was playing.

Munson was unapologetically a homer for Georgia. That's one of the things that made him great. The aspect that made him the greatest was his tendency to say the most unconventional things when something big happened. Sometimes, it was head scratching and sometimes it seemed too revealing and honest. The reality is that it was brilliant and always on target. Most people have heard "Run Lindsay" or "We just stepped on their face with a hobnailed boot," or "Oh you, Hershel Walker." Those plays, and the calls associated with them, are legendary. I am going to share a few of my favorite examples that will hopefully give folks some insight into what it was like listening to a Georgia game called by Larry Munson.

> "My God...a freshman!" - after Hershel Walker scored against Tennessee in 1980.

> "We're going to try to kick it a hundred thousand miles." - before Kevin Butler's 60-yard field goal against Clemson in 1984.

> "Oh, look at the sugar falling out of the sky" - as the clock wound down against Auburn in 1982. After the same game - "We are going to do something to Opelika."

➢ "Now, you got 105 seconds to hang on. Don't celebrate now for God's sake" - after Georgia scored to take the lead in 2006 versus Georgia Tech. It was Munson's last game on the call.

➢ "Get the picture," "Old Lady Luck," and "Whatchagot Loran" - multiple games.

He was so excitable listeners didn't know what he would say next. He would say "My God" so dramatically that it was fair to wonder if someone had just jumped out of the press box. Munson would urge on the team by growling "Hunker Down!" He counted out yard lines every five yards and even counted the clock down per second. He was Georgia football to so many in the South.

The game was played fairly conservatively in the beginning. A Blankenship field goal gave Georgia a 3-0 advantage after its second possession. Later in the quarter, a Texas A&M punt pinned Georgia at its own 1-yard line. The Bulldogs weren't able to dig out of the hole and were forced to punt from deep in their own end. It was a good punt, but a nice return set A&M up in Georgia territory.

As the second quarter began, the Aggies kicked their own field goal to knot the score at 3-3. Georgia quickly answered with another field goal from "Hot Rod." The unbelievable 49-yard kick, in driving rain, put Georgia up 6-3. After the Texas A&M offense was forced to retreat, Georgia's offense attacked through the air. A couple nice receptions moved the Dawgs into scoring position. A final reception placed them in the end zone. The Texas A&M offense couldn't gain much traction in the rain versus the aggressive Georgia defense. Georgia's offense seemed ready to break out, but there was always a slip up that would stop the momentum. The half ended with the Dawgs leading, 13-3.

The heralded Georgia defense continued its assault in the third quarter. On Texas A&M's first possession of the second half, safety Richard LeCounte caused and recovered a fumble. The advantageous field position assisted Georgia in extending the lead to 16-3. The Bulldogs attempted a surprise onside kick, but Texas A&M wasn't fooled. The Aggies offense began to click, working the ball down to Georgia's 26-yard line, where it faced a third-and-one. The Dawgs defense stood tough on third and fourth down. A&M had decided to go for it on fourth down, but they were halted by the stingy UGA defense.

Texas A&M took advantage of good field position during its next possession. A nice completion by quarterback Kellen Mond and a penalty against the Georgia secondary helped A&M reduce the deficit to 10.

With the score 16-6, Georgia quarterback Jake Fromm answered with a long pass to wide receiver George Pickens. That started a nice drive, but it crumbled with a crucial penalty. The quarter ended with Georgia facing a fourth-and-seven inside Texas A&M's 15-yard line.

The time between the third and fourth quarters of any Georgia football game is very lively. When the game is in Sanford Stadium, it is dynamic. After a few quiet seconds, the band breaks into "Krypton." The fans love and embrace it. They hold up four fingers and their phones, with flashlights beaming, and then wave them up and down with the music.

This has become Georgia's newest tradition. "Light Up Sanford" gets the crowd amped and shows the players that Bulldog Nation is supporting them. Afterward, the band played "Glory, Glory" and a hype video was shown on the video board. Around that time, red LED lights synchronized to the music illuminated the stadium. It was as if a red dawn had infiltrated the place. It was certainly something that the fans enjoyed, and I see it continuing for a long time.

As the game resumed, Rodrigo Blankenship made his fourth field goal to increase Georgia's lead to 19-6. From there, the Texas A&M offense came out firing. It was inconsistent to start the drive, but the Aggies were able to convert a couple third downs. The A&M offense finally started stringing completions together that resulted in it eventually reaching the end zone.

The next few possessions saw both offenses move the ball, but not enough to result in a score. Georgia received the ball back with four and a half minutes to play. Senior running back Brian Herrien made a tough run to convert the initial third down. Then, talented runner D'Andre Swift took over the game. He made brilliant runs one after the other. The Georgia offense ran out the clock as it moved the ball down the field. Final Score: Georgia 19, Texas A&M 13.

Under the glow of the video board revealing "Dawgs Win," the soggy mass of people slowly made its way out of the stadium. They orderly made their way back to their parking spots. Some resumed the party while others headed for home. Many were organizing plans for a night out in Athens. It's a place that students and alumni love to experience.

Loran Smith would know. He has been in Athens for over 60 years. He studied at UGA and was a star on the track team. His time working in multiple capacities for the University of Georgia gives him a unique insight. Smith noted, "It's kind of a tradition to come back for the game and enjoy Athens." Loran has been all around the SEC and collegiate athletics, and he knows that Athens is a special place. He explained, "People love their alma mater and spending time in small towns. They like coming back to Athens."

That's the truth, and why wouldn't they love it. It's a great school, in a wonderful town with plenty of fantastic traditions. It will make your spirit sing, "Glory, glory to Ole Georgia!"

Georgia Bulldogs

Defensive Linemen

Geno Atkins
(2006-09)

Freddie Gilbert
(1980-83)

Bill Goldberg
(1986-89)

Charles Grant
(1999-2001)

Quentin Moses
(2003-06)

Jimmy Payne
(1978-82)

David Pollack
(2001-04)

Richard Seymour
(1997-2000)

Bill Stanfill
(1966-68)

Marcus Stroud
(1997-2000)

My favorite players to watch at other defensive positions:

LB - Mo Lewis (1987-90)

DB - Champ Bailey (1996-98)

DB - Thomas Davis (2002-04)

LB - Richard Tardits (1985-88)

Running Backs

Nick Chubb
(2014-17)

Terrell Davis
(1992-94)

Todd Gurley
(2012-14)

Rodney Hampton
(1987-89)

Garrison Hearst
(1990-92)

Knowshon Moreno
(2007-08)

Frank Sinkwich
(1940-42)

Lars Tate
(1984-87)

Charley Trippi
(1942, 1945-46)

Hershel Walker
(1980-82)

My favorite players to watch at other offensive positions:

WR - Hines Ward (1994-97)

QB - Eric Zeier (1991-94)

WR - A.J. Green (2008-10)

OL - Ben Jones (2008-11)

Fan Favorites: RB - Hershel Walker, DB - Champ Bailey, DL - David Pollack

15

THE AUBURN FAMILY

Week of the November 30, 2019 game against Alabama

The Auburn community considers itself a family. It shares good and bad memories, breakfast hang-outs, rituals, Toomer's lemonade and of course an admiration for Auburn sports. As most close-knit families do, they also share many of the same values. Each person's values are individually prioritized according to their hopes, dreams and life experiences. The Auburn Family's values are, at least partially, rooted in the Auburn Creed.

The Auburn Creed was penned by George Petrie, a Montgomery native who spent more than 50 years working at the school in multiple capacities. Petrie was a historian who served at Auburn University as a professor and administrator. He is also credited with organizing and coaching the first football team in school history. In November of 1943, just over a year after retiring and becoming a widower, Petrie's admiration for Auburn flowed from his passionate thoughts through his fingers and onto the paper in the form of the Auburn Creed.

The Auburn Creed

I believe that this is a practical world and that I can count only on what I earn. Therefore, I believe in work, hard work.

I believe in education, which gives me the knowledge to work wisely and trains my mind and my hands to work skillfully.

I believe in honesty and truthfulness, without which I cannot win the respect and confidence of my fellow men.

I believe in a sound mind, in a sound body and a spirit that is not afraid, and in clean sports that develop these qualities.

I believe in obedience to law because it protects the rights of all.

I believe in the human touch, which cultivates sympathy with my fellow men and mutual helpfulness and brings happiness for all.

I believe in my Country, because it is the land of freedom and because it is my own home, and that I can best serve that country by "doing justly, loving mercy, and walking humbly with my God."

And because Auburn men and women believe in these things,

I believe in Auburn and love it.

The words of the Auburn Creed can be found meticulously carved into stones, precisely etched onto plaques and artfully painted within murals. Since 1943, it has motivated students, inspired industry leaders and endeared itself to the community. It's a glimpse into the responsibilities of being a mature adult. It's a beacon that helps lead the members of the Auburn family to its individual paths. It's the model that helps form their character. It is woven in the spirit of Auburn. It is the essence of the Auburn Family.

Coach Pat Dye is one of the most successful coaches to lead student-athletes at Auburn University. He excelled as Auburn's athletic director and head football coach for over a decade. Dye won SEC Coach of the Year honors on three different occasions and was inducted to the College Football Hall of Fame in 2005. When Coach Dye first read the Auburn Creed, he noticed two specific phrases ("I believe in work. Hard work," and "... a spirit that is not afraid") and he thought to himself "Hey, that's me. I believe in those things too." It was then that he knew Auburn was right for him and that he was right for Auburn. Coach Dye used hard work and "a spirit that is not afraid" to change Auburn football's culture and the SEC forever. His experiences also changed him for the better and made him the Auburn man he is today.

Being an Auburn man or woman is not something that one achieves by displaying a logo on a cap or a sticker on a truck. It is not as simple as just declaring an allegiance. It's not something that one can buy. Auburn men and women have been molded and refined over the years as those who approach life with a sincere sense of the Auburn Spirit. The Auburn Spirit is difficult to describe, especially for those who haven't spent significant time there. It is something that one has to experience and live out individually. It has to permeate one's being. When the Auburn Spirit touches the soul, then it will be forever transformed.

David Housel speaks of the Auburn Spirit: "It is indefinable. It's just something to where we take care of each other."

Mr. Housel should know. He has been an Auburn man since 1965. His roles at

Auburn, AU

School Colors:

Blue & Orange

Traditions:

Tiger Walk

War Eagle Flight

Toomer's Corner

Singing "God Bless America"

The Auburn Creed

Auburn Marching Band

Fight Song - War Eagle

Glory To Ole Auburn

Tiger Rag

Favorite Battle Cries:

War Eagle

Go Tigers

Auburn have ranged from student to professor to athletics director. Housel relates the Auburn Spirit to, "a joyful attitude: an attitude of kindness, camaraderie and of a human touch." Joyful is the inescapable word when he describes Auburn. "A joyful place. A joyful attitude." Coach Dye would certainly agree, as he was quick to point out that Auburn was "ranked No. 1 when it comes to the happiest student body in the country."

That isn't the only thing for which Auburn has received high marks. *U.S. News and World Report* lists Auburn's Veterinary Medicine program as 14th best in the nation, along with Rehabilitation Counseling at No. 15 and Pharmacy at No. 25. *The Princeton Review* named Auburn a "Best Value College" in 2020. The university was established in 1856. In 1872, Auburn became the South's first school to be designated a land grant institution. The school has since added sea grant and space grant status and become a leader in research initiatives. The university has also produced many industry leaders, and with an enrollment of more than 30,000, that trend is sure to continue.

Housel and Dye are two important figures in Auburn history. Dye forever changed Auburn Football, as he brought a courage and toughness to the university and the city of Auburn when they sorely needed it. Coach Dye wouldn't back down from anybody, and he made it clear the Auburn faithful needed to stop worrying about everyone else and focus on Auburn. He was a rural boy from Georgia who knew hard work. He had survived the wrath of his older brothers, so he was certainly tough. Dye won an SEC championship as an All-American player at Georgia and five more as an assistant coach at Alabama. Coach Dye conquered four more SEC titles as the head coach at Auburn. With three consecutive conference titles, from 1987-89, Coach Dye became only the fourth coach in SEC history (Neyland, Bryant, Dooley) to accomplish the feat. Steve Spurrier and Nick Saban have since accomplished the feat.

Perhaps Dye's most indelible mark was more about a location than an outcome. The Iron Bowl (the game between Auburn and Alabama) had been played at Legion Field, in Birmingham, since the rivalry was renewed in 1948. After 41 consecutive years in Birmingham, Dye followed through on his promise to have the game played at Auburn in 1989.

There is a whole story behind everything it took to get the game moved to Auburn. To me, the most fascinating story is how having the game played on their campus helped remove the yoke of oppression felt by the fans and citizens of Auburn. In a sense, it put Auburn on the same plane as Alabama in the state. It has been likened to the Israelites finally reaching the Promised Land. The Iron Bowl and Auburn have never been the same since December 2, 1989. For the record, Auburn beat No. 2 ranked and undefeated Alabama 30-20 that day. The Iron Bowl has eventually become a true home-and-home series that is played on both campuses.

I asked David Housel what 1989 was like. His face locked into a huge smile and he admitted, "It was special." He struggled to find the perfect words and uttered, "There's been nothing like it before or since."

I inquired if the biblical comparison was overstating it. Housel grinned at me and responded "You can only be delivered to the promised land once!"

Housel has been part of many of the biggest events in Auburn history. His talents and knowledge have led him to be a popular speaker, and his favorite topic is the Auburn Spirit. He takes pride in telling how the town takes care of the kids, and how the Auburn students are ready to go to work when they graduate. He knows that Auburn University will help its students grow past their potential. They will be better prepared for a career, better prepared to start a family and better human beings. When talking to the parents of potential students or newly-enrolled freshmen, Housel leaves them with his most prideful observation: "When you send them to Auburn, they'll never come home the same."

On my first day on Auburn's campus, I wondered how many parents were confirming Housel's proclamation. It was Thanksgiving week. The students had the week off, and the vast majority of them had already gone home. The most interaction I had, other than in the bookstore, was from two maintenance workers talking trash about the upcoming game. One was wearing an Alabama cap and hollering about the Crimson Tide. The other showed up and defended his Auburn Tigers. The Alabama fan continued with a confident arrogance. The Auburn man decided it was time to put up or shut up. A $100 wager was offered. It was good to see someone with a spirit that was not afraid to defend his team. As I walked on, I heard "I don't want to take your money," to which the Auburn man comfortably said, "Don't worry. You won't!"

It was very serene walking through the "loveliest village on the plains" without crowds of students rushing to get somewhere. I leisurely strolled over to College Street and set my direction toward Toomer's Drugs. Their famous lemonade would be a perfect refresher on this beautiful sunny day. As I arrived at Toomer's Corner, a few signs with small orange letters informed me that those particular trees should not be rolled. A few years earlier, a fire had stunted the maturity of the young oaks at this historic spot. They simply were not yet ready to endure the stress of being rolled. Rolling refers to the tradition of people blanketing trees, light posts and power lines with toilet paper after momentous Auburn victories.

The origins of the cherished tradition come from just across the intersection of College St. and Magnolia Ave. Toomer's Drugstore has resided there since 1896. It was and still is one of the places to go in town. In the early days, before there were radios and televisions, it was difficult to find out the scores of the Auburn road games. Toomer's had the town's only telegraph machine, and they would regularly receive messages with the score of the game. If the Tigers were victorious, then the workers would take the ticker tape outside and throw it over the power lines. That way the whole town knew when Auburn had won. It has developed into one of the most storied traditions in all of college sports.

I stood and imagined the scene when the whole corner was covered in streams of toilet paper. I thought about the games that precipitated such a celebration. I pondered the other activities that accompanied a rolling like that. I contemplated the possibility of it happening the very week that I was visiting. I examined other viewpoints to take it all in. Hey, wait a second. I still haven't gone over to get my lemonade. I made my way across the intersection only to find that Toomer's Drugstore was closed until after Thanksgiving. I would have to wait another four days for their famous elixir. For now, I was pleased to admire the Tiger Trail of Auburn. Stone plaques of Auburn greats laid into the brick-lined walkways.

Auburn is a quaint picturesque little town, or should I just say it's "the loveliest village on the plains." Beautiful buildings with manicured storefronts lined the clean streets. It's almost difficult to determine where the campus ends and the town begins. It all blends together in perfect symmetry. As I would come to learn, that scenic symmetry is a microcosm of the relationship between the school and the town. They both toil independently, but they also work in unison to help each other thrive. As I continued to explore the town, it was inevitable that I popped up back on campus. Maybe it was the lack of people during the holiday week or the fantastic autumn weather, but this was the easiest and most pleasurable time that I had finding my way around a town and campus.

I made my way to Samford Avenue and meandered toward Swingle Hall. I sent some pictures of Swingle to my brother, who is a Fisheries Biologist. Homer Swingle, whom the building is named after, is considered the godfather of fisheries management. In fact, because of Swingle, Auburn became the first school to offer graduate and undergraduate courses in fisheries management. Homer Swingle worked on the faculty at Auburn from 1929 until his passing in 1973. His work at Auburn and around the world revolutionized the fishing industry. He attracted an array of students from foreign destinations to come and learn from him at Auburn. It has been widely documented that his work and discoveries directly led to pond and lake management and the introduction of the catfish farming industry.

My self-guided tour continued as I worked my way toward the campus bookstore, where I knew it was possible to purchase a bottle of water and check out the deals on Auburn gear. From there, it was time to venture into Jordan-Hare Stadium. But first, I realized that I was standing on Heisman Drive. John Heisman was the Auburn football coach for five years at the end of the 19th century. Of course, he is the man whose name is attached to the coveted Heisman Trophy. Auburn is the only school in the country able to boast about having John Heisman serve as coach and also have a Heisman Trophy winner (three to be exact). Heisman Drive hugs around three-quarters of Jordan-Hare Stadium. On the southeastern side of the stadium, there's a bust of John Heisman and a statue of Auburn's three Heisman winners: Pat Sullivan, Bo Jackson and Cam Newton.

Walking into the stadium was as fun as it was at every school. Every stadium has its own character and it tells its own story. I love seeing the old teams and players represented. If I looked at the pictures and plaques long enough, they came alive. I could see the players converging for the championship team picture. I could hear the radio call of each game-shifting play. I felt the buzz of a locker room during a coach's emotional post-game address. My ears picked up the echoes of a humbled acceptance speech.

My adrenaline levels rose with every recollection of where I was in those particular moments or similar moments that I shared with my teams. My mind ventured to imagine what this very spot where I am standing was like when those moments occurred. Was it crowded? What were the sounds? What were people wearing? Who were they with? Was anyone even here if it was a road game? Does the stadium sense their tenants' accomplishments when it happens at a sister stadium? It's all a moot point, but it sure is fun to imagine!

The day was getting late, so I walked up a ramp into the stadium. The first thing I noticed was that the middle of the field, from goal line to goal line, was dirt. There was already a plan to re-sod the field, but the previous weekend's deluge required it to be completed now. The inside of the stadium revealed markings for the legendary players, undefeated seasons and national championships. My eyes perused the classic stadium, checking off landmarks as they came into focus. I envisioned the eagle flight. I replayed Terry Beasley running under a deep ball for a touchdown, Kevin Greene finishing off a sack, Ronnie Brown breaking a long run and, of course,

Jordan-Hare Stadium

Pat Dye Field

Surface: Grass

Built in 1939

Capacity: 87,451

Record Attendance: 87,451 - Multiple Times

Nickname: Tigers

Mascot:

Costumed – Aubie the Tiger

War Eagle: War Eagle VIII - Aurea (Golden Eagle) and Spirit (Bald Eagle)

*Fans' Favorite Home Games:

Won 30-20 over Alabama in 1989

Won 34-28 over Alabama in 2013

Chris Davis catching and returning a certain missed field goal.

Orange seatbacks stamped with the Auburn logo peppered the expansive bleachers. I examined the hedges that shield the benches as well as the thicker hedges that converge with the wall. One of the iconic things that I did not see were the huge posters of the all-time players at the top of the end zone. They had been removed a few years earlier to make room for the gigantic new video board and new press box. On the opposite end, it was actually pretty cool to see the smaller old school scoreboard. As I exited and started the journey to my truck, I walked by two flatbed trailers filled with large rolls of new sod. The crew would work through the night to install the new turf.

The next couple of days were similar to the first. The Auburn campus had mostly beautiful weather, tranquil scenes and a lot of interesting discoveries. It would have been nice to experience Auburn University in full swing, but it was a relief to finally be alleviated from the fight for parking and the hurried mobs of students. It was surreal to be able to go back and forth across campus without the threat of being late for an appointment or interview. I was able to revisit areas and places that I normally wouldn't have had time to. The student rec center was one place that I wanted to revisit. I learned that they have a golf simulator, so I wanted to schedule a round, but it didn't happen. They would only let me do it if a student sponsored me.

My Augusta plans were foiled again! As it turns out, I would have had to settle for Pebble Beach anyway because the Augusta National course isn't on the simulator.

Across the street sits Auburn Arena. It is an attractive building, but it is the Final Four banner and Charles Barkley statue that really catches the eye. There is a lot to see in Auburn Arena. There are plenty of Auburn signs and murals, the practice facility, pictures of the SEC Championship and Final Four rings, locker rooms and party lounges. On the concourse level, there is a museum-type setup that honors all of the sports at Auburn. It is a dynamic area where visitors can learn a lot about the history of Auburn Athletics and the Auburn Spirit. My favorite element is where all of the championships are displayed. I stood in a circular area and looked up to see the War Eagle flying across the sky. Narrow orange and blue banners streamed down around me. Each blue banner is dedicated to a Southeastern Conference championship while the orange banners are dedicated to national championships. It is awesome and unique.

There are so many things that Auburn has to offer. There is a breathtaking arboretum that features the Founders' Oak. There is Samford Hall, where one can hear the carillon in the clock tower play "War Eagle" every day just after noon. There is great architecture and meticulous landscaping. On this day, Auburn's maintenance staff was decorating the campus for Christmas.

I walked through a village of tents left in place for the upcoming weekend's tailgating. Many of them are identifiable as from the Tailgate Guys (who originated from Auburn). Each unique title entertained me as I walked through the tailgate ghost town. The one that made the biggest impression on me boldly stated, "THEY'RE NOT GONNA KEEP 'EM OFF THE FIELD TONIGHT".

I retreated to my Airbnb in Chambers County for a Thanksgiving break. As it turns out, Chambers County is where the great boxing legend Joe Louis was born in 1914. LaFayette, the county seat, is also where JaTarvious "Boobie" Whitlow, the Auburn running back, played high school football. My stay was in a private room in a beautiful historic home. It included a television that gave me access to the SEC Network on demand. My "Charlie Brown" Thanksgiving consisted of turkey Hot Pockets and catching up on the *Saturdays in the South* series. There was some work completed, but the holiday provided a relaxed and entertaining break.

It was back to work on Friday, and Auburn was bustling. Families were touring the campus and having photo shoots at various landmarks. Groups were parading through the shops and streets of downtown. Toomer's Drugs was open and the line for their famous lemonade wound around the store and out onto the sidewalk. I found my place at the end of the line and was pleasantly surprised to have the lemon juice and sugar concoction in hand within five minutes. Fathers were tossing footballs with their sons on the lawn in front of Samford Hall. Tailgaters were delivering supplies to their pre-game destinations. More RV's and tents found their posts. The *SEC Nation* set had been constructed and was now attracting fans. Auburn was invigorated!

As the day wore on, the activity only increased. People were arriving in town, linking up with their hosts and beginning to commence with the festivities. Auburn University gives the fans a free look at the game day facility on Friday afternoons, so many Auburn fans (and Alabama fans for that matter) took advantage. They used the opportunity to tour the facility, take pictures with a Heisman Trophy, visit the locker room and even walk out to the field. It was a nice family atmosphere, but there was still a feeling that a big game was less than 24 hours away.

A college football Saturday in Auburn is special. When Alabama is in town, it has the potential to become epic. This Saturday showed great potential from the start. A vibrant blue sky invited the sun to climb to its peak. All types of people acknowledged each other with warm greetings. A sea of tents was unapologetically decorated in team colors. Televisions boldly displayed football content. Enticing aromas and festive music soon filled the air. Divided families relished in an atmosphere that felt right to all. There wasn't nervousness or animosity. It was an anticipation for what everyone seemed to know would be a great event. It was a celebration of college football.

Similar scenes played out all over the campus. It felt like Thanksgiving had paused on Thursday and picked up again on Saturday, as friends and family came together again to celebrate good times and traditions with each other. The *SEC Nation* set was packed with people watching the show. As I approached, they began to run a piece about the Bramblett family. I stopped at attention out of respect for their story. I wasn't the only one. It seemed as if the whole campus was in one big living room watching the feature together. Rod Bramblett was an Auburn radio announcer for years. He and his wife Paula had died in an automobile accident six months earlier. The story explained the events, but it conveyed more about the Auburn Spirit than anything.

Make no mistake - Rod and Paula Bramblett are a significant part of the Auburn Family. This would be the first Iron Bowl since losing them. That is noteworthy because his call at the end of the 2013 Iron Bowl may just be the most iconic radio call in college football history. When the story concluded, many people had to compose themselves. The show and the campus slowly and gently moved forward. As I continued on, my mind kept replaying Rod exclaiming, "They're not gonna to keep 'em off the field tonight!" after the 2013 Iron Bowl.

In one of the RV lots near the stadium, I noticed a flagpole with three distinctive flags being flown. On top was the American Flag, and the bottom displayed an Irishman lying across letters spelling "Harrigan." Sandwiched between the two was a flag declaring a house divided among Auburn and Alabama fans. I met Patrick, an Auburn man, and his wife, who is an Alabama lady. They attend games at both schools each season, and they told me that they decided long ago that the Iron Bowl outcome would not affect their relationship or their kids. I wondered how realistic that was. I must say that I witnessed a loving family even with some spirited ribbing about the game.

With noon fast approaching, the sidewalks on Donahue St. began to overflow with people. They were staking a claim to their spot for the Tiger Walk. Almost every school has a version of it now, but Auburn has engaged in this tradition since the 1960s. The fans were very excited about it and insisted that I must witness it. The anticipation and the crowd built as the minutes rolled by. A large mass of humanity surrounded the intersection at

Donahue and Heisman. I almost felt like that's where the game was going to be played. Loud cheers and "U ... S ... A" chants followed the military personnel down Donahue like a line of dominoes tumbling over. The team wasn't far behind. As the team walked through, the cheers were intense and constant. Watching the coaches and players walk into the stadium usually doesn't thrill me, but this spectacle was impressive. And it wasn't over. My hosts for Tiger Walk alerted me that, "The band will be along in a few minutes."

The crowd thinned slightly as people retreated to their tailgates for more consumables. I posted up near a bank of televisions to catch up on the scores of Rivalry Week. Suddenly, I heard music and turned to see the band playing and dancing. People rushed back to see four masses of the band melding together at that same intersection. It was raucous and fun. When I bragged on it, my new buddy told me "This has nothing on '89."

The 1989 Iron Bowl was the first time it was played at Auburn. The Tiger Walk that day was legendary. There are still framed photographs of it hanging in people's homes and offices. For Pat Dye, the Tiger Walk was just something that happened when they were entering the stadium to prepare for the game. But he confirmed to me that the 1989 version was special. Dye recalled, "People held their babies out for you to touch, and there were people with tears streaming down their face."

That reminded me that they were going to recognize the 1989 team during the game as part of the 30th anniversary of the first Iron Bowl at Auburn. It was time for me to get a sandwich, check the scores one last time and make my way to the stadium. I didn't want to miss any of the pre-game events at the Iron Bowl. As I broke loose from the crowd and approached the slightly more desolate area around the gates, I heard it run through my mind again.

"They're not gonna keep 'em off the field tonight!"

I thought it was just my admiration for the call. It was catchy. Like saying "War Eagle" or "Go Tigers." It couldn't happen today could it? That would just be over the top with everything else that was going on. I made my way through the gate, up the ramp and to my area. I'm here. I'm finally going to witness an Iron Bowl in person.

I watched the stadium fill up as the teams completed their pre-game rituals. I noticed that people lined the edges of the ramps. An energy ran through our corner of the stadium as people noticed Bruce Pearl (the Auburn men's basketball coach) entering the opposite side of our section to watch the game. I continued looking up toward the top corners of the stadium. I wanted to make sure that I saw Aurea's (War Eagle VIII) pre-game flight. It happened fast. The PA announcer told the crowd to turn its focus above section 12 in the southwest corner. By the time I figured it out, Aurea was in the air. I managed a decent video of the event and a lasting memory. Another lasting memory was watching the band form the letters "USA" and display an American Shield. Flags from every state were presented around the perimeter of the field. They played "God Bless America" while the audience delivered a heartfelt rendition of the lyrics. It sure made me proud to be at Auburn and proud to be an American!

I was excited to see the 1989 SEC Champion Auburn Tigers honored before the current team took the field. I was again tempted to try to imagine what it was like here on December 2, 1989. I snapped back when I saw the massive video board play a message from Pat Dye to the Auburn faithful. Nothing I saw gets the Auburn fans more ready for battle than words from Coach Dye. The teams charged the field, and it was time for the Iron Bowl. As expected, the crowd was juiced for the start of the game.

The game itself was a little slow to start. It was almost like two prized fighters feeling each other out in the opening rounds. Jordan-Hare had a fun and energetic atmosphere in the first quarter. The stadium really went wild when an Alabama touchdown was called back because of a penalty.

While the crowd stayed lively throughout, the teams finally followed suit midway through the second quarter. With the score tied, Auburn's defense produced points with a pick-six. The crowd was jubilant, at least until Alabama returned the ensuing kickoff for a touchdown. After the teams traded touchdowns again, the scored was locked at 24-24. Alabama took the lead on another touchdown with 33 seconds remaining in the half. Auburn put a couple decent plays together, but the clock ran out before they could squeeze in another play. The clock was set at 20:00 for halftime, and the PA announcer even reported the halftime score as Alabama 31, Auburn 24.

But the officials just weren't ready for halftime yet. They determined that the clock should have stopped to set the chains for a first down. It took a while to sort out, but the officials placed 0:01 back on the clock. While Alabama argued the ruling, Auburn placed its field goal team on the field. The clock would start when the officials blew it ready for play. Alabama eventually put its unit on the field, the whistle blew and the ball was snapped before the horn sounded. The holder placed the ball down and Auburn kicker Anders Carlson drilled a 52-yard field goal.

Actual halftime score: Alabama 31, Auburn 27.

The second half was filled with more big plays from each team. One of the most crucial happened in the third quarter with Alabama threatening to extend a 1-point lead. A pass into the end zone went off the back of one of the Crimson Tide players, and Auburn linebacker Zakoby McClain grabbed it out of the air and darted 100 yards to the end zone, giving Auburn the lead. Alabama responded, though, with a touchdown drive. Auburn came right back with a field goal. The third quarter ended with Auburn leading, 40-38.

Alabama went on a 90-yard drive to score a touchdown and take a 45-40 lead. Auburn reciprocated with an 11-play touchdown drive. Quarterback Bo Nix completed a two-point conversion to receiver Shedrick Jackson to give Auburn a three-point cushion.

The clock ticked and the fans grew restless. Alabama started to move down the field and attempt to take the lead. But Auburn's defense bowed and forced Alabama to attempt to tie the game with a short field goal with two minutes left. The fans watched the 30-yard attempt almost as if conceding the points. As soon as the kick collided with the upright, arms and drinks went flying, shakers bounced back and forth and people were screaming with excitement.

The possibility that Auburn might pull this off started to hit home. People were high fiving each other, but some did so with guarded enthusiasm. I was high fiving Ainsley Kathryn. She was a two-and-a-half year old who sat in front of me and watched me over her parents' shoulders throughout the second half. She must have thought that we were on the same level of maturity. Once, when everyone had stood up, she wanted to stand on the bleachers. I assisted her in climbing onto the seat, and she was then my buddy forever. When the game-tying kick was missed, Ainsley Kathryn wanted someone to celebrate with. I let her give me a high five. I acted like it hurt my hand, and she was hooked. She must have repeated it 50 times before Auburn ran its next play. I watched the final minutes holding Ainsley Kathryn while she continued to "give me five."

When the fourth quarter clock ran out, the scoreboard read Auburn 48, Alabama 45. It ran through my head as the fans ran on the field: "They're not gonna keep 'em off the field tonight!"

I watch the revelers for a few minutes with Ainsley Kathryn in my arms. It wasn't riotous like in some places. It was a celebration. I decided that I needed to be a part of it. Little Ainsley Kathryn and her older sister gave me a hug, I exchanged pleasantries with their parents and I was on my way to the field. It took me a while to navigate the lines of people looking to do the same thing. While working through the maze, I heard the Auburn fans vocalize their versions of Dixieland Delight and the Rammer Jammer Cheer. As you can imagine, both revisions mention beating Alabama.

Right about the time that I reached the wall. A suggestion to exit the field was announced over the PA system. I was just getting to the wall, and they were not gonna keep me off the field tonight. So I continued forward and launched myself outward and landed feet first like a javelin at the end of its flight. I walked around and absorbed the moment. People were hugging each other and taking pictures. It was a joyful place. After another 10 minutes or so, the next request to exit the field was announced. This time, I complied. I congratulated Brad Rapacz, Auburn's director of football equipment, on the victory, and I climbed back up the stands. It was time for me to venture over to Toomer's Corner.

When I left the stadium, there wasn't a mad rush to Toomer's Corner. Maybe it had already occurred while I was matriculating my way to the field. In any case, fans were taking pictures with the Heisman statues, saying goodbye to their game companions and some that had gone back to tailgating. I tucked in with a group who was headed toward Toomer's Corner. At one point, we found ourselves behind a building where we had to choose to go left or right. A man suggested, "They missed the kick off of the left upright, so let's go left." We all agreed and continued winding through campus. As we neared the area, some students came out of their dorms with large packs of toilet paper. They gave the rolls (and some suggestions) to all of the kids arriving. When the kids thanked them for the help, the students told them "That's what we do here at Auburn."

Around the corner, there were people everywhere, and many of the structures were already adorned with toilet paper. In front of Samford Hall, it was mostly families taking pictures and watching the kids toss the toilet paper into the trees like they were shooting hoops in their driveway. At Toomer's Corner, it was a throng of college kids relishing a darn good reason to party. They were perched on walls, sitting on shoulders, leading cheers, taking selfies and just having a good time. I happened to be standing near the spot where I imagined this scene earlier in the week. It wasn't much different than I envisioned, but it's always better to see the real thing. It looked impossible to reach Toomer's Drugs through all of the people. I made my way down Magnolia past a crowded Southeastern and a couple fraternities. There were still some good parties going on throughout campus. I rejoined a few tailgates as I winded my way back.

There was one more stop that I wanted to make - I wanted to visit the divided family that I met earlier that day. The party was going stronger now than when I was there before the game. Harrigan's buddies, Jim McInnish and Mike Bruner, brought energy and amusement to the setting. The group of guests eventually dissipated, and I stood there talking with Patrick and watching the late games. It was a nice relaxed end to a long day. Mrs. Harrigan stepped out from the RV and announced that she was headed to bed. There were no jabs or gloating about the outcome. I took it that Patrick wasn't going to sleep on the couch. I guess being a divided family can work after all.

We parted ways, and I started the mile walk back to my truck. During that walk, I realized that this was the last campus of my journey. I had completed my mission of visiting all 14 schools during one football season. There was a sense of relief and a freedom of burdens. It hadn't always been easy.

It was also bittersweet. I had met a lot of wonderful people, seen some beautiful places and attended some historic events. It was truly *A Season of Homecomings*. Thank you, Auburn family. It truly was an epic Saturday.

Thank you, Southeastern Conference family. It was an epic regular season.

Auburn Tigers

Defensive Linemen

Derrick Brown
(2016-19)

Nick Fairley
(2009-10)

Tracy Rocker
(1985-88)

Aundray Bruce
(1986-87)

Quentin Groves
(2004-07)

Gerald Robinson
(1982-85)

Reggie Torbor
(2000-03)

Marlon Davidson
(2016-19)

Donnie Humphrey
(1979-83)

Zeke Smith
(1957-58)

My favorite players to watch at other defensive positions:

DB - Brian Robinson (1993-94)   DB - Carlos Rogers (2001-04)

LB - Karlos Dansby (2001-03)   LB - Takeo Spikes (1995-97)

Running Backs

James Brooks
(1977-80)

Stacy Danley
(1987-90)

Bo Jackson
(1982-85)

Ronnie Brown
(2000-04)

Stephen Davis
(1993-95)

James Joseph
(1986-90)

Carnell Williams
(2001-04)

Joe Cribbs
(1976-79)

Brent Fullwood
(1983-86)

Tre Mason
(2011-13)

My favorite players to watch at other offensive positions:

OL - Marcus McNeill (2004-05)   QB - Stan White (1990-93)

WR - Frank Sanders (1991-94)   QB - Jason Campbell (2001-04)

*Fan Favorites: RB - Bo Jackson, QB - Pat Sullivan, QB - Cam Newton

16

2019 SEC Championship Game

Week of December 7, 2019 game between Georgia and LSU

Atlanta, Georgia is a world-class city that is the heartbeat of the South. Atlanta began as a railroad town that connected the South with many of the other regions in the country. Those connections have expanded through the air. Hartsfield-Jackson Atlanta International Airport has developed into the world's busiest airport. The airport is one of the reasons that Atlanta has attracted so much corporate activity. A large percentage of Fortune 1000 companies conduct business in the metropolitan area. Sixteen Fortune 500 companies have headquarters that call the area home. This combination has led Atlanta to maintain one of the most robust economies in the world.

Atlanta is also home to major media outlets - CNN, TBS, and The Weather Channel all reside in the greater metropolitan area. The state of Georgia, and Atlanta in particular, have recently seen an influx of film and television production as well. Atlanta has been a featured setting in both television shows and on the big screen. The city contains a plethora of landmarks, museums and history. Tourists will find the National Center for Civil and Human Rights, the Carter Presidential Library and Museum, Georgia Aquarium, the Martin Luther King Jr. Center, World of Coca-Cola and Centennial Park.

Atlanta has a diverse professional sports scene with franchises in the NFL, MLB, NBA, MLS, and WNBA. The city has hosted several major sporting events like the Olympics, Super Bowls, Final Fours, PGA

Championships, 2003 NBA All-Star weekend, 2008 NHL All-Star Game, 2000 MLB All-Star Game and many important college football games. Running events are so popular in and around Atlanta that the city has adopted the self-claimed moniker, "Running City, USA." Motor sports also enjoy great racing venues with both the Atlanta Motor Speedway and Road Atlanta located just outside the city.

The city of Atlanta has had a major impact on Southeastern Conference athletics. The "Deep South's Oldest Rivalry" (annual Auburn-Georgia football game) was first played in 1892 at Atlanta's Piedmont Park. As a matter of fact, the first ten installments were played in Atlanta, including the 1895 and 1896 games that featured coaches Glenn "Pop" Warner (Georgia) and John Heisman (Auburn). The teams split the two meetings. One of those early games against Georgia in Atlanta is also believed to have been the genesis of Auburn's beloved War Eagle tradition. The Peach Bowl, the College Football Playoff and, of course, the conference's football championship game have all been played multiple times in Atlanta stadiums.

With Atlanta's sports history, it was no surprise that the College Football Hall of Fame decided to move there. The current location opened in 2014 and encompasses more than 94,000 square-feet of space. It sits next to Centennial Park and is surrounded by many of Atlanta's most popular attractions. On Thursday, I was afforded the opportunity to visit. I met up with my friend Dave, who is a fellow author and college football fan. We took the MARTA train into downtown and took a pleasant walk to the shrine of college football excellence.

The grandeur is evident the minute you enter the Chick-fil-A College Football Hall of Fame. There is a magnificent three-story helmet wall that displays the helmet of every NCAA and NAIA football team. There 818 helmets in total, and they are all randomly arranged. Each visitor's experience is tailored to his or her affiliation. Part of the experience is having the helmet of your team illuminated on the wall. It's really fun to decipher what teams' fans are visiting the same day as you. I had the fortune to have the helmets of every school where I coached get illuminated while I was at the museum.

On an adjoining wall hung a mural revealing players, coaches, rivalries and moments throughout college football history. It is crafted to represent many different time periods, and it is fantastic. On the base level of the museum, there is an indoor playing field where people can practice different skills. It's all set on a turf field, and I am sure that many parents have unleashed kids there while they observed the exhibits. Dave and I decided to hold off until we had a chance to view the rest of the offerings.

We encountered a 52-foot touch screen that allowed you to relive moments from your favorite team and explore the history of others. As I said, the experience is catered to your team, but visitors aren't limited to just that school. The touch screen recognizes the badge you're wearing and loads content based on your school affiliation. It's pretty cool not to have to search for your school's contributions. From there, one can always manually choose another team or subject to view.

Major team and individual trophies were also on display in that area. For instance, I saw the trophy naming Tua Tagovailoa the 2018 Walter Camp Player of the Year.

Just around the corner, we found a room dedicated to the newest inductees. Dave and I had fun reliving memories of many of the newest members. We were actually surprised that some of the guys weren't already members before this year. SEC schools had three players included in the 2019 class. Texas A&M was represented by defensive lineman Jacob Green, who played from 1977-79. Darren McFadden (running back) of Arkansas and Patrick Willis (linebacker) of Ole Miss were the other two Southeastern Conference representatives. It's awesome that those two are going in together because they would both be on my all-time SEC team.

There is a section that allows fans to have a game day experience. There is interactive face painting and mock *College GameDay* hosting. There are also places to design and call a play, sing a school's fight song and even play a timed trivia game. All of it gets recorded on your account connected to the badge around your neck and is accessible from a home computer.

Next to that area is a wing dedicated to rivalries. There are iconic rivalries (Alabama-Auburn) that are showcased. Three interactive screens let visitors look up any school and research their rivalries. The series information is remarkably current. For the Kentucky-Louisville rivalry, the blurb ended with "Kentucky won 45-13 in 2019."

Wait a minute. That happened only five days ago when I was at Auburn. Pretty cool, huh?

We finally made it to the third floor where the actual Hall of Fame is located. It is simple yet elegant in its design. The large rotunda has a lot of open space around the interactive flat screen displays. One has the ability to learn about every coach or player that has been elected into the exclusive club. Around the edges are glass panels with every class etched on its irradiated face. Circling above are multiple large screens that show highlights of the honored members.

It was disappointing to hear the closing announcements broadcast over the speakers as 5:00 pm approached. We didn't have much time left. I slipped off into the Game Day Theater. There was a large panoramic screen with a booming sound system. The room closed and began a montage that placed the audience in the middle of the action on Saturdays around the country. It was basically a hype video for college football, and it worked! I was ready to run through a tunnel somewhere. Anywhere!

Alas, it was closing time, and we had to go. Sadly, neither Dave nor I were able to show off our skills on the indoor playing field.

It was a gray overcast sky with an idle threat of rain on Friday. Fortunately, the majority of my day would be inside. It was the first time that I had been in Mercedes-Benz Stadium. The place is unbelievable. I'm not sure that there is a better stadium in America. Behind both sidelines are luxurious field level lounges. They are a vast space with sleek modern decor. The building had an array of SEC decorations. Every SEC school had its logo on banners circling the stadium. The SEC Football Championship logo was presented in various places from high in the rafters to curtains in the tunnels underneath the stands.

The Mega-Column was a unique feature. It is a 101-feet tall video display behind the west end zone, and it rotated SEC content. The participating teams' logos appeared in many formats. Sometimes, the whole column would be exclusively Georgia or LSU. My favorite had to be when it had the SEC circle logo at the top with every member institution's logo displayed under it. Speaking of unique, the Halo Board at Mercedes-Benz Stadium is a genius design. It gives spectators a phenomenal view from any seat in the place. It isn't intrusive, and it has a vibrant resolution. It was enjoyable to watch the SEC commercials on it from different parts of the stadium.

I attended the press conference with the coaches. They were both obviously proud to represent their school in this environment, and they showed a lot of respect for their opponent. To accentuate the challenge of making the SEC Championship Game, coach Kirby Smart stated, "In the SEC, these games are essentially championship games every week...'cause if you don't win 'em, then you're not in the championship."

Coach Ed Orgeron had a similar view, but a recruiting question pre-empted the most entertaining answer of the event. While explaining how he enjoys recruiting in Louisiana, he said, "I am going to be in about 18-22 homes next week, so that means about 18-22 gumbos ... It's kind of a party when I get there." It must be good to be king in Louisiana!

Commissioner Sankey also had a press conference. His opening statement was essentially a State of SEC Football address. He discussed the success and competitiveness of SEC football in 2019. Sankey expressed, "I'm of the opinion that we have the most intense competition of any level of sport in America on a consistent basis, particularly starting, myself, with what happened on CBS, beginning with Auburn's game at LSU and every week thereafter, the last seven weeks of the season, were almost like playoff games on our campuses." He spoke on the league members' opinions about scheduling. He detailed the league's replay procedures and addressed the "name, image, and likeness" issue. Many of the questions for Commissioner Sankey were about those three topics.

After the press conference, I walked over to the Georgia World Congress Center. That's where the Dr. Pepper SEC FanFare event was taking place. SEC FanFare is a must attend event for any SEC fan. It is a celebration of every school in the Southeastern Conference. The approach to the event is clad with SEC markings. On the left, the western division was represented with a long banner listing the teams on that side of the conference. A column was lettered with SEC, Western Division, and the names of all the schools. The right side mirrored the left, but represented the Eastern Division. Between the two sides was a banner that had the SEC logo, and underneath it simply stated, "IT JUST MEANS MORE."

The entrance provided a dramatic introduction to the SEC. A large SEC banner hung overhead encircled with spotlights. The spotlights showcased the football uniforms of each Southeastern Conference team. Mannequins clothed in every team's home uniform stood next to sturdy posters declaring the school and its emblem. The number 19 emblazoned every uniform except Texas A&M which donned #12 (Home of the 12th Man). The West division team uniforms were on the left, and the East were on the right. The LSU and Georgia displays had a more forward and centered location as the representative of their respective division in Atlanta. It was a popular spot for people to take pictures next to their favorite team. Banderoles announcing the SEC, its teams and its sponsors filled the rafters.

The *SEC Nation* set was constructed to the left. The designated space provided ample room for fans to observe the inner workings of the shows they dutifully watched. The exhibit hall was filled with interactive activities. Fans could attempt to kick a field goal, push a blocking sled, throw passes, practice on a tackling dummy or even run a 40-yard dash. There were numerous turf fields where young fans played flag football games. Each field had a PA announcer that excitedly called the game. On the other side of the expansive hall was a stage where fans could watch interviews with past SEC greats. Those presentations were scheduled throughout the day and into Saturday.

The event was the culmination of a great season for the corporate sponsors. The companies that had backed SEC football all season were present to continue their support for the SEC fans. The sponsors offered prize give-aways, food and drink samples, and picture opportunities. It was my final time to get a ceremonial picture with "all of 'em" (the emblems of every school). This was, however, the first opportunity that I had to take a picture with the SEC Championship game trophy. In the far corner, there was even a temporary SEC store. There was something for every age group and every fan base. It was a glorious jubilee for the SEC faithful.

The weekend also included the SEC Legends Dinner on Friday night. It's where representatives from each school are officially introduced as SEC Legends. The 2019 class included:

Alabama-Ray Perkins
(WR 1964-66, HC 1983-86)

Florida-Jevon Kearse
(OLB 1996-98)

Arkansas-Dennis Winston
(LB 1973-76)

Georgia-Vince Dooley
(HC 1964-88)

Auburn-Karlos Dansby
(LB 2000-03)

Kentucky-Oliver Barnett
(DT 1986-89)

LSU-Johnny Robinson
(HB 1957-59)

Missouri-Jeremy Maclin
(WR 2007-08)

Mississippi St-Barrin Simpson
(LB 1996-99)

South Carolina-Fred Zeigler
(F 1967-69)

Ole Miss-Jonathan Nichols
(K 2001-04)

Tennessee-Darwin Walker
(DL 1997-99)

Texas A&M-Ed Simonini
(LB 1972-75)

Vanderbilt-Jovan Haye
(DE 2002-04)

Saturday morning was cooler than it had been all week, but it didn't keep people from enjoying the festivities. The Home Depot Backyard is a green space located outside of Mercedes-Benz Stadium. It has a park and a pavilion, and it was transformed into a terrific tailgate spot. A culmination of cars, tents and flags jammed the convenient location. Up a long outdoor escalator, there was another green space that contained a slew of vendors. It was also the location of the ESPN's *College GameDay* set. I spotted fans wearing hats, shirts and hoodies of every SEC team on that chilly morning.

People from all over the South were there to celebrate the Southeastern Conference. After talking with a man and his teenage son who were both wearing Kentucky gear, I worked my way toward the Georgia World Congress Center.

Large masses of people were migrating back and forth between the two locations. The location of *SEC Nation* hosted the party inside the massive showroom that contained SEC FanFare. The Georgia and LSU bands made appearances. Each band transformed into an enormous blob of people, as they moved about the exhibit hall. They cheered, chanted, and took videos of the performances. Enthusiasm gushed from confident supporters of the Dawgs and Tigers. School spirit permeated every corner, and the battle lines were beginning to form.

The LSU Tigers and Georgia Bulldogs were the only teams that I saw play more than twice during the 2019 season. There was the obligatory home game on each school's campus. Plus, these two were the only teams that I saw more than once on the road. Now, this neutral site matchup would mark the fourth time that I was able to observe each team in person during 2019. The Dawgs fans confirmed their reputation for supporting their team. The place was crawling with UGA folks, just like the other places that I joined them. The Tigers fans solidified their status as one of the most festive fan bases in the country. They fully and gladly embraced the festivities.

As I entered Mercedes-Benz Stadium, it reminded me of Times Square at noon on December 31st. The preparations were ready for a momentous occasion, but everything sat in an anticipatory mood. There was a security presence at every corner, and there were early stragglers peppering the stands. I went to the press box to locate my assigned seat. While I was there, I sat with a group of guys to have lunch and watch some of the Big 12 title game. Familiar faces migrated in and out of the large assembled space. One of the guys at the table assessed the cornbread. He said that it was "Yankee cornbread" because it was sweet. Before the opinion could be analyzed, the head of the group received a phone call requesting their presence on the field.

After I finished the meal, "Yankee cornbread" and all, I left my supplies at my seat and headed down to the field. There weren't many people at first, but the traffic continually increased as game time neared. As I stood behind one of the goalposts, I recognized a man who walked by. He was a member of the chain crew and part of the group which I had shared lunch. Players from both sides began to enter the field for their warm-up. Steadily, the stands were filling up, and it had all transformed into pregame mode. I had a few conversations with some acquaintances, wished them luck, and then went back up to the press box.

While the teams were on the field for their pregame routine, the bands participated in their own jousting match. One played iconic school melodies to energize the fans, and then the other reciprocated. The impromptu battle of the bands seemed to call people inside the stadium. When the bands vacated their seats to go to the field, it left a huge gap in the mass of people in the stands. Sticking with the theme of the day, the pregame show focused on Georgia and LSU, but maintained references to the entire conference. Also, the field had a special touch that honored all of college football. The "College Football 150" logo was used as the numbers at the 50-yard line. This was the first time that I had seen that done.

Both school's band performed a pregame routine. "The University of Georgia Redcoat Marching Band" did the traditional formation of the Arch, while "The Golden Band from Tigerland" spelled out LSU. Both bands performed the Star-Spangled Banner together. For the Anthem, the official colors were presented at the 50-yard line on the home sideline. A mighty American flag waved at mid-field with numerous American flags behind it. Along the sides was a flag for each Southeastern Conference member. A sizeable SEC banner was pulled tight at the numbers. The Halo Board played hype videos for each team before they entered the field. Everyone was ready for the culminating game of the 2019 SEC football season.

LSU won the toss but deferred its choice until the second half. Georgia was going to get the ball first. On the first play, Jake Fromm had the tight end open right away in the middle of the field, but he passed that up to go deeper. He threw an absolute strike, but the receiver dropped the perfect pass. Georgia's offense had been criticized coming into the game for its perceived lack of production. The Bulldogs also entered with a broken roster from injuries and suspensions. It was obvious from the start that they were going to take their shots in this game.

On the flip side, LSU's defense had faced the same criticism and injury situation earlier in the year. The LSU defense proved to be more stable on the first series. After a Georgia punt, the LSU offense had its first opportunity.

In 2019, Joe Burrow was the most consistent and unflappable player that I had seen in a long time. Many people were predicting him as the Heisman winner coming into the game. On his third play, he completed a pass to himself. The pass was deflected back at him, and he caught it and then ran for a 16-yard gain. I commented to my media neighbor that Burrow may have just had his "Heisman moment." That was until five plays later. Burrow had good time in the pocket. He went through his progressions and maneuvered to buy more time. At the last opportunity, he fired the ball into a tiny window for a touchdown. That scoring play gave Joe Burrow the record for touchdown passes thrown in an SEC season, and it put LSU ahead, 7-0.

The teams traded punts, which left Georgia with the ball at their own 44-yard line. After pushing into LSU territory, the Dawgs settled for a long field-goal attempt. Rodrigo Blankenship is usually a pretty good bet, but he missed the 52-yarder. LSU took the ball back and let Joe Burrow sling it around the field. The strategy worked as the Tigers increased the lead to 14-0. Georgia regained possession as the first quarter expired. The Dawgs started fresh in the second quarter with a nice drive. After penetrating LSU's 25, the drive slowed, and Blankenship made good on his second chance from 39 yards out.

The teams traded punts again before LSU pieced together another drive into Georgia territory. The Dawgs defense stood up and forced a field goal by LSU kicker Cade York. Then, Fromm quickly connected on two nice gainers through the air. But an attempt to hit a third one backfired. Tiger corner Derek Stingley Jr. intercepted the pass at the LSU 13-yard line. LSU put together a rapid 10-play drive that left them attempting a field goal from 48 yards out. This time York couldn't connect, and the score remained, 17-3 LSU at halftime.

The second half kickoff eliminated a player for both teams. Linebacker Walter Grant, from Georgia, was injured on a play that was confirmed targeting. Grant didn't move for a while, and everyone in the stadium was concerned. LSU players even came off the sideline to show their support. Thankfully, he was able to regain his wits and walked off of the field. When the game resumed, the LSU offense methodically picked away at Georgia's defense. The Tigers marched inside the 5 before a sack and an incompletion forced York to tack on three more points.

When UGA had its opening possession of the second half, running back D'Andre Swift recorded one of his two carries of the afternoon. He was battling an injury, but he made the most of this carry, as he took it around the left end for 13 yards. Even without a healthy Swift, the Dawgs drove down to the Tigers' 19-yard line. That's where a 37-yard field goal was missed. The Bayou Bengals looked to capitalize, and did they ever.

On the first play, Joe Burrow delivered his ultimate Heisman moment. As a blitzer came free, Burrow jab stepped to his right and spun back to his left leaving the defender scrambling. As the defender recovered, and another approached, Burrow stepped back (to his own five) and exited the pocket to the right. As Burrow reached the sideline, he launched a strike to receiver Justin Jefferson, who took it inside the Georgia 10. It was a 71-yard completion and the fourth longest pass in SEC Championship Game history. Three plays later, Burrow would throw his third touchdown pass. LSU's lead had ballooned to, 27-3.

After the kickoff, Stingley Jr. didn't waste any time getting the ball back for his offense. On the first play, he pilfered the pass and took it to the Dawgs' 13-yard line. Burrow quickly delivered his fourth touchdown pass. With Georgia getting another opportunity on offense, the third quarter ended with LSU leading 34-3.

Between the third and fourth quarters is special for fans in the SEC. LSU's band jumped in right away with "Touchdown for LSU." Georgia's Redcoats quickly followed with "Krypton." The remaining Georgia fans did represent with their flashlights, but many of the UGA faithful had left already. The Tiger backers accentuated that with a strong and proud chant of "L S U, L S U."

Georgia still had the ball as the fourth quarter commenced. Still fighting, the Dawgs worked the line of scrimmage down to the LSU 2-yard line. From there, Fromm connected with wide receiver George Pickens for the touchdown. Those points revised the score to 34-10. LSU running back, Clyde Edwards-Helaire responded with some nice runs that put LSU back in scoring position. Then, York hit another field goal - this one from 50 yards out. After that score, the teams were stalemated the rest of the quarter. The game ended with a final score of LSU 37, Georgia 10.

As the fourth quarter crept toward the finish of the game, I made my way down to the field level. I stood on the LSU sideline as its offense expired the clock. While cheerleaders, photographers and fans rushed to the middle of the field, I strolled out on the playing surface and observed the reactions of the players and the fans in the stands. A male cheerleader waved a massive purple flag with the Tiger head logo on it. About the time that I reached the numbers, air cannons blasted blue and yellow streams of confetti into the air from all four corners.

In the middle of the field was a celebration of those closely involved with the LSU football program. Coaches went around to hug and congratulate their players. Some of the players did interviews while others shared the moment with their teammates. People hurried around the mass giving players black championship caps and purple championship t-shirts.

One of the purple SEC Championship shirts was lying on the field next to me. I bent down to pick up and give to a player next to me. My arm was extended as I straightened back up, but the player was already pulling one of the shirts over his shoulder pads. I commented to him that I thought that it was one that he had dropped. He replied, "Yeah, I was going to take two of 'em." I went to hand it over when he continued, "Unless you want one?" Of course I did, but I hadn't done anything to earn it. He quickly followed up with "I'm good, man. You take it." I threw it over my shoulder, shook his hand and congratulated him. It was very gracious of him, and I just wanted to tell him again publicly. Thank you!

I didn't seek out any of the players for comment, but I did congratulate many of them that were around me. They were a good bunch of guys that showed appreciation. Some even gave me the 'ol "man hug" in appreciation. My response was always something to the affect of "Now, go do something with it. Go get one for the SEC!" or "Represent for the SEC in the playoff!" The reaction was regularly "Oh, yes sir!" or "You already know!"

I felt good about this LSU team. I knew they had enough talent to win the whole thing. What made me confident in their destiny was the focus that they had shown. During a teleconference at the beginning of the week, I heard it in their voices. They were excited about the opportunity to win the SEC, but it was obvious to me that they wanted more. It's not something that you can fake. They were focused on winning it all. It was the same vibe that I felt from them that night after winning the SEC Championship Game. Yes, they were going to celebrate, but they were far from being done. I already marked it down that I would hear it again during the playoffs. Hear what? S ... E ... C, S ... E ... C, S ... E ... C!

AFTERMATH

GEORGIA BULLDOGS

The Georgia Bulldogs had a tough time at Mercedes-Benz Stadium. There were injuries, near misses and some mistakes. Teams can only experience a limited amount of those things and still have much of a shot against the 2019 LSU Tiger team. It was a tough loss, but Georgia is still a fine ball club. The Bulldogs actually didn't fall far in the rankings. UGA had a great season, and the program was rewarded with a trip to New Orleans to play in the Sugar Bowl. It would be a chance at redemption for the previous year's loss in the same game. They would face a Baylor team that also fell short in its conference championship game.

The Sugar Bowl is a great bowl game that usually features an SEC team. There is a long history between the SEC and the Sugar Bowl. At least this time, there wouldn't be any other bowls in the same time slot. As a kid, I always looked forward to watching the SEC Champion represent in the Sugar Bowl. We only had one TV in the house, and my dad would come in and turn it to the Orange Bowl halftime show. I didn't have any say, but I always thought, "What is wrong with him!" To start, I would rather see any football game than a halftime show. Secondly, the SEC Champ was playing. How could you ever want to watch another game?

Georgia participated in the game without fourteen of its players, and at least half of those missing were starters. There were various reasons for them not being available. Many of the cases were because of injury. It's always tough to deal with injuries, but teams don't expect as many for the bowl game. UGA battled injuries throughout the 2019 season. The talented offensive line rarely played at full strength. They were regularly shuffling guys around to compensate for a missing component most of the year. At least they would have a month to prepare for the Sugar Bowl.

The Bulldogs obviously utilized their time to prepare. The UGA defense continued their stellar play, holding the Baylor offense scoreless in three of the four quarters. Fromm had a nice swan song, and the Georgia offense averaged over five yards per play. My wife and I watched the Dawgs handle Baylor by a score of 26-14, and I didn't have to worry about any halftime shows (or chick flicks for that matter). The Georgia Bulldogs completed a 12-2 season as the Sugar Bowl Champions!

S ... E ... C, S ... E ... C, S ... E ... C!

LSU TIGERS

After winning the SEC Championship, the College Football Playoff Committee ranked LSU as the No. 1 team in the country. They were going to play No. 4, which turned out to be Big 12 Champion Oklahoma. Because it earned the highest seeding, LSU was afforded the opportunity to choose which semi-final location it wanted. The Tigers were going right back to Atlanta to play the Peach Bowl in Mercedes-Benz Stadium.

During the layoff between the SEC Championship and bowl games, there is the infamous "awards dinner circuit" that players and coaches have to work around, and LSU representatives were sure busy during that time. Head coach Ed Orgeron won the Home Depot College Coach of the Year award while co-offensive coordinator Joe Brady was named the Frank Broyles Award winner as the best assistant coach in college football. The LSU Tigers also had a lot of players honored with various national post-season awards. Grant Delpit won the Thorpe Award as the nation's top defensive back. The Biletnikoff Award went to Ja'Marr Chase as the best wide receiver in the country. The LSU offensive line was presented with the massive and coveted Joe Moore Award recognizing the best offensive line unit in the country.

Joe Burrow won about every award in which he was eligible. Those honors included the Davey O'Brien Award (Best Quarterback in the Country), Walter Camp Trophy (National Player of the Year), Maxwell Award (Best Player in America), Manning Award (Top QB in the country) and Johnny Unitas Golden Arm Award (nation's top quarterback that best exemplifies character, scholastic and athletic achievement). He was the Associated Press Player of the Year as well.

Of course, Burrow also became the 85th winner of the Heisman Trophy. It wasn't even close, as Burrow eclipsed records for the highest percentage of first-place votes, the highest percentage of possible points and for appearing on the most Heisman ballots. His margin of victory was the largest in the storied history of Heisman Trophy winners. He is the second player from LSU to ever win the Heisman Trophy. The other was Billy Cannon 60 years prior, in 1959.

There were so many other LSU players that received multiple All-SEC and All-American designations. It was definitely a successful regular season for the Bayou Bengals. It can be difficult for a team to stay focused on the task at hand when they have all of that going on. It's even more difficult to just find time to get the work in while they're traveling around the country hearing how wonderful they are.

But like I said earlier, I felt like this team was different. They weren't done yet. They wanted more. Much more!

To accomplish what they set out to do, the LSU Tigers had to win the playoff game against Oklahoma. They returned to Atlanta to play the 12-1 Sooners in the Peach Bowl. Mercedes-Benz Stadium had been good to LSU in the SEC Championship Game, but that didn't compare to what occurred on December 28, 2019. The Tigers had a historic first half that buried the Sooners before anyone could even contemplate what had happened.

Burrow zipped the offense up and down the field faster than a comet passing the earth. LSU's offensive production in the first half alone might not be matched again until Halley's Comet comes back around in another 40 or so years (the comet was last seen in 1986). Of LSU's eight possessions in the first half, seven of them went for touchdowns. Only one drive took more than six plays or longer than three minutes to score a touchdown. That possession was a nine-play drive that only took 3:10 off of the clock. It went for 75 yards which was only its third longest drive of the half (in terms of yardage). When the purple and gold streaks of exhaust finally settled at the intermission, LSU led No. 4 Oklahoma by a score of 49-14.

Burrow's stat line included 21 of 27 passing for 403 yards and seven touchdowns. Wide receiver Justin Jefferson had nine catches for 186 yards and four touchdowns. Both players broke several game records. Wait, did I mention that both of those stat totals were only for the first half of play? Jefferson accumulated five more catches and 41 yards in the second half. Burrow continued his efficiency and added a rushing touchdown in the third quarter.

Of the four possessions in the second half, LSU scored two touchdowns, missed a field-goal attempt (after gaining 47 yards) and ran out the clock on the last series. LSU put up mind-boggling offensive numbers, especially for a national semi-final contest. Four runners averaged five or more yards per carry (three did it on multiple carries). Six receivers averaged double-digit yards per catch (five did it on multiple receptions). Ja'Marr Chase was able to accomplish both feats (5.0 ypa and 30.5 ypr), although he did not score a touchdown. The Tigers posted 692 yards of offense and scored touchdowns on nine out of their twelve drives. LSU beat Oklahoma, 63-28.

The LSU Tigers were going to play for the National Championship for the first time since 2011. The game would be played in New Orleans just an hour from the LSU campus. This would be the fourth National Championship game for LSU since 2003, and every one of them has been played in New Orleans. The three previous games yielded two national championships. This one would be played against the winner of Ohio State and Clemson.

In one of the best games of the year, Clemson completed a comeback victory to earn a shot at defending its title. It would be two southern teams playing for the national championship in one of the most renowned cities in the South.

National Championship Game

The National Championship was a matchup of schools who use Tigers as their mascot, and who both claim their home as "Death Valley." Both teams entered the game with a 14-0 record. Clemson came in as the defending national champions with a 29-game winning streak and a quarterback who had never lost a college game.

LSU entered with a record setting offense, the Heisman Trophy winner and two successive thrashings of the 4th-ranked team in the country.

The Mercedes-Benz Superdome was set for an epic collision on January 13, 2020.

Clemson received the ball to start the game, and the LSU defense immediately sent them backwards on first down. After that, Clemson showed off its talent with two big plays that carried them to LSU's 27-yard line. But the LSU defense steadied and pushed Clemson back. After taking a 5-yard penalty, Clemson punted the ball down to the LSU 7.

The record-setting offense started out with a bang. A completion to tight end Thaddeus Moss went for 38 yards. As quickly as it happened, though, it was brought back even quicker. An illegal man downfield nullified the positive opening play and pushed LSU closer to its own goal line. The offense sputtered after that and forced LSU to punt the ball back to Clemson. The Clemson offense went three-and-out, and then the Clemson defense forced the same from LSU.

Clemson regained the possession and hit a huge gainer on the first play. An illegal block was called against the orange-clad Tigers, but it was after the catch. When it was sorted out, Clemson still had the ball at the LSU 40-yard line. Four plays later, Clemson quarterback, Trevor Lawrence, was running into the end zone. The Clemson Tigers had the first score and a 7-0 lead.

LSU received the kickoff and looked to break free from the oppressive Clemson defense. The LSU Tigers were able to get one first down, but soon had to punt back to Clemson again. All year long, people were asking me about my opinion of Burrow. My response was always that the most impressive thing to me was that I never saw him get rattled. In the first quarter, I saw him uncomfortable for the first time all year. Brent Venables has been one of the best defensive coordinators in college football for a long time. His multiple disguises of the Clemson defense had LSU's offense frustrated.

LSU's defense had been questioned many times throughout the year. Dave Aranda's unit had given up a touchdown already, but they were also forcing Clemson away from some of the things that they wanted to do. The defense gave up one first down because of a penalty, but then it forced Clemson to punt again. It gave the LSU offense an opportunity from their own 30.

LSU put together some positive plays earning a first down. A nice run from Clyde Edwards-Helaire left LSU with a second-and-two at its 48. Joe Burrow followed that play with a throw that led a streaking Ja'Marr Chase right into the end zone. The 52-yard touchdown tied the game at 7-7.

Clemson's offense also found some momentum, and it used its possession to drive the ball into LSU territory as the first quarter ended. When play resumed at the start of the second quarter, Clemson's offense wasn't able to convert another first down. They called on their kicker who blasted a 52-yard field goal. The three points put Clemson ahead 10-7. Clemson's defense found strength with the lead and forced LSU to punt within four plays.

The punt was tremendously executed and pinned Clemson at their own 4-yard line. But Lawrence alleviated the poor field position on the first play with a 24-yard completion to receiver Justyn Ross. Clemson running back, and Louisiana native, Travis Etienne then contributed a couple positive runs of 29 and seven yards to put the ball at LSU's 36. The fourth play of the drive was a reverse to wide receiver Tee Higgins. He ran through a few tackles and finished the run in the end zone. Clemson executed a quick 96-yard drive and built a 17-7 lead.

Some LSU fans started feeling nervous, but I was confident in this team. I witnessed many of the big things LSU had accomplished this year, and I couldn't help but remember the focus and desire they had for winning THIS game. I told the people around me that LSU would be leading by halftime. Burrow and Chase helped back up my statement.

Two consecutive connections between the two put LSU at Clemson's 3. On third down, LSU scored with a quarterback draw out of an empty set. It was the same play that sealed the Auburn game, converted a key fourth-quarter third down at Alabama and opened up the flood gates against Georgia.

Clemson began the next drive running the ball. After the second play, Clemson was in LSU territory again. It came after an effective Etienne run that ended with a facemask penalty against LSU. Three straight ineffective pass attempts undermined the Clemson drive, and they had to punt back to LSU. The punt left LSU 87 yards away from taking the lead.

That wasn't a problem for this LSU offense. On the sixth play of the drive, Burrow laid a pass over Chase's left shoulder. Chase wrapped his hands around it for a 14-yard touchdown catch and a 21-17 LSU advantage. Clemson had the ball back again, but couldn't do anything with it against Aranda's troops. A huge punt now left LSU backed up even further, starting at its own 5-yard line.

Again, no problem for the LSU offense. It just took a few more plays than usual. Edwards-Helaire started the drive with a huge 25-yard run to the 30. The LSU Tigers sputtered a bit, but were given new life on a pass interference penalty on Clemson. LSU eventually faced a third-and-ten at Clemson's 35 where they would utilize the quarterback draw again. The

Heisman winner rambled for 29 critical yards, and LSU scored on the next play. The LSU Tigers led the Clemson Tigers 28-17 at halftime.

Normally, my predictions don't happen the exact way that I say them. For instance, when Brett Favre left the Packers in 2008, I said they would be fine with Aaron Rodgers and still make the playoffs. The Packers were talented that year, and I felt that Rodgers was good. They ended up having a load of injuries and did not make the playoffs, but I think we can all agree that the Packers ended up being fine with Rodgers. This time, it happened just the way I predicted. LSU had even stretched the lead before half. They did it with three straight touchdown drives, each one longer than the previous one (75 yards, 87 yards, and finally 95 yards).

LSU opened the third quarter with the ball. The offense was stagnant starting the second half as it has many times this season. A fair-catch interference penalty on the punt gave Clemson the ball at midfield. The defending champions weren't going away quietly. They drove the ball into the end zone to cut the lead. After receiver Amari Rodgers caught the two-point pass attempt, the Clemson Tigers had pulled within a field goal, 28-25.

The score was locked over the next two series as both teams traded punts. Then, LSU was finally able to get the offense cranked back up. Another big play to Chase for 43 yards set them up in scoring position. Another touchdown pass to Moss moved them back ahead by double digits. LSU's defense was able to record an interception on the next series, but a pass interference call against them wiped the pick off the board. Three more ineffective passes had Clemson punting right back to LSU.

Right away, Jefferson contributed with a clutch 35-yard reception. The offense couldn't muster much afterward, and LSU had to settle for a field-goal attempt. The kick to increase the LSU Tigers lead to thirteen was no good.

Despite the missed opportunity, LSU's defense pushed the Clemson Tigers back and forced another punt. The LSU offense had good field position and gained a first down as the third quarter ended.

As the last quarter of the college football season began, the Tigers in purple and gold looked to take another step closer to completing their quest. The productive passing game peppered with the occasional run had LSU close to the red zone. On second-and-nine, Clemson brought its inside linebackers on the rush. LSU's offensive line fit up perfectly with the rush to give Burrow a clean pocket. His pass headed into the end zone and into the hands of a leaping Terrace Marshall Jr. The lead was now 17 points.

Clemson's offense tried desperately to get back into the game. After Clemson achieved a first down, each team committed pass interference. With the ball reset at its own 37, Clemson wasn't able to get any traction offensively. After receiving the punt, LSU's offense drained more than five minutes off the clock. LSU then punted back to Clemson, giving them the ball with less than five minutes to play.

The Clemson Tigers proceeded to move the ball down the field. First, they had a 12-yard run from Lawrence, and then a 21-yard catch from Higgins. Lawrence ran for another 12 yards, but the LSU defense ended that run with a fumble recovery. Grant Delpit hit Lawrence and caused the fumble that Derek Stingley Jr. recovered. The LSU offense took the ball inside of Clemson's 10, and then ran out the remaining time.

The LSU Tigers won the National Championship Game 42-25.

LSU fans and players alike made the most of the celebration. The team was supremely talented and used an extraordinary focus to conquer all challengers. At 15-0, almost half (7) of the teams they beat were ranked in the top ten at the time. Their schedule, before the playoffs, included nine bowl teams.

In the final polls, LSU had played and defeated five of the seven teams behind them in the top eight. All of them had 11 wins or more, and only one of the games was in Baton Rouge. The other two teams (in the top eight) lost to teams that LSU had beaten during its run.

A dream season in the Bayou ended with the LSU Tigers winning a national championship for the state of Louisiana in New Orleans. They did it in classic Louisiana style by using hard work to make it happen.

Their leaders were overlooked as components that could win a championship. Few people believed that Ed Orgeron could take a team to the next level. National pundits thought LSU had made a mistake in appointing him the permanent head coach. Joe Burrow was a transplant from Ohio. There were questions about his ability to even play at the FBS level, and some schools denied offering him an opportunity.

Both Orgeron and Burrow had been told by other institutions that they weren't good enough. Despite showing ability, they were both denied opportunities to prove it at other schools. They believed in their capabilities, and they never gave up the fight.

They proved their abilities, but even more they proved their leadership qualities. They helped elevate the other players' performances. The defensive linemen, running backs, and offensive linemen were thought to lack the ability LSU needed to compete for a championship. They all proved what could be accomplished as "One team. One heartbeat."

The national championship trophy is now enjoying its own homecoming back in the Southeastern Conference as our ears welcome the sweet melody of:

S ... E ... C, S ... E ... C, S ... E ... C!

17

SUNDAY SUPPER

One of the South's most treasured family traditions is Sunday supper. It's a family gathering for a meal that usually occurs in the early afternoon after church services. Many people were raised with this tradition, and plenty of folks still carry on its legacy. The menu might include country ham, collards, and cornbread or fried chicken, mashed potatoes, and biscuits. The buffet of homemade comfort food is sure to please, especially if it is accompanied with peach pie or a blackberry cobbler. Everyone looks forward to the flavorful cuisine, but it is the time spent with family that makes Sunday supper such an important tradition.

Often, these suppers are the only times that families get to spend together. Thus, many meaningful conversations take place at these get-togethers. Loved ones come together to share their accomplishments, talk out their challenges, and help each other set focused paths toward further success. Now that we've had a main course at each campus, let's go back out on the porch and visit a little bit.

The Southeastern Conference is the premier football conference in America and it has been for a *heckuva* long time. We don't need to argue about it or let any "shock jocks" get us riled up. The numbers are indisputable.

The SEC is consistently at the top of the list when it comes to the number of bowl teams, bowl victories and ranked teams at the end of the year. Since the top 2-ranked teams began matching up in the postseason, the SEC has led (or tied for the lead) in at least one of those categories for 24 of the 25 years. The only time the SEC was not the leader in either bowl teams, bowl victories or ranked teams was at the end of 2002. There has only been 6 years (including 2002) when the SEC failed to be at the top in at least two of those categories. On the flip side, the SEC has led or tied for the most in all three standards eight different times since 1995.

Some people believe that a national championship is the only thing that defines a season. The SEC is even more impressive in that context. In the same 25-year period, the SEC has 19 national championship game appearances. SEC teams have won 13 times with an average margin of victory of more than 14 points. Two of the six defeats were actually to fellow SEC teams. The 13 national titles by five different schools dwarfs the next best totals of four titles from three schools by the Big Twelve (the ACC has four championships from two schools).

Over the last 15 years, the SEC has ruled non-conference games against the other Power 5 conferences as well. One Power 5 conference (Big Ten) has bested the SEC in three of those seasons, while the other three major conferences have managed a winning record against the SEC only twice in those 15 seasons. Some pundits considered the 2019 season "a down year" for the SEC, but it still managed a 16-8 record against non-conference Power 5 opponents. Ten of those games were in the post-season, where the SEC recorded eight wins. That brings me to the first topic of discussion.

Scheduling

My thoughts and hopes for scheduling reform have nothing to do with anything people in the media or other conferences say about the SEC. As was just outlined, the SEC has already solidified its place atop the mountain. My feelings on scheduling are about making the SEC and college football better as a whole. These concepts would increase the enthusiasm of the fans, coaches, players, students, recruits and television networks.

The first idea is to have a conference challenge with SEC football similar to the ones in college basketball. One proposal would be to rotate the challenge, so the SEC could take on the Pac-12 in 2021, the Big Ten in 2022, the Big 12 in 2023, and then the ACC in 2024. The games should all be played on campus.

My preference would be to set up home-and-home series with Power 5 opponents, so the SEC matches up with a conference two consecutive years before it moves to the next one. For example, the SEC would play six road games and six home games against the Pac-12 in 2021. The away teams would then host the games in 2022. The challenge would be replicated with the Big Ten in 2023 and 2024, the Big 12 in 2025 and 2026, and then the ACC in 2027 and 2028. Of course, the number of games would depend on the number of teams that the other Power 5 conferences have in their leagues.

The challenge could be scheduled during the first week of the season or one of the subsequent weeks in September. Or what if it was spread throughout the season? There could be four or five challenge games in each of the months of September and October and then it could conclude with a couple games in the first two weeks of November. There are plenty of ways to construct it, and it would undoubtedly provide more excitement and produce more revenue.

Furthermore, traditional non-conference rivalries should be rekindled. Fans are disappointed that these games are not on the schedule. Games such as Texas versus Texas A&M, Kansas versus Missouri, Tulane versus LSU, Indiana versus Kentucky, Georgia Tech versus Auburn, and Miami versus Florida should be played every year. Games like East Carolina versus South Carolina, Memphis versus Ole Miss, Northwestern versus Vanderbilt, Southern Miss versus Mississippi State can be great annual opponents.

Speaking of rivalries, we have to alleviate the dismissal of some of the great conference rivalries that are now only scarcely played. One example is Auburn versus Tennessee. I've met many people throughout the years who consider that game as a primary rival of both of the schools. To play these rivalries more frequently, there has to be a ninth conference game added. The only thing better than SEC football is more SEC football. The coaches, players, and constituents want it. I am sure the networks wouldn't be opposed either. It could be another permanent crossover rival or an additional rotating game against the other division. It would at least cut the idle time of not playing that school in half.

Why not have nine conference games on the 12-game schedule? There used to be an 11-game schedule with eight conference games and other rivalries on the slate. That's what it was when Commissioner Roy Kramer added the SEC Championship Game. It was met with opposition because it was perceived that the SEC would knock itself out of national championship contention. In reality, it helped the SEC become stronger, and that was before No. 1 and No. 2 were contracted to play one another. Today's college football landscape is much different than it was then. There are now over 40 bowl games and a four-team playoff. This past season, nine SEC teams made bowl games, while LSU beat 11 bowl teams and seven top-10 teams on its way to a 15-0 national championship season. Quality SEC teams can handle it, and they won't be in danger of being left out of the playoffs or bowl games.

Respect for Injuries

Football is a physical game and injuries are inevitable. If a player goes down and eventually jogs off the field or comes back into the game, then it doesn't mean that he was faking an injury. It's disgusting for fans to "boo" a player when the game is stopped for an injury timeout. There was one instance at a game I attended in 2019 when the visiting team's offensive player was booed for being injured. His team had the lead and was driving to score again. I don't think that it was part of the game plan for him to get injured and stymie his own team's momentum. When he jogged off the field, the disdain from the home crowd grew louder. For the record, that player missed the next game. The automatic assumption that an injury is fake only serves to make fans look foolish. You know what they say happens when you assume something.

The health and well-being of the players is paramount, and it is taken seriously by most. We should believe the validity of an injury when a player is down. When a team exploits that concern to gain an advantage, it is bush league. I witnessed one obvious example this season. It's embarrassing when coaches and players use that tactic. This is the SEC, and there is no reason for it to occur. If it is proven that a player's distress was fabricated, then I believe that the coach should be fined and the player should be suspended for the next game. For now, though, fans should be respectful of fallen players, and if they fake it, then shame on them.

Targeting

Fans at every game had grown restless with the execution of the targeting rules. Everyone understands the importance of the rule for safety purposes. Sure, some fans are just plain biased and dislike when their team is penalized. Most people are exasperated with the inconsistency in the enforcement of the rule. It was surprising how I saw targeting upheld one week (changing my perspective) and then overturned the next with the same components as the week before. It became confusing from game to game, and I understand why the fans get aggravated. I also saw an offensive lineman flagged for targeting. Replay overturned the call, but it brings up an interesting angle. Is it not targeting when an offensive player initiates contact with the crown of his helmet? There is too much subjectivity involved especially when part of the penalty is an ejection for the player. When replay is utilized, the rulings should be more consistent.

Replay

Instant replay has been a fantastic enhancement to the game. Officials are human and are prone to mistakes. Every rational person understands that. The replay system has helped them make sure the rulings are valid. The

SEC has been at the forefront of instant replay reform for college football. Their new efforts toward transparency are a refreshing change that we enjoy as supporters of the conference. There are two enhancements that I would like the SEC to institute. The first is being consistent with showing replays in the stadiums. Some schools show multiple replays while others don't show any. Even during games, some replays are shown while others are not. That inconsistency inevitably leads fans to consider a conspiracy. The solution is consistency. Either show all the replays or none of them. I believe that SEC schools should have the same procedures or at least stay consistent with their own processes throughout the game.

The other thing that I would love to see the SEC take the lead on is to create a way to get more accurate spots. It is frustrating to watch a quarterback sneak or run up the middle that ends in a big pile and the officials make a crucial call only after deconstructing the stack. There is no way that those officials know if the ball crossed the line before the ball carrier was down. Why can't college football use a system similar to the "Hawk-Eye" system in tennis, particularly on the goal line? The Hawk-Eye system utilizes multiple high performance cameras around the court. In the SEC, there are already HD cameras all around the field so it shouldn't be too big of a transition. I would even be for a system that puts a chip in the ball. Of course, the cost is a consideration, but replay must assist the officials on the field to be as accurate as possible.

Veteran Tributes

It is a source of pride that so many schools pay tribute to veterans through the duration of the season. Schools in the conference honor veterans each week. It makes perfect sense because many of our schools have roots in military service. It is special when the pilots from the flyover or the guys who parachute the game ball into the stadium are able to receive adulation from 60,000 to 100,000 grateful citizens. In many of the SEC stadiums, there are seats dedicated to POW/MIA veterans or POW/MIA flags flying high atop the event. Good for the athletic administrators in the SEC who recognize our veterans. It is because of their sacrifice that we can enjoy fall Saturdays in the SEC. Thank you to all of the men and women who provide us with those freedoms.

Coaches/Players

All around the conference, it is common to see statues honoring coaches and players who have made an impact on their school's football program. It is a terrific tribute to those who have shaped the history of the SEC. It is impossible to fully comprehend the effort and sacrifice it took to accomplish all that they did. Lest we forget all of the other players and coaches that themselves have given as much for the university. We should always respect and honor the contributions they've made so that we can be entertained on Saturdays. Their diplomas, lettermen's jackets and rings are invaluable to them. They have as much if not more pride for their school than we do. It doesn't matter if they were a walk-on, an All-American or a 1st round draft pick. We should always respect their efforts and share our adulation for their commitment.

Traditions

I have an affinity for traditions. It is definitely one of the major reasons that college football differentiates itself from other sports in this country. I believe that it's also one of the biggest reasons for the popularity of the sport. I am impressed by all the traditions at schools in the SEC, and those traditions are much more than just rituals. It is a way of life for the fans. It's a crucial part of the experience. It's one of the most heartfelt ways that a fan base can show its support of the student-athletes, coaches, band members, alumni, each other and the university itself. The vast majority of the traditions in the league are timeless and based on showing loyalty to the school and its teams.

Some traditions are under fire or have been scrapped all together. Each of those censured traditions have their own set of circumstances around its criticisms. The arguments for and against each will claim to be in the name of progress. I am all for being progressive as long as it doesn't unnecessarily take away from a positive experience and it's done for the right reasons. Let's make progress in the form of education and appreciation. I implore the fans and universities to work together to maintain a positive and spirited legacy for all the honored traditions at their schools.

There are some terrific new traditions around the conference. Singing "I Won't Back Down" at Florida and "Don't Stop Believin'" at Mississippi State are two great examples. Everything involved with the "Lone Trumpeter" at Georgia makes it feel like an age-old tradition. The significance and emotion make it one of my favorite newer traditions in the SEC. The long-standing traditions are just as wonderful and important. Whether it is wearing houndstooth at Alabama, celebrating on the "Cockaboose Railroad" at South Carolina or LSU playing on "Saturday Night in Death Valley," the traditions are unique and significant to the spirit of the SEC.

College Football

College football has no rival in my opinion. There is nothing like the passion and traditions that are linked to Saturdays in the fall. There is no other event that has the pageantry of college football. The three-and-a-half-hour games have developed into all-day celebrations. There are so many events linked to game days that entertainment companies all over the world have tried to emulate the atmosphere. But it's impossible to recreate because it's organic. The reunions, tailgates, homecomings, school and team pride, pregame shows, team arrivals, band performances, rivalries, traditions and so much more are what make college football unique and special.

That's not even considering the game itself. College football has an energy that is unique from all other sports. Since attending my first college football game in 1986, I have surmised that there is nothing better than game day on a college campus. My experiences over the last 34 years have done nothing but confirm that conclusion. The games are exceptional events whether or not the team is ranked or the quarterback is in the running for the Heisman Trophy. Sometimes, we get the joy of watching programs that aren't traditional powers produce great teams and talents. There have been plenty of examples of that across the country.

An unexpected college program that has produced exceptional talent is Kansas. The Jayhawks boast alumni such as Gale Sayers, Nolan Cromwell, Todd Reesing, John Riggins, Dana Stubblefield, Dezmon Briscoe and Chris Harris. In terms of team accomplishments, the 1990 college football season presented two great occurrences. Colorado went 11-1-1 (5-1-1 against the final Top 25), including a win in the Orange Bowl rematch with Notre Dame (10-9). Also that year, Georgia Tech toppled then No. 1 Virginia in November and finished 11-0-1 with a Citrus Bowl victory over Nebraska (45-21). Colorado and Georgia Tech both stake a righteous claim to the 1990 national championship.

Those are great examples of what the non-elite programs have done. What about the traditional powers such as Southern Cal, Michigan, Florida State, Nebraska, Notre Dame, Miami (FL), Oklahoma, Ohio State, Texas, or Penn State? Those schools are responsible for a large amount of the exciting history of collegiate football. It isn't just the win totals or award winners that make them an integral part of this great game we love. They all provide us with many of the unique traditions and rivalries that help make college football sensational. Without those programs, college football just isn't as grand, and with them, one can see where some conferences begin to make a case for their relevance.

College football thrives on traditions like tailgating, homecomings, and debates. Hopefully, it is apparent that I appreciate other schools and conferences, but I have to be honest, I am of the opinion that there is no other conference that approaches the contributions that the SEC provides to collegiate athletics. We are fortunate to live in the United States where college football was founded, and I am thankful to be from the South where college football has darn near been perfected. Without the Southeastern Conference, college football is a sunless day. I believe more unbridled passion, stimulating environments, cherished traditions and riveting rivalries reside in the SEC than anywhere else!

See what I mean by debates?

The South

Many proud Americans claim the South as their home. Whether or not they still live there, it is still home to them. My grandfather, who introduced me to SEC sports, passed away 17 years ago. One of the few possessions that I have of his is a shot glass that reads "American by Birth, Southern by the Grace of God." It really sums up how many of us feel about the region that will always be our home. *A Season of Homecomings* took me around the SEC during the 2019 season, but it also brought me back home.

It was back to the values that I hold dear, the landscapes that are burned in my memory and the people that I cherish. Southern folks are as diverse as the towns from which they came. Their dialects, religious denominations, food choices and even habits are usually influenced by their hometowns. The combinations are as eclectic as the sayings you'll hear around the South. In Texas, I was told "We'll treat you so many ways that you'll like one of 'em." And in Tennessee, Abby Early showed her affinity for Dolly Parton when she advised that she abides by the mantra "WWDD - What Would Dolly Do?"

The music choices in the South will differ, but the preferences will be respected. Not all Southerners sound alike, but they'll be polite. The dinner tables won't always have the same fare, but no one will leave hungry. Not everyone is from the same town or state, but we recognize each other as Southerners. The reality is that people in the South have a strong "sense of place." One of the most appropriate examples of that "sense of place" is with the passion and affinity for SEC football. Some may even go as far as saying "Southern by Birth, SEC Fan by the Grace of God."

The Southeastern Conference

The SEC has a long list of athletic accomplishments outside of football. Its teams have dominated both the indoor and outdoor track and field seasons for many years. As of the latest (March 9, 2020) gymnastics poll on usagym.org, eight SEC teams were ranked in the top 18 in the nation. By the way, those eight are the only schools in the conference that have gymnastics teams. Even in sports that are relatively new to the conference, they are making their presence felt. The SEC has 13 schools that sponsor softball, and all 13 teams have made the NCAA tournament each of the last three years (2017-19). As for the other two of the "Big 3" men's sports, the SEC makes a strong case there too.

The SEC has a storied history in college baseball. Each year, eight teams advance to Omaha, Nebraska for the College World Series. There has only been five times in history where a conference was represented by four of the eight teams in the CWS. The SEC is responsible for four of those instances. Since the baseball tournament was expanded to 64 teams in 1999, the SEC has dominated the field. The conference has had 12 teams make a total of 46 appearances in the CWS. The next best conference has had eight teams with 38 appearances. In that same time period, the SEC has won more national championships (7) and recorded more runner-up finishes (9) than any other conference in America. The last *Baseball America* poll of the suspended 2020 season lists eight SEC teams in the Top 25.

Many people in the country don't consider the SEC to be very competitive in men's basketball. The numbers show otherwise. The Final Four is a universal measure of success for college basketball teams. When looking at the tournament since it expanded to 64 teams in 1985, the SEC has had seven different programs make the Final Four. That is tied for the most among Power 5 conferences. Compared to those same conferences, the

SEC has the second most national championships. Not too shabby for a conference that is said to have only two sports - football & spring football.

When we assert the SEC chant, it is our way of showing pride in our conference brethren. Our teams have been through the battles with each other, and we understand the trials that have been overcome. We are vocalizing the respect for the accomplishments of our fiercest opponents and our closest allies. It's an appreciation for those who don the orange and blue, black and gold, maroon and white or red and black. Where it is appropriate to dress in purple and gold stripes or orange and white checkers. When blue opposes crimson or the times when it all flows together into a red, white and blue medley.

It is not about race, political party, background, religious beliefs or economic status. It's for the people who proclaim "Geaux Tigers," "Hail State" or "Roll Tide." For those that "give their all for Tennessee" or do a "Missouri Waltz" through the heart of America. It's the anticipation of the "calling of the hogs" or the crow of a "Gamecock." It's support from a "12th Man" when the "War Eagle" flies and we need to "Anchor Down." It's a "Hell Yeah, Damn Right" when we hear the "Battle Hymn of the Bulldog Nation" or "My Old Kentucky Home." Because "In all kinds of weather," we are forever ... S ... E ... C, S ... E ... C, S ... E ... C!

Acknowledgements

I was driving in November 2018 when I heard on Sirius XM radio that the 2019 college football regular season would be 14 weeks long. I had been so busy that I hadn't had the time to look up the future schedules. That night I verified the 14-week season, and I decided that 2019 would be *A Season of Homecomings*. It took a considerable amount of time to figure out the schedule. I needed to see every SEC team at home, and I decided that I would make each one a conference game. For months, I tried to alter it (to include different games) only to realize that I already had the most inclusive combination.

The trip took a full 15 weeks on the road, as I also attended the 2019 SEC Championship Game. I added more than 15,000 miles on my truck, and (according to the app on my phone) I walked more than 650 miles during the journey. I live in South Texas, so it was impossible to drive back and forth during the small breaks that I had between campus visits. I stayed at all different types of places during the trip. There were Airbnb's, a few decent hotels and some not so much.

During a couple of the breaks between stops, I was able to stay with my brother James and his family. It was great to see them and much easier to do laundry. Thank you for always being so accommodating. In Arkansas, I was invited to stay at the home of friends from UK (Damon and Stephanie). I had fun hanging out with you guys, and I am thankful that you opened your home to me. Will Poole in Oxford always found a place for me to stay. I appreciate your efforts and thanks for letting me use your office. Don and Susan Crowther were fantastic hosts in Baton Rouge. It was nice getting to know you, and I am grateful that you allowed Josiah to stay as well.

The trip was full of others that helped me along the way. Some in an official capacity and others just to be good people. Thank you to all of the tailgate hosts that welcomed me into your circles especially Travis Thomas, Patrick Harrigan, David Lawrence, Austin Ramirez, Brian Alford, Phil Nichols, Kyler Hecke, the Hailgaters, Matt Fletcher and Gene Plauche. And to all the campus parking officials that helped make the journey without one violation. Thanks to all of the Airbnb hosts that put up with me. You are all different, but all wonderful people.

Thank you to legendary coaches Pat Dye and Vince Dooley for taking the time to speak with me about your experiences in the SEC. Thank you Mike Anderson for a great lunch and terrific conversation. Thank you Wanda Poole for being so gracious with your time. To Sam Ball - I appreciate all that you've done for UK and the state of Kentucky. Also to John Schlarman - thank you for the tickets, but also thank you for being a good friend. Thank you Randy Ross for providing access in Fayetteville.

Thank you to Dion McInnis and Ashton Vara for welcoming me and teaching me the procedures of Student Bonfire.

Thank you Trent Woods for sharing a lot of fun and welcoming me into your trusted group.

I appreciate the Day family for all the support in Baton Rouge. William, John, Patricia David, Diana and Susan. You guys were phenomenal, and I enjoyed being around your family. To Joe Simmons - Thank you for the tickets and the access.

I am grateful to you Brad Bradway. I am thankful for your generosity, but more so for the laughs and friendship that we share.

To the fellow writers, historians and media members who took the time to talk through things with me - Langston Rogers, Sue Owen, David Housel, Tommy Ford, Loran Smith, Chris Harry, Pat Dooley, Ryan Brown, Ken Gaddy, Colin Castleberry, Cliff Kuo and Jamie Morrison. Thank you for imparting your wisdom into this process.

I am indebted to many of the SIDs and other university representatives that helped me through my quest. I would especially like to thank Mike

Wright, Claude Felton, Kirk Sampson, Kyle Campbell, Michael Bonnette, Charles Bloom, Susan Lax, Brad Marquardt, Alan Cannon, Kyle Parkinson, Bill Martin, Ken Crain, Allen Sitzler, Brad Rapacz, Tyler Fondren, Jake Taccone, Larry Waters, Ryan Dunn, Steve Orlando, Victoria Adams, Grant Kauvar and Adrienne Pace.

I want to thank the SEC communications staff for all of the great work you do to bring us information about the conference and its members. I am especially appreciative of the efforts of Herb Vincent. Thank you Melinda Calderini for being a great representative of the professionalism in the SEC offices.

To my editor Dave Holcomb. Thank you for combing through and fixing so many of my mistakes. I appreciate your expertise and friendship.

Thank you to all my family and friends who believed in me throughout this endeavor. It wouldn't have been possible without your support.

Thank you Nora for your patience and allowing me to be me. I am blessed to have you as my wife. You always believed in my vision and let me convert you into a full-blown SEC fan. Now that this book is complete, I guess that you will want to send me off for another three months.

I will inevitably forget to include people whose actions were a tremendous benefit to me. Please know that it wasn't intentional and that I am indebted to each of you. I am very grateful for all the wonderful SEC fans who I met over that 15-week period. It truly was a joy that you shared your experiences with me, and it is my honor to share this book with you.

About The Author

Ron Lang was born in Louisville, Kentucky. A coaching career took him across the country before he eventually settled in South Texas with his wife Nora. Under his tutelage, his players earned multiple All-Conference and All-American accolades. Since leaving the coaching ranks, Ron has owned businesses in the insurance and financial services industries.

When he isn't writing or doing speaking engagements, Ron loves watching any and all college sports. His other hobbies include playing golf, fishing, reading and cooking. He has volunteered for a number of organizations that assist children in improving their lives by overcoming their personal obstacles. He also enjoys helping the many children in his family to become more productive students and better prepared athletes.

Even before he attended and graduated from the University of Kentucky, Ron was enthralled with SEC sports. He has followed, supported or participated in the SEC for 40 years. That passion for the SEC led him to writing *A Season of Homecomings*. It is his third published book, and he is dedicated to producing books that deliver positivity and inspiration. You can find his other works by searching for Ron Lang on Amazon.com or do a Google search for:

Relative Genius: Lost in Transition

or

Unveiling Success: Reveal It For Yourself

Made in the USA
Coppell, TX
23 May 2020

26349333R00217